# GOD'S HAND IN OUR LIVES

*Teacher's Notes for Lessons on the New Testament*

*God's Hand In Our Lives*
*Teacher's Notes for Lessons on the New Testament*
Copyright © Church of The Lutheran Confession. Used by permission.

Reprinted by South Asia Lutheran Mission, 2025.
Is licensed under CC BY 4.0
ISBN: 978-1-960840-36-3

Cover artwork by Kelly Schumacher of Agnus Dei Liturgical Arts, AgnusDeiArts.com
Interior and cover design by Zeshan Asghar.

Scriptures marked NKJV are taken from the NEW KING JAMES VERSION (NKJV): Scripture taken from the NEW KING JAMES VERSION®. Copyright © 1982 by Thomas Nelson, Inc. Used by permission. All rights reserved.

SouthAsiaLutheranMission.com

# TABLE OF CONTENTS

## STORY
Zacharias - Luke 1:5-25, 57-80

## TEACHER PRAYER
Dear Father in Heaven, we are all on a journey of faith where we must simply trust your promises and lay aside our reason and doubts. Help me, O Lord, to trust that you will bless Your Word as I speak it to the students in my care. Help us to see that you do indeed keep all your promises to us so that we firmly believe that you also forgive us our sins through Jesus' work and will bring us through life to eternity with You in heaven. Amen.

## VOCABULARY
*lot* - different colored stones from which one was selected at random; this was a way the Lord used at that time to show whom He had selected.

## OUTER AIM
God sends John as a messenger to prepare for Jesus' coming.

## INNER AIM
God keeps His promises.

## BACKGROUND
*(Rupprecht Bible History References Vol. 2, pp. 2-11)*
About 4,000 years had passed since God gave His first promise of the Savior to Adam and Eve. Through the years God had revealed increasingly more information about the coming Savior, but it had been 400 years since the Lord had last given information through Malachi the prophet. Malachi, besides speaking of the Savior coming, also prophesied that God would send a messenger ahead of Jesus to prepare the people for His coming (Mal 3:1). This story tells of the events surrounding the birth of that messenger, John the Baptizer.
Below are notes on each verse of the account:
v. 5
▸   John's parents: Zacharias: a priest of the course (or division) of Abijah (Abia in Greek).
▸   Each course of priests took turns ministering in the Temple for one week.
▸   There were about 2,000 priests at the time of Jesus.
▸   Elizabeth: "God her oath," descendant of Aaron and relative of Mary— though of a different tribe.
v. 6
▸   Both parents are described as "righteous before God, walking .. blameless" which describes believers in the coming Savior.
v. 7
▸   They had no children, which in those days was considered shameful.
▸   Children were regarded as a great blessing of the Lord.
▸   Because of their age, it seemed impossible to sire and bear children.
vs. 8-10
▸   Zacharias was chosen to perform for one week the twice daily public ceremony of prayer and of burning incense in the temple.
▸   God had given this ceremony to picture how Christ would bring the people's (that is the Jews) prayers to God.
▸   Their prayers would rise to God like the smoke of the incense.

vs. 11-12
- An angel suddenly appeared beside the altar where Zacharias was worshiping.
- Zacharias, knowing his own sinfulness, was immediately afraid in the presence of the holy angel.

vs. 13 - 17
- But the angel told Zacharias not to fear, for he was bringing joyous news.
- The prayers of Zacharias and Elizabeth and other believers of Israel were indeed being heard.
- A special son would be born to them who would be dedicated as the forerunner of the Lord.
- Malachi prophesied (Mal 4:5), John would go before the Savior to prepare people's hearts to believe in Jesus.
- John would be great as a Spirit-filled preacher boldly calling people to repent and believe in the Lamb of God who takes away the sins of the world.

vs. 18 - 20
- Zacharias' human reason got in the way of his believing God's message, causing him to doubt Gabriel, the messenger from the very presence of God.
- For that reason the angel chastised him by taking away his voice until the Lord should fulfill also this promise.
- Gabriel was also the "messenger of God" sent to Daniel and Mary.

vs. 21-22
- Zacharias' loss of voice also became a sign for the people who had gathered outside to pray.
- They perceived that he had seen a vision.

vs. 23-25
- Zacharias was allowed to continue his service at the temple before he returned home to his wife with the good news.
- As the Lord promised, she conceived.
- Then she hid herself for five months, perhaps to be a picture of how— for a time, but not permanently — the Lord's blessing had seemed hidden to them.

vs. 57-58
- About nine months later, when the full time after Elizabeth had conceived had passed, as God had promised, she gave birth to a boy.
- This brought much rejoicing from neighbors, friends, and relatives for this blessing.

v. 59
- Through the rite of circumcision, the child entered into the life of the nation of Israel and into the covenant made with Abraham.
- God had commanded circumcision (Gen 17:10-14) (Baptism had not yet been instituted.) to be performed on the 8th day after birth; the child was customarily named then as well.
- Children were often named after their parents or close relatives.

vs. 60-63
- But in testimony to their faith in God's message sent by the angel, both parents insisted that his name was John.
- "John" was an unusual name for them to pick, going against the custom of their day, since they didn't have any relatives by that name.

vs. 64-66
- As soon as Zacharias demonstrated his faith by declaring the God-given name of John, the promise was fulfilled to loose his tongue.
- Praises, with no hint of blame, flowed from his heart toward God.

- All those around them were awed by God's amazing work causing them to wonder what God had in mind for this child.
- We notice that the hand of the Covenant Lord blessed John as he grew up into the role the Lord had preset for him.

vs. 67-75
- The Holy Spirit moved Zacharias to proclaim in joyous prophecy that the Lord indeed was keeping His greatest promise, that of the coming Savior.
- God was now fulfilling all His ancient promises for deliverance from the spiritual enemies of His people.

vs. 76-79
- Zacharias prophesied of John's important role in God's plan.
- John would proclaim Jesus to the people and show them how they would find light and peace in Jesus to replace the darkness and trouble of sin.

v. 80
- John became strong in the Spirit, learning from the O.T. Scriptures to prepare for the role set for him.
- Until age thirty, when he would be allowed to preach to Israel, John chose as his home the solitude of the deserts between Jerusalem and the Dead Sea.

## STUDENT PRAYER

Dear Father in Heaven, We have learned that You keep all Your promises to us. When our reason would make us doubt Your Word and our patience wears thin, overcome our doubt and strengthen our faith to believe Your promises will be fulfilled according to Your wise plans. Send Your Holy Spirit on us that we may be bold in believing Your promises of forgiveness, of life and salvation in Jesus and so reach the home You have promised to all who believe in Jesus. Amen

## PRESENTATION

Ask the children to think of promises that they have made or that others have made to them. Sometimes these human promises are broken by circumstances, forgetfulness, or their impossibility. When people break promises, they hurt each other and cause mistrust. But God never breaks His promises to us. God showed this when He kept His promise by sending John to Zacharias and Elizabeth. For God had promised them a son when He foretold, some 400 years earlier, that He would send a messenger to prepare people for Jesus.

Briefly review the previous story as time allows. Make links to the new story when possible. Tell the story: Teachers, be encouraged to tell the story in your own words while remaining faithful to the scriptural account. When scripture records the story in more than one place, you may want to harmonize the accounts (including extra details found in each account.) Let the students know where they can find the additional details in the Bible.

Discuss the story: While reviewing the major events of the story, discuss the possible applications to the students' lives. Ask questions that make them think about the story and show that they understand the story.

## APPLICATIONS

1. God made many important promises in the Old Testament about Jesus. Those made about His life on earth have all been kept. He promised that Jesus would suffer and die to take away the sins of the world and Jesus did that. And God promised that by believing in what Jesus has done for us, we too will have eternal life in heaven. This is God's promise to us. Can we trust God's promise to us? Why?

2. What is faith? It is trusting or relying on God's promise, even if our human reason doubts God's message. Discuss Heb 11:1; 12:1-2.

3. God has promised that He will be with us always, in every trouble or problem that we face. And He promises that all things work together for good to them that love God, to those who are called according to His purpose. Can we believe those promises? Why is it good to look back over our lives to see how God has kept His promises to us? How does that help us face the future?

4. What are some other promises that God has made in His Word? Have we seen all of them fulfilled yet?
   - a. Noah - no more great floods.
   - b. Continuous seasons of sowing and harvesting.
   - c. Christ coming as a man.
   - d. Christ coming a second time.
   - e. Abraham having countless children.
   - f. God's promise to never leave or forsake His people.

## PASSAGES

These passages can be assigned as memory work or simply discussed in class as to how they fit the lesson.

Lower
John 3:16 - For God so loved the world that He gave His only begotten Son, that whoever believes in Him should not perish but have everlasting life.
Matthew 28:20 - Jesus said, "Lo, I am with you always, even to the end of the age." Amen.

Middle any of the above and...
Joshua 1:9 - Have I not commanded you? Be strong and of good courage; do not be afraid, nor be dismayed, for the LORD your God is with you wherever you go.
Hebrews 11:1 - Now, faith is the substance of things hoped for, the evidence of things not seen.

Upper any of the above and...
Romans 8:28 - And we know that all things work together for good to those who love God, to those who are the called according to His purpose.
Hebrews 13:5 - Let your conduct be without covetousness; be content with such things as you have. For He Himself has said, "I will never leave you nor forsake you."
Malachi 3:1 - Behold, I send My messenger, and he will prepare the way before Me.

## HYMN CHOICES

"Let the Earth Now Praise the Lord" (TLH 91 1-4)
"We Have a Sure Prophetic Word" (TLH 290 1-4)
"I Am Trusting Thee, Lord Jesus" (TLH 428 1-6)

## STORY
Announcing a Miracle Child - Luke 1:26-56, Matthew 1:18-25

## TEACHER PRAYER
Dear Father in heaven, the truths I am about to present with this lesson are doubted and attacked so mightily today, yet they are so important in assuring Your children that Jesus is indeed their Savior. Bless me, Your servant, as I carry Your Word to those in my care. May the students' faith in Your amazing power and love be strengthened and move them to praise You with faith, word, and deeds, now and into eternity. Amen

## VOCABULARY
*Galilee* - The northern province of Israel during Roman occupation, with King Herod allowed to rule.
*Nazareth* - means "verdant" or "offshoot" and brings to mind the prophecy in Isaiah 11:1 that Jesus would come from the stem or shoot of the tribe of Jesse (cf. Matthew 2:23).
*Betrothed* - pledged to be married, the commitment had already been made to be husband and wife."
*found with child"* - she was pregnant.
*public example* - charge her with adultery and refuse to marry her.
*Jesus* - the name literally means "Savior".
*Immanuel* - literally it means "God with us", a testimony that Mary's Son would be God in human flesh.

## OUTER AIM
God announces the miracle of Jesus' birth.

## INNER AIM
Believers show faith in the miracle within Jesus' birth.

## BACKGROUND
*(Rupprecht Bible History References Vol. 2, pp. 11-16)*
When everything was ready, God sent forth His Son, born of a woman (Gal. 4:4). (The study of how human history converged to make this the right moment is beyond the scope of this lesson.) Jesus' forerunner, John, was on his way. So God sent His angel to a humble virgin (unmarried girl) of the tribe of David. (cf. Isaiah. 7:14 "Behold a virgin shall conceive and bear a son...."). Various events emphasize how the birth of Jesus fulfilled Old Testament prophecies and reveal that Jesus was the promised Messiah and Savior.

Below are notes on each verse of the account:
Luke 1:26
- ▸ in the sixth month of Elizabeth's pregnancy.
- ▸ Gabriel: the same angel sent to Zacharias (and Daniel).

v. 27
- ▸ betrothed (see above) to Joseph of the house of David: note that both mother and stepfather were of the house of David, just as God has prophecied.
- ▸ Joseph's family tree is traced in Matthew 1:1-18 and Mary's in Luke 3:23-38.
- ▸ Virgin : repeated twice to emphasize the fulfillment of God's prophecy of Isaiah 7:14.

v. 28
- ▸ Rejoice, highly favored one: (sometimes "Hail, Mary") The angel's greeting to Mary has been twisted to support the worship of Mary, a modern idolatry in some churches.
- ▸ The greeting announces that Mary should rejoice because of the blessing God is giving her.

v. 29

- ▸ Troubled : Mary was perplexed, confused about the angel's words;
- ▸ considered : She thought intently about the unusual greeting.

vs. 30-33

- ▸ Do not be afraid, Mary : Like all sinful people, Mary was afraid in the presence of the holy angel.
- ▸ Jesus : Savior, Redeemer cf. with Matt 1:21.
- ▸ Called the Son of the Highest : Son of God because Jesus is exactly that.
- ▸ Throne of His father David : Jesus would be a descendent of King David according to promise and would rule over the house of Jacob (spiritual Israel) forever.

v. 34

- ▸ How can this be? : Mary was confused about the means how this would be accomplished, because pregnancy could only happen by sexual intercourse.

v. 35

- ▸ Holy Spirit shall come upon you, ...overshadow you : the Third person of the divine trinity would accomplish this mysterious miracle of uniting God with human flesh.
- ▸ So the Son of God from eternity also took on human flesh and became God and man, the Holy One, Jesus, the Incarnate (in flesh) Son of God.

vs. 36-37

- ▸ barren: without having children and assumed unable to have children because of age.
- ▸ This message was given as encouragement to Mary that God has the power to do anything.

v. 38

- ▸ maidservant of the Lord : Mary's humble acceptance of her miraculous conception demonstrates a humble willingness to take God at His Word and to serve in faith according to it.

vs. 39-40

- ▸ with haste, to .. Judah, hill country : Mary hurried the 80 miles or so to be with Elizabeth, pregnant with John, to share the good news with someone.

v. 41

- ▸ the babe leaped : John, a human baby at 6 months, reacted favorably to the mother of Jesus greeting his mother.
- ▸ Elizabeth's words show that the Holy Spirit revealed the nature of God's blessing upon Mary.

vs. 42-45

- ▸ Elizabeth spoke out : With exuberance, Elizabeth rejoiced with Mary, humbly accepted the fact of the miracle taking place within Mary and marveled that Mary should be visiting her.
- ▸ Elizabeth also encouraged Mary in her faith that the Lord would indeed fulfill His promised blessing.

vs. 46-55

- ▸ My soul magnifies the Lord : declares the greatness of the Lord in awe of His amazing blessing.
- ▸ Mary looked with joyful faith to the special baby in her womb to save her also from sin.
- ▸ All but one of the statements in Mary's song were from the Old Testament.
- ▸ has regarded the lowly state : Mary in humbleness praised God for the honor given her, despite what might be considered her low position in the world's eyes.
- ▸ Mary realized that God with great mercy was fulfilling His centuries-old promises of a Savior for her and all believers.

Matt 1:18-19

- ▸ birth of Jesus Christ : the unusual circumstances surrounding Jesus' birth needed to be explained, especially to Mary's intended husband who would be Jesus' stepfather.

‣ Before they were formally married, Mary was known to be expecting a baby.

‣ In all other circumstances, that would have been considered a sin which according to Mosaic Law (Deuteronomy 22:13-21) could have meant her death or at least a private divorce.

vs. 20-21

‣ in a dream : God chose to send Joseph a message this way.

‣ Joseph should not fear the consequences of accepting Mary as his wife because God was working a special miracle here.

‣ Mary had conceived by the Holy Spirit, resulting in a boy to be named Jesus.

‣ Notice that the message emphasizes Joseph is David's descendent and that Mary is his wife.

‣ Jesus' name fits His sole purpose on earth, namely, to save His people from their sins.

vs 22-23

‣ that it might be fulfilled which was spoken by the prophet : Matthew was writing to the Jewish people, showing them that Jesus was their Savior.

‣ Matthew, by the Holy Spirit, quoted Isaiah 7:14 to emphasize that Jesus had to be both "God with us" and conceived of a virgin in fulfillment of God's promise.

vs 24-25

‣ Joseph, .., did as the angel of the Lord commanded him : Joseph also believed the miracle within Jesus' birth and followed the instructions of the Lord.

‣ They called Mary's firstborn son, "Jesus."

## STUDENT PRAYER

Dear Father in Heaven, You teach us today that Jesus is both Your only-begotten Son and also a human being born of a virgin named Mary. This miracle made Jesus both God and Man and so our perfect, holy Savior; we know this is a matter of faith. O Lord, strengthen our faith in this and all other mysteries of Scripture, that we may remain Your children now and into eternity. Help us to show our faith with words of praise and deeds of obedience that blessing may come through us as Your servants. In the name of Jesus, our Savior, we pray. Amen.

## PRESENTATION

Discuss the different ways that Christians show their love and faith in God's Word: read and meditate on the Bible; hear it in church; live, believing God's sometimes difficult truths and obeying Him in their lives; being kind and helpful to friends, relatives and neighbors. Mary and Joseph (and Elizabeth) showed that they believed God's Word. As Mary told the angel that she believed what he had told her, she praised God for this great blessing; Joseph also did as the angel said and married Mary.

Briefly review previous story as time allows. Make links to the new story when possible.
Tell the story: Teachers, be encouraged to tell the story in your own words while remaining faithful to the scriptural account. When scripture records the story in more than one place, you may want to harmonize the accounts (including extra details found in each account.) Let the students know where they can find the additional details in the Bible.

Discuss the story: While reviewing the major events of the story, discuss the possible applications to the students' lives. Ask questions that make them think about the story and show that they understand the story.

## APPLICATIONS

1.   As the announcement of John's birth showed that God keeps His promises, this one shows us that God is able to do so in seemingly impossible ways, if He chooses. We learn that His power and love, although hard to grasp intellectually, are acceptable in faith. Only by faith do we understand that Jesus is indeed both God and human according to God's plan (Galatians 4:4-5). As a human being He could die in payment for our sins; as God His obedience and sin-payment could be flawless, holy and acceptable.

2.   Faith in God's Word shows itself in praise of God for His amazing Grace and in obeying His directions in our lives. What blessings can result when we live God's way! We show our faith in the way we treat everyone around us. God blesses our lives and others as we live according to His Word.

## PASSAGES

These passages can be assigned as memory work or simply discussed in class as to how they fit the lesson.

Lower
Matthew 1:21 - "And she will bring forth a Son, and you shall call His name JESUS, for He will save His people from their sins."
Luke 1:37 - "For with God nothing will be impossible."

Middle any of the above and...
Isaiah 7:14 - "Therefore the Lord Himself will give you a sign: Behold, the virgin shall conceive and bear a Son, and shall call His name Immanuel."
Galatians 4:4 - But when the fullness of the time had come, God sent forth His Son, born of a woman, born under the law.

Upper any of the above and...
Galatians 4:4-5 - But when the fullness of the time had come, God sent forth His Son, born of a woman, born under the law, to redeem those who were under the law, that we might receive the adoption as sons.
1 Timothy 3:16 And without controversy great is the mystery of godliness: God was manifested in the flesh.

## HYMN CHOICES

"Savior of the Nations, Come" (TLH 95 vs. 3-4)
"Praise We the Lord This Day" (TLH 274)

## 3

## STORY
The Birth of Jesus - Luke 2:1-20

## TEACHER PRAYER
O Lord, Dear Father in heaven, you have given us, who in no way deserved it, such an amazing gift, Your own Son, to be our Savior.  His humble birth hides the grand and noble work You sent Him among us to do.  This baby, Jesus, became our perfect Savior, although it meant He would leave the glories of heaven to live within the confines of the Law which we cannot keep and then would suffer the desolation and agony of hell and death instead of us.  Help me, Oh Lord, to share the joy and amazement at this wondrous gift You have given to us.  And grant that the peace through forgiveness in Jesus given for all of the world would come to each of our hearts in every season.  In Jesus saving name, I pray. Amen.

## VOCABULARY
*Caesar Augustus* - the Roman Emperor or ruler of the Roman Empire.
*Quirinius or Cyrenius* - this governor's name gives many people trouble.
*host* - a very large group or army, too many to count (of angels, people)

## OUTER AIM
Jesus Our Savior is Born

## INNER AIM
Jesus, the Promised Savior, is Born!

## BACKGROUND
(Rupprecht Bible History References Vol. 2, pp. 23-34)
Galatians 4:4 - "When the fullness of the time was come (when everything was ready), God sent forth His Son, made of a woman, made under the law, in order to redeem them that were under the law, that we might receive the adoption as sons."

This sums up the plan and purpose of God in connection with the birth of Jesus.   God arranged history so everything would be ready.  The Jews no longer ruled themselves as God had prophesied (Genesis 49:10).  So a Roman Emperor, looking for more taxes, served God's plan to have Joseph and Mary in Bethlehem (Micah 5:2) just in time for Jesus' birth.  Joseph and Mary registered there because they were descendants of the family of King David.  But the birth of the King of Kings was anything but royal.

There was no room in the inn, so Mary and Joseph found themselves in a stable, possibly a cave for the animals.  Jesus' first bed was the feeding crib or manger.  Jesus' humble birth was in keeping with His work as Messiah - not to rule as an earthly monarch, but to serve under God's law and to finally give His life as a ransom for all. Below are notes on each verse of the account:
Luke 2:1
▸    Caesar Augustus : the first Roman Emperor ruled from 27 BC to 14 AD.
▸    Registered :This was a census in the Roman empire to be sure nobody was overlooked in taxes.
▸    To do this, the people of Palestine returned to the city of their family or heritage where family records were kept.
v. 2

- Quirinius or Cyrenius: the Roman form and the Greek form of the name for the same man.
- He ruled over Syria including Palestine (twice) from 7-2 BC and again 6-9 AD.
- The census or registering took place during his first term in the office.
- (Note: We don't know the exact date of Jesus' birth, nor do we need to. The early church began celebrating Christmas in contrast with a Roman holiday which followed the shortest (darkest) day of the year - December 21.)

vs. 3-5
- Joseph also went up.: He traveled among crowds of people, each going to the city of his family to obey the command to be registered.
- Mary, his betrothed wife, also needed to be registered, so she went along despite her condition.

vs. 6-7
- Her firstborn son: Compare with Matt 1:25 (and the previous lesson) to recall the miracle within this simple, humble birth.
- Swaddling cloths: Strips of cloth wrapped securely around the Babe, as the angel had identified Jesus for the shepherds.

V. 8
- Shepherds living out in the fields: Shepherds protected their flocks by remaining in the fields with their sheep.
- These particular sheep were raised to be temple sacrifices.
- The lowly birth, matching the humble purpose of Jesus' coming, was first announced, not to royalty, but to rustic shepherds.

V. 9
- An angel of the Lord: The Lord's holy messenger produced fear in the hearts of these shepherds.

V. 10
- Do not be afraid: Perfect love casts out fear.
- The angels had Good News of God's love to bring,.
- which will be to all people: the tidings of great joy are not meant to be hoarded but shared and enjoyed by all people.

V. 11
- Born to you this day: The Savior of the world is born for you today.
- He is Christ, the long awaited Messiah, the Lord, who was promised to become your Savior.
- The most important news in all of history is brought first to humble shepherds.

V. 12
- Shall be a sign to you: The angels wanted the shepherds to see this great event for themselves, so they enabled them to find Jesus.

V. 13
- A multitude of the heavenly host: Countless angels of heaven filled the sky around these shepherds singing their praises of God.
- Amid the lowliness of Jesus' birth, the glory of His person shone through in the choir of angels that proclaimed Jesus' birth that night.

V. 14
- Glory to God: God's greatest glory is his working out our salvation by His grace.
- This salvation, the forgiveness of sins, alone brings peace to human hearts and reestablishes good will between God and mankind.
- Surely it is worth singing about!

V. 15

▸ Let us now go to Bethlehem and see: They wouldn't wait, but convinced each other to see the event announced by the angels on God's behalf.

V. 16

▸ And they came with haste: Their hurried search was rewarded with the joy of finding the Babe as the angels had said.

V. 17

▸ They made widely known: Probably for a long time to come they told people all about the angel's description of this one special child, for His coming was great news of joy for all Bible-believing people.

V. 18

▸ All of those who heard it marveled: The shepherds carried amazing news that caused everyone whom they told to be amazed.

V. 19

▸ But Mary: Mary stored all these events in her heart and thought about them over and over again as she discovered more and more about God's wonderful plan of Salvation through the baby Jesus.

▸ Surely the Lord had given her and gives us much to think about.

V. 20

▸ The shepherds returned, glorifying and praising God: They returned to their duties but with joy in their hearts which they gladly shared with others.

## STUDENT PRAYER

O Lord, dear Father in heaven, though we did not deserve it, You gave us such an amazing gift, Your own Son, to be our Savior. His humble birth hides the grand and noble work You sent Him among us to do. Jesus became our perfect Savior. He left the glories of heaven to be born a human baby and to live within the confines of the Law which we cannot keep. Then He also suffered the desolation and agony of hell and death instead of us. Help me, Oh Lord, to know and to share the joy, the amazement, and the peace sent through this wondrous gift You have given to us. In Jesus' saving name, I pray. Amen.

## PRESENTATION

You might begin the lesson by asking the students what is the first thing that comes to mind when they think about Christmas. Then move from there into the greatest gift given which is God's own Son our Savior. The real meaning of Christmas is God's undeserved gift of a Savior for us. It is a cause for amazement and joy because of the salvation and peace that Jesus brings.

## APPLICATIONS

1. How do we express our joy at Christmas? We anticipate Christmas with Advent services and celebrate with special services on Christmas Eve and Christmas Day. We decorate our homes and churches. We send religious cards sharing the message with family and friends.

2. Christmas decorations have a message. An evergreen tree signifies everlasting life, because it stays green through winter; the lights on the tree signify Jesus the light of the world and His children who are to share that light with the world. Giving gifts reminds us of the greatest gift ever given, Jesus, the Savior of the world.

3. The many outward customs of Christmas carry a danger. Our time, energy, thoughts, and finances can be soaked up by the outward festivities of Christmas, while our meditating on and rejoicing in the birth of

Jesus gets buried in the background. We want to make sure that our children realize that Christmas is not Santa Claus and exchanging presents but a very special time set aside for celebrating the greatest Gift of all.

4. We, too can be shepherds. The joy of Christmas is in the peace of conscience that God gives for all people through Jesus. The shepherds were the first Christian missionaries, telling what they had heard and seen concerning Jesus. We get the privilege of bringing this gift to others, too. May we share our joy as the shepherds did.

## PASSAGES
These passages can be assigned as memory work or simply discussed in class as to how they fit the lesson.

Lower
Luke 2:11 - For there is born to you this day in the city of David a Savior, who is Christ the Lord.
Titus 2:11 - For the grace of God that brings salvation has appeared to all men.

Middle any of the above and...
1 John 4:9-11 - In this the love of God was manifested toward us, that God has sent His only begotten Son into the world, that we might live through Him. In this is love, not that we loved God, but that He loved us and sent His Son to be the propitiation for our sins. Beloved, if God so loved us, we also ought to love one another.

Upper any of the above and...
Isaiah 9:6 - For unto us a Child is born, Unto us a Son is given; And the government will be upon His shoulder. And His name will be called Wonderful, Counselor, Mighty God, Everlasting Father, Prince of Peace.
Micah 5:2 - But you, Bethlehem Ephrathah, Though you are little among the thousands of Judah, Yet out of you shall come forth to Me The One to be Ruler in Israel, Whose goings forth are from of old, From everlasting.
Galatians 4:4-5 - But when the fullness of the time had come, God sent forth His Son, born of a woman, born under the law, to redeem those who were under the law, that we might receive the adoption as sons.

## HYMN CHOICES
"From Heaven Above to Earth I Come" (TLH 85 1-4 and any other verses)
"A Great and Mighty Wonder" (TLH 76 1-4)
"Hark! the Herald Angels Sing" (TLH 94)

## 4

## STORY
The Wise Men - Matthew 2:1-23

## TEACHER PRAYER
O Lord, You led the wise men with Your Word and a star to find and worship the Savior of the world. Help me to use Your word as a guiding star for the students entrusted to my guidance.  Give all of us a desire to seek You as our Savior and King and to worship you with our gifts.  Guide us.  Protect us from evil.  And let Your light shine to and through us all.  I come to you in the name of the Light of the World, my savior, Jesus. Amen.

## VOCABULARY
*Wise Men or Magi* - a certain group of priests or advisers to rulers of eastern countries.  They studied philosophy, the sciences, astrology, and astronomy.  Daniel was such, but did not practice the wicked art of astrology or sorcery.  (See Rupprecht, page 46)
*Frankincense* -a dry resin with a strong smell and white or yellowish color valued because it burns long with a sweet odor.  Like incense today.
*Myrrh* -a scented gum from thickened sap of a low thorny tree which grows chiefly in Arabia.  It was used for precious ointments, embalming, and perfume.
*Ramah* - a small town near Jerusalem, near the later city of Bethlehem.
*Gentiles* -all the non-Jewish people of the earth.

## OUTER AIM
God led the wise men to Jesus.

## INNER AIM
God reveals the Savior of all people.

## BACKGROUND
*(Rupprecht Bible History References Vol. 2, pp. 45-54)*
This story stresses that the salvation which God prepared in Jesus was not only for His people Israel (the Jews) but also for the Gentiles (non-Jews).  God revealed the birth of the Savior to these Gentile astronomers through a special star.  He has also revealed this Jesus to us (Gentiles) through His Word.
Below are notes on each verse of the account:
Matthew 1:1
▸ The event took place probably within two years of Jesus' birth.
▸ We do not know the country where the wise men came from (the East), nor how many there were (there were three gifts).
▸ Jerusalem was the capital city and seemed a likely birthplace for a king.
v. 2:
▸ His Star: Numbers 24:17 speaks of the Star of Jacob.
▸ Evidently these wise men learned the scriptures from Jews (Daniel, others) who had been carried away captive to Babylon and perhaps beyond.
▸ The wise men traveled a long journey to find and worship this King.
v. 3:
▸ Herod was paranoid, constantly afraid that someone was going to take his throne and power away from him.
▸ To hear that a new king was born who might take his power deeply worried Herod and also people of Jerusalem, who knew Herod's ruthless reputation.
▸ Fear to lose what he treasured caused Herod and others to miss out on a far greater treasure.

v. 4 :
- Herod, "The Great," did not know the scriptures well enough to know the answer and had to ask his advisers about the scriptures.

vs. 5-6:
- Herod's advisers searched the scriptures and found the answer.
- Micah 5:2(-5) names the birthplace of the Ruler King who would shepherd the wayward flock of Israel.

v. 7:
- In private he questioned the wise men from the east to learn important details

v. 8:
- Herod's words sounded good, but we find his heart plotted evil. So Herod in his selfishness misses a great opportunity to find salvation.

v. 9:
- The wise men heard the information and continued their search, but God still led them so they wouldn't make a mistake.
- Many have fruitlessly speculated about the star.
- What was it and how could it lead them to the very house where the Christ Child lived?
- God's miracles, always used with good purpose, humble us before His greatness.

v. 10:
- They were exceedingly joyful that God was leading them to their goal.

v. 11:
- God led them right to their goal.
- Notice that Jesus and family were now living in a house.
- The wise men were not too proud to fall down in humble worship before God, giving Him their hearts and their precious gifts.
- Gold would immediately prove useful to Mary and Joseph as they served the Lord by traveling to Egypt.
- The frankincense and myrrh also were expensive materials that could be sold, if not used.
- Note Isaiah's prophesy of these gifts (60:6).
- Many have seen symbolism in these gifts: frankincense of pure faith and prayers ascending to heaven, myrrh to be used to bury Jesus after His crucifixion, and gold for the exalted king.

v. 12:
- God again guided the wise men who willingly obeyed and served God as He protected Jesus from Herod.

v. 13:
- Jesus needed further protection.
- God also instructed Joseph through a dream to flee to Egypt because Herod, blinded by sin, would seek to destroy the innocent child.

v. 14:
- Without questioning the need for the long journey, Joseph immediately left in secret for the safety of Egypt.

v. 15:
- Details, yet God announced them over 500 years before through Hosea 11:1 that all might know their Savior when He was revealed. v. 16: although Herod tried to deceive the wise men and God, Herod got angry when the tables were turned.

▸ Misusing the information of the wise men, Herod's horrible, evil anger was thorough as he destroyed all the children two years or younger, not only in Bethlehem but all the surrounding areas as well.

vs. 17-18
▸ Although God knew about the evil that would come He did not cause it.
▸ His messenger, Jeremiah (31:15) warned of the great misery caused by the crime.
▸ Rachel, one of Jacob's wives, died at the site of Bethlehem giving birth to Benjamin.

vs. 19-20
▸ Herod died, (despite his attempts to remain on the throne) and God called for His Son through a dream to Joseph.
▸ The one who ordered the "search to destroy mission" against Jesus was dead, so the whole family could return to Israel.

v. 21:
▸ Again, Joseph obediently traveled at God's instruction to God's goal.

v. 22:
▸ Archelaus, Herod's son, was just as wicked and dangerous as his father.
▸ So God directed the family to the safety of Galilee.

v. 23:
▸ And yet God's plans were not thwarted by the schemes of men, rather they were fulfilled despite the wicked people of the world.
▸ This prophecy is more subtle and not actually a direct quotation.
▸ "The name Nazareth is derived from a Hebrew word meaning a branch or tender offshoot. Thus the Messiah is called in Isaiah 11:1" (Rupprecht. p.54)

## STUDENT PRAYER

O Lord, You used a star and Your Word to lead the wise men to worship before Jesus. You made known that Your Son is the Savior for all peoples. We thank and praise you for leading us also by Your Word to worship our Savior Jesus. Continue to enable Your Word to lead people to their Savior and to protect your Church from the attacks of all evil. Bless each of us with joyous, generous hearts, willing to give our gifts for Your work in the world. In the name of the Light of the World, our Savior Jesus, we pray. Amen

## PRESENTATION

How could people from a far country find the house where the Child Jesus was so that they could worship Him? God helped lead them, not only with a star, but with His Word, so they went right to Jesus.

{Some illustrations of the events might help present it (e.g the throne room of the wicked king Herod whom God continually thwarted; The wise men traveling far to then bow with their gifts before the Lord Jesus; The parents of Jesus carrying Him to and from Egypt.). God's hand is seen throughout, guiding the wise men to Jesus and protecting Jesus from Herod.}

Briefly review previous story as time allows. Make links to the new story when possible.
Tell the story: Teachers, be encouraged to tell the story in your own words while remaining faithful to the scriptural account. When scripture records the story in more than one place, you may want to harmonize the accounts (including extra details found in each account.) Let the students know where they can find the additional details in the Bible.

Discuss the story: While reviewing the major events of the story, discuss the possible applications to the students' lives. Ask questions that make them think about the story and show that they understand the story

## APPLICATIONS

1.    As God led the wise men to Jesus, so God has led us to find Jesus. He uses different ways to lead us to Jesus but always the same means or tool does the work - God's Word. Where in the story did God use His Word to point people to Jesus? (God's Word told about the star, locations, and events in connection with Jesus; other people shared His Word). We seldom have a star guiding us to find Jesus; but, parents, family, friends, personal study, teachers, pastors, and others bring God's Word to us, revealing where we may find Jesus to worship Him.

2.    We also can help others find Jesus in God's Word and show them that Jesus is everyone's Savior. We can even help people far away, across the world, find Jesus when we send them Bibles or missionaries to carry God's Word to them.

3.    With joy in their hearts, the wise men gave of their best! They gave expensive gifts of gold, frankincense, and myrrh. Giving any gift to God is to be done with joy and love for our Savior and then no gift is too great or too small when given in faith. Some have said that we should give to our Lord the "gold" of faith, the "frankincense" of prayer, and the "myrrh" of repentance.

## PASSAGES

These passages can be assigned as memory work or simply discussed in class as to how they fit the lesson.

Lower
Psalms 37:5 - Commit your way to the LORD, Trust also in Him, And He shall bring it to pass.
Isaiah 49:6 - Indeed He says, "I will also give You as a light to the Gentiles, That You should be My salvation to the ends of the earth."

Middle any of the above and...
Isaiah 60:2-3 - For behold, the darkness shall cover the earth, And deep darkness the people; But the LORD will arise over you, And His glory will be seen upon you. The Gentiles shall come to your light, And kings to the brightness of your rising.

Upper any of the above and...
Micah 5:2 - But you, Bethlehem Ephrathah, though you are little among the thousands of Judah, yet out of you shall come forth to Me The One to be Ruler in Israel, Whose goings forth are from of old, from everlasting.
Psalms 2:2-4 - The kings of the earth set themselves, And the rulers take counsel together, Against the LORD and against His Anointed, saying, "Let us break Their bonds in pieces And cast away Their cords from us." He who sits in the heavens shall laugh; The LORD shall hold them in derision.

## HYMN CHOICES
"Hail, Thou Source of Every Blessing" (TLH 129 1-3)
"As with Gladness Men of Old" (TLH 127 any or all)
"O Jesus, King of Glory" (TLH 130 1-4,6)

## 5

## STORY
Twelve-year-old Jesus in the Temple - Luke 2:40-52

## TEACHER PRAYER
Dear Father in heaven, send Your Spirit among us to show to us, Your Son Jesus as a young man, eager to do Your will, to hear Your Word, and to obey not only You but also His earthly parents. Let them see Jesus' love for them as He carried out also this part of Your plan to save sinners. May His love for us draw us to Him in repentance and faith, trusting in Him for salvation and inspiring us to live according to Your will. In His name we pray, Amen

## VOCABULARY
*Feast of the Passover* - God commanded this week-long annual feast. As part of the events of Israel's exodus from Egypt, the Passover pictures how a lamb (Christ) would save believers from eternal death. (cf. Ex 23:14-17, Dt. 16, v16)
*"was subject"* - Jesus placed himself under the authority of His earthly parents in obedience to the 4th commandment to keep also this commandment for us.

## OUTER AIM
The boy Jesus came to do His heavenly Father's business.

## INNER AIM
Jesus willingly treasured God's Word perfectly for us.

## BACKGROUND
*(Rupprecht Bible History References Vol. 2, pp. 54-62)*
This is the only event from Jesus' childhood recorded for us in the Canonical Scriptures. The Holy Spirit purposely shows us that even as a young child Jesus knew He was here to carry out God's plan that He would be the Savior of the world. In this account Jesus followed His Father's plans in a number of ways: a) Jesus kept the third commandment through His desire to study the Word of God and also as He kept the Old Testament Feast of the Passover even as a young boy. b) Jesus kept the 4th commandment as He respectfully answered His mother, Mary, and also "was subject" or perfectly obedient to His parents. In this and other ways Jesus grew in favor with God as our perfect substitute. Below are notes on each verse of the account:
Luke 2:41
- According to the Law of Moses, every adult Jewish man was obligated to attend three annual feasts in Jerusalem: The Feast of the Passover, the Feast of Weeks, and the Feast of Tabernacles.
- Often the entire Jewish family would make the journey, as was the case in this episode.

v. 42
- Customarily, male children began their formal education in the Scriptures at the age of five years.
- From five to ten years of age, their religious education focused only on the Scriptures.
- Then from the ages of ten to fifteen, instruction began to include the "traditions of the elders" or commentary notes on the Bible.
- At twelve years the boy was considered responsible for his religious instruction in a way similar to our modern custom of Confirmation.

v. 43
- The feast of the Passover lasted for an entire week before families would return to their homes.

► In one of those incidents that sometimes happens at some point in many families, the parents assumed that when they were leaving, their entire family was with them.

► But Jesus remained behind in Jerusalem without his parents immediately realizing it.

v. 44

► Traveling on foot with all the other people returning from the feast, Mary and Joseph began looking for Jesus near the end of the day.

► They searched the likely places among relatives and friends.

v. 45

► It took them another day to return to Jerusalem as they continued their unsuccessful search for Jesus.

v. 46

► Three days included two days of traveling and another day searching in Jerusalem.

► The temple (including sanctuary and mall) was a large group of buildings including an area customarily used for education and discussions with the priests and other religious teachers.

► There, as a diligent student of the Word, Jesus listened to the teachers and asked them questions to learn more and more.

v. 47

► Jesus greatly astounded the people who were listening in on the discussions.

► His insight or understanding and answers to questions put to Him astounded them.

v. 48

► When Joseph and Mary found the boy Jesus, they were overwhelmed by the situation.

► Mary rebuked Jesus for causing both His father and mother such painful anxiety from having to search for Him for so long.

v. 49

► But Jesus hadn't done anything they shouldn't have expected Him to do.

► He hadn't disobeyed them (for that would have been a sin and disqualified Him as our Savior).

► Jesus reminded them that it was necessary that He be doing the things His (heavenly) Father had asked Him to do.

v. 50

► But His earthly parents didn't understand what He meant by those words.

v. 51

► Nevertheless, Jesus obediently returned with His parents to Nazareth and was subject to them, as a perfect child would be to His parents.

► But Mary remembered the event and, along with the other unusual events of Jesus life, as she saw Jesus' life and mission unfold.

v. 52

► Jesus grew up physically but also intellectually, gaining knowledge and learning how to correctly apply it.

► As Jesus did all things perfectly while growing up (hard for us sinners to imagine), both God and those people around Jesus were favorably impressed with Him.

## STUDENT PRAYER

Dear Father in heaven, even as a little child, Jesus did Your will and worked for our salvation. Help us to live thankful lives, eager to hear Your word, and to obey not only You but those whom you have placed over us for our care. And when we fall, bring us back to You in repentance and faith, trusting in Your forgiveness and the Salvation that Jesus, Your Son through His perfect obedience, gained for us. We pray, trusting in Jesus, Amen.

## PRESENTATION

You might begin by asking the students what kind of child they think Jesus was. Direct their thoughts to His attitude to God and church and also His obedience to parents. Help the students to realize that Jesus grew up as a child like us but unlike us was perfectly without sin throughout. Even as a child, Jesus knew that his mission in life was to save the world from their sins.

Explore the concept of "tempted in all points like as we are," yet without sin (Heb. 2:17-18 and 4:15).

Or possibly use the festivals of the New Testament Church: 1) which are the main festivals (three), 2) whether God commands them or not and 3) why do we celebrate them and also Sunday?

Jesus went to church as a young man.

Briefly review previous story as time allows. Make links to the new story when possible.

Tell the story: Teachers, be encouraged to tell the story in your own words while remaining faithful to the scriptural account. When scripture records the story in more than one place, you may want to harmonize the accounts (including extra details found in each account.) Let the students know where they can find the additional details in the Bible.

Discuss the story: While reviewing the major events of the story, discuss the possible applications to the students' lives. Ask questions that make them think about the story and show that they understand the story.

## APPLICATIONS

The teacher may have to choose among a number of possible applications from this story:

1.     Jesus teaches children how important God's Word is for their life as well. For God's Word tells them about Jesus their Savior. This leads to other applications: a.) We will want to hear and learn from God's Word regularly, whether at home, or church, or in church school. b.) We will want to live God's Word in our lives by believing it, repenting of our sins and looking to Jesus for forgiveness, and following God's will for our lives.

2.     When we have the opportunity or privilege to hear God's Word, we will want to listen carefully to learn from God. We don't want to become guilty of despising God's Word by fooling around, not paying attention, disrupting other people who are listening, by daydreaming, or dozing. Luke 11:28

3.     It is good to remember that our salvation was earned not only by Jesus' death on the cross and resurrection back to life, but also by His perfect life of obedience. This story shows Jesus keeping the 1st, 3rd, and 4th commandments of God. Because Jesus grew up just as we, yet without sin, we know that His death also pays for the sins of our childhood and youth, because Jesus perfectly kept the Law also in this time of His life.

4.     W.D.J.D.? What did Jesus do? Jesus spent His entire earthly life doing His Father's will which was saving us from our sin. His perfect life gives us many examples to help us see how we can express our thankfulness to Him by doing God's will in our lives.

## PASSAGES

These passages can be assigned as memory work or simply discussed in class as to how they fit the lesson.

Lower

Luke 11:28 - (Jesus said) "Blessed are those who hear the word of God and keep it!"

Psalms 119:105 - Your word is a lamp to my feet And a light to my path.

Middle any of the above and...

Psalms 84:10 - For a day in Your courts is better than a thousand. I would rather be a doorkeeper in the house of my God than dwell in the tents of wickedness.

Hebrews 7:26 - For such a High Priest was fitting for us, who is holy, harmless, undefiled, separate from sinners.

Upper any of the above and...

Hebrews 4:15 - For we do not have a High Priest who cannot sympathize with our weaknesses, but was in all points tempted as we are, yet without sin.

John 5:24 - "Most assuredly, I say to you, he who hears My word and believes in Him who sent Me has everlasting life, and shall not come into judgment, but has passed from death into life.

## HYMN CHOICES

"O God, Thou Faithful God," (TLH 395 1-3)

"One Thing's Needful; Lord, This Treasure" (TLH 366 1 & others)

"Abide, O Dearest Jesus" (TLH 53 1-2,4)

## 6

## STORY

The Ministry of John and Baptism of Jesus - Matthew 3:1-17
(Note: the focus is on the baptism of Jesus and less so on the work of John the Baptist)
(Also see for John's ministry: Mark 1:1-8, Luke 3:1-8; John 1:19-28;)
(Also see for Jesus' baptism: Mark 1:9-11; Luke 3:21-22; John 1:29-34)

## TEACHER PRAYER

Dear Father in Heaven, in this world today many teach that people can be saved by any religion.  Yet at
the Baptism of Jesus, you proclaimed that Jesus is Your Son and that He is the only Savior of the world.  Only Jesus kept the law perfectly in our stead, then suffered the punishment of our sins to purchase our forgiveness.  Help me to teach the students in my care to trust only in Jesus for forgiveness, the One You have declared to be our Savior.  In Your name  I pray, Amen.

## VOCABULARY

*John the Baptist* - He was the first one whom God authorized to baptize.  If the students get this confused with "the Baptists", you might refer to John as "John, the one who
baptized" or "the Baptizer".  You may need to distinguish between John the Baptist and John the Apostle, the inspired writer of 5 books of the New Testament.

*Baptize* - literally means "to apply water".  The method of baptism isn't clear in scripture beyond that meaning.  Apparently Jesus was in the water of the Jordan River for His baptism (cf v 16) but nowhere
 are we directed to immerse for a proper baptism.

*Pharisees and Sadducees* - Two groups of religious leaders of the Jewish people of Jesus' time. They are often portrayed in scripture as leaders who falsely claimed they kept the laws of God perfectly and expected perfection of the people. They became enemies of Christ, eventually orchestrating His crucifixion.

*Brood of Vipers* - very poisonous, dangerous snakes.

*Repentance* - Sorrow over sins and faith in Jesus Christ for the forgiveness of sins.

*Winnowing fan, purge, chaff* - At harvest time, grain was purged (cleaned) by hand using a method called winnowing - to separate the kernels of grain from the chaff, husks, and extra leaves that were thrown away.  The winnowing fan was used to pick up the mixture of grain and other items to throw it in the air so the wind could blow away the chaff, while the grain fell back down to the threshing floor.

*Messiah* - (the term is not in the scripture itself but used in the Inner Aim.) the Old Testament word for
the New Testament Word "Christ".  Both words mean "Anointed One."  Anointing was the symbolic ceremony used to place a person into an official office: Prophet, Priest, or King.  Jesus served in all three
of these offices.

*Triune* - The special quality of our God of being three distinct Persons in one True God.

## OUTER AIM
Jesus was baptized to publicly begin His ministry as our Savior.

## INNER AIM
God declared Jesus to be the Promised Messiah, our Savior.

## BACKGROUND
*(Rupprecht Bible History References Vol.2, pp. 64-74 and pp. 75-78)*
When Jesus was thirty years old, it was time for Him to begin the public journey that would lead Him to the cross. The baptism of Jesus marks the beginning of His ministry (His service for us) and identifies Him as the promised Messiah. Review the story of the birth of John and what it means that he was the forerunner of Jesus, i.e., to prepare the way for Jesus.

\*\*\* John's ministry \*\*\*
(Note: Because the focus of this lesson is on the baptism of Jesus, the notes for John's ministry are only based on the account from Matthew 3:1-17 and not other references.)

Matthew 3:1
 This verse marks the beginning of a new time period, the beginning of the ministries or public service of John the Baptist and (about 6 months later) Jesus. Jewish law didn't allow men to publicly teach or preach until they were 30 years of age or older.
v. 2
 ▸     John preached both the Law and the Gospel.
 ▸     The Law shows the people their sins, calling them to repentance and preparing their hearts for Jesus, their Savior.
 ▸     The Kingdom of heaven is God's ruling activity over our hearts and lives through the Good News of Jesus, Who was already on the scene.
v. 3
 ▸     Isaiah proclaimed God's promise that God would send a messenger who would preach in the wilderness to prepare the way for God Himself to come to people's hearts.
v. 4
 ▸     John's clothing and food showed the simple, humble life he led as one whom God had dedicated to the special mission of preparing people to meet their Savior.
vs. 5-6
 ▸     People from a wide area around the Jordan and Southern Palestine went to hear John's message.
 ▸     God blessed his ministry so that the people not only heard but responded to his important message.
v. 7
 ▸     Scripture in various places exposes the Sadducees and Pharisees as hypocrites who acted holy but were not truly holy.
 ▸     John's harsh words were meant to break down their trust in their own holiness.
 ▸     They needed to repent of their sins and seek forgiveness so  they wouldn't be condemned by God's anger against sin.
vs. 8-9
 ▸     The Pharisees and Sadducees often trusted that because they were descendants of Abraham, God would forgive them their sins.
 ▸     John told them that true repentance with faith shows itself in works that demonstrate genuine sorrow over sinfulness and faith in God's forgiveness.

v. 10

▸ This was a picture of how God condemns to the fires of hell those who do not repent of their sins through faith in Jesus.

▸ True repentance and faith show themselves with the good works.

v. 11

▸ John here spoke of Jesus coming among them.

▸ John's work was to prepare people to know Jesus when He came.

▸ In humility John realized that he did not deserve to serve Jesus in even the simplest way because Jesus was greater than John.

▸ Jesus would bless the people with the Holy Spirit and powerful faith.

v. 12

▸ (see vocabulary) The wheat God would keep, but the chaff or waste from the winnowing process would be gathered for burning.

▸ This pictures God separating the repentant believers from unrepentant unbelievers, sending the former to heaven and the latter to hell.

*** Jesus' Baptism ***

v. 13

▸ Galilee was the northern region of Palestine where Jesus spent a good part of His ministry.

▸ John was baptizing along the Jordan river east of Jerusalem. See a map.

v. 14

▸ John recognized that Jesus was the Son of God.

▸ John knew his own sinfulness and need to repent and be cleansed by Jesus, so John questioned why Jesus wanted John to baptize Him.

v. 15

▸ John's baptism was a Means of Grace that bestowed the forgiveness of sins, similiar to the baptism later instituted by Jesus.

▸ Jesus was without sin, and did not need the forgiveness offered by baptism.

▸ Jesus urged John to permit Him to be baptized because it was the right thing to do.

▸ When Jesus explained that it was intended to "fulfill all righteousness", John baptized Jesus.

v 16

▸ As soon as Jesus was baptized, some amazing events followed that marked the beginning of Jesus' public service or work for us.

▸ Luke 3:21 mentions that Jesus was praying when the events took place.

▸ The heavens were opened in a way that scripture leaves to our imaginations, not giving distracting details.

▸ Both Jesus and John (and others probably) saw the Spirit of God (the Holy Spirit) in the form of a dove (see Luke 3:22) descending and landing on Jesus. (cf. John 1:32-34 also: Acts 10:38, Luke 4:18ff, Is 49:8,9; 61:1,2).

v. 17

▸ And at the same time, a voice from heaven (God the Father) announced that God was well pleased with Jesus, His beloved Son.

▸ This was God's public stamp of approval on Jesus as the Messiah and Savior at the beginning of His ministry.

▸ Compare also Jesus' transfiguration (Lesson 16).

## STUDENT PRAYER

Dear Heavenly Father, thank you for showing us that through His baptism Jesus is Your Son sent to be our Savior. Help us to picture in our hearts Jesus' baptism and how He kept the Law for us to be our perfect Savior. When we sin, call us to repentance and faith that Jesus Christ, Your Son, washes us clean from all our sin, just as our baptism reminds us. We ask this in Jesus' Name. Amen.

## PRESENTATION

Note: Whole sermons are preached on the work of John the Baptizer. In this story, time constraints may require you to summarize John's work and mission. God sent him to prepare people's hearts for Jesus. He did that by preaching the law that showed people their sins, calling for them to repent with words and deeds. John also preached the Gospel when he pointed them to Jesus as their Savior. The focus of the lesson will be on Jesus' baptism which marks the beginning of Jesus' public ministry as our Savior.

## APPLICATIONS

1.      Why was Jesus baptized? Jesus was baptized to obey the Law of God perfectly for us because we are not able to do that. He was acting in our place in order to be able to be punished for our sins in our place. How does your baptism compare? Our baptism cleanses us from sins through faith that Jesus forgives us our sins because He suffered for them already on the cross, although Jesus was not guilty of any sin.

2.      God told us at Jesus' baptism that Jesus was His Son so that people then and now would know He is the Savior whom God sent to save the world from sin. There is no one else like Jesus!

## PASSAGES

These passages can be assigned as memory work or simply discussed in class as to how they fit the lesson.

Lower
John 3:16 - For God so loved the world that He gave His only begotten Son, that whoever believes in Him should not perish but have everlasting life.

Middle any of the above and...
1 John 1:7, 9 - The blood of Jesus Christ His Son cleanses us from all sin. If we confess our sins, He is faithful and just to forgive us our sins and to cleanse us from all unrighteousness.

Upper any of the above and...
Ephesians 5:25-26 - Christ also loved the church and gave Himself for her, that He might sanctify and cleanse her with the washing of water by the word.
Galatians 4:4-5 - But when the fullness of the time had come, God sent forth His Son, born of a woman,
born under the law, to redeem those who were under the law, that we might receive the adoption as sons.

## HYMN CHOICES

"On Jordan's Bank the Baptist's Cry" (TLH 63 1-3)
"God Loved the World so that He Gave" (TLH 245 1,4,5)
"He That Believes and is Baptized" (TLH 301 1-2)

## 7

## STORY
The Temptation of Jesus - Matthew 4:1-11

## TEACHER PRAYER
Dear Heavenly Father who loves us all, enable me to overcome the temptations the devil throws at me. Forgive me for those times when I failed to use Your Word and fell into sin. Thank You for the times when You have prevented me from falling into temptation. I know that the students in my care will, throughout their life, also face many powerful and dangerous temptations. Help me to impress upon them how with Your Word and the victory Christ has won, they, by Your grace, have the resources to overcome the temptations they face. Forgive them when they fall and lead them to appreciate it when You give them the victories in Christ, in whose name I pray. Amen.

## VOCABULARY
*Fasted* - not eating anything and perhaps not drinking anything. In this case, going without food for 40 days and nights.

*Tempter* - another name for the Devil, or Satan. Here it describes what the Devil was doing to Jesus.

*Pinnacle* - cf Rupprecht - a wing or high point on the temple, speculated to be 600-700 ft high.

*opportune time* - another favorable time to tempt Jesus such as in Gethsemane.

## OUTER AIM
Jesus did not sin when the Devil tempted Him.

## INNER AIM
Jesus overcame the Devil for us.

## BACKGROUND
*(Rupprecht Bible History References Vol.2, pp. 78-82 and cf. Spokesman, August 1997, pp. 6-8)*
The Devil is that fallen angel who was thrown out of heaven and seeks his revenge by introducing and expanding sin into the world. Read Genesis 3 and Revelation 12:7-12, esp v 11.

The devil also tempted Jesus, as we see here and in Hebrews 4:14-15. If the Devil could have successfully led Jesus to sin, then Jesus could not have been our Savior and no one else could deliver us from sin, death, and the power of the Devil. Thanks be to God who gives us the victory over the Devil.

Harmony note: Matthew and Luke record the same temptations, though in a different order. The wording in Matthew suggests the order, and nothing in Luke contradicts that order, so it is the one generally used.

Matthew 4:1
▸ Immediately (Mark 1:12) after Jesus' baptism (Luke 4:1), Jesus was led by the Holy Spirit into a wilderness (location unknown) to be tempted by the devil.
▸ No one was there to come to His aid.
▸ He would face the temptations alone.
▸ This too was part of God's plan of salvation as a real and valid testing of Jesus' human nature and His determination to save us by His self-sacrifice.

v. 2

▸ Jesus became genuinely hungry because He was truly human.

▸ To be our true substitute and Savior, in no way could Jesus use His Divine nature to withstand these temptations, but relied upon the resources available to Him as a human being.

▸ He was to be tempted in the same way we are, yet without sin.

▸ Mark 1:13 and Luke 4:2 add that those 40 days included continual temptation by the Devil.

▸ God chose to tell us of only three of the temptations used as prime examples of all the other temptations.

v. 3

▸ The Devil used multiple approaches here.

▸ Knowing Jesus' weakness as a result of fasting, he encouraged Jesus to use His divine power for His own bodily needs instead of acting as our true human substitute under the laws of nature.

▸ The Devil used Jesus' hunger and human limitations to suggest that Jesus serve Himself instead of being so self-sacrificing.

v. 4

▸ Jesus quoted Deuteronomy 8:3 which, especially in its context, shows that even when physically hungry, we should obey God and continue to trust that God will sustain us according to His Word.

▸ The Word of God is the best tool available to a human fighting the Devil.

▸ The goal of this temptation, as in the others, was: to get Jesus to think of His needs, His "rights", and what He "deserves", (rather than ours). After all, the Devil reasoned, why should God lower Himself to go through with this "self-sacrifice"?

v. 5

▸ God permitted Jesus to be taken by the Devil to the Holy City, Jerusalem, onto a high point of the temple.

v. 6

▸ Again we see how tricky the Devil was.

▸ He also knew and thus misused scripture to tempt Jesus. But the Devil left out the important words "to keep you in all your ways," which remind us that the promises of the passage apply when we walk in the paths that God has appointed for us.

▸ Again the Devil challenged Jesus' position as the Son of God.

▸ Some commentators say that the Devil was trying to get Jesus to seek the popularity of the people with a miraculous demonstration of self-preservation. If Jesus could survive the jump from 600 ft, the crowds below would give Him celebrity status without Jesus having to fulfill His mission as our Savior, an easy out.

▸ This was the issue again. The Devil tried to tempt Jesus: "Why not get the honor and acclaim you deserve by a miracle (rather then going through all that self-sacrifice?)"

v. 7

▸ Jesus' reply, again from the Scriptures, turned back the Devil's temptation again.

▸ Notice Jesus used "it is written," instead of speaking on His authority as God.

▸ From Deuteronomy 6:6 Jesus warned that we are not to tempt God by our own foolishness and expect Him to deliver us.

v. 8

▸ Many have speculated on which mountain this occurred without having any scripture to confirm their guesses. No mountain by itself provides a view of all the kingdoms of the world and their glory. So that implies the Devil has the power to create visions for deceitful purposes. Jesus actually saw them through whatever means the devil had to reveal his version of them.

v. 9
- ▸ This temptation connected to the many prophecies that Jesus would rule over all the earth.
- ▸ The Devil was again offering an easy out. Instead of Jesus having to live a perfect life, to suffer and to die, the devil suggested Jesus could have such power by an easier way.
- ▸ Of course the Devil doesn't own anything on earth, for the earth is the Lord's and the fullness of it.
- ▸ His rulership as the Prince of Darkness exists only as people's hearts are ruled by him.

v. 10
- ▸ Jesus' reply, again from Scripture, included also the command for Satan to leave.
- ▸ Jesus not only overcame Satan's temptation but reaffirmed His own commitment to serve His heavenly Father, even to the death of the cross in order to be our self-sacrificing Savior.

v. 11
- ▸ The Devil left Jesus alone when Jesus ordered him away, for Jesus had won all of these battles, even as He would remain the Ultimate Victor keeping a perfect record even with His death.
- ▸ Notice Luke mentions that at other favorable times through Jesus' life, the Devil tempted Jesus (compare Matthew 16:23, Maundy Thursday).
- ▸ After these temptations, God sent His angels to serve Jesus with praise and such needs as they could meet.

## STUDENT PRAYER

Dear Heavenly Father, even as we pray in the Lord's Prayer, "Lead us not into temptation, but deliver us from evil," so deliver us from temptation and evil. Strengthen our faith and increase our knowledge of Your Word so that we, by Your Grace, may overcome the Devil through Jesus' victory for us. Help us to see and use the escape from temptation that You have promised to provide us. Forgive us for the times when we have fallen into temptation. May we be thankful when You give us each victory, so that when our battles are ended, You will have brought us through this life to share in the Victory that Jesus won for us. We pray, believing in the name of Jesus our Victorious Savior, Amen.

## PRESENTATION

Briefly review previous story as time allows. Make links to the new story when possible.

Tell the story: Teachers are encouraged to tell the story in their own words while remaining faithful to the scriptural account. When a story is recorded in more than one place in Scripture, teachers may want to harmonize the account (including extra details found in each account.) When harmonizing, let the students know that the story is found in more than one place in the Bible. Then they can see the additional details are also found in the Bible.

Discuss the story. While reviewing the major events of the story, discuss the possible applications to the students' lives. Ask questions that make them think about the story and show that they understand the story.

## APPLICATIONS

1. What are temptations that children particularly face? (Examples can be drawn from family life, friendships, and general review of the commandments). What are some of the weapons that God has given us to use when we are faced with those temptations? Consider passages like Ephesians 6:10-18; 1 Corinthians 10:13: (Be both general and think of specific passages that could be used.)

2. Why does the Devil work so hard to tempt us to sin? What would happen if we just gave in to temptations and stopped fighting to do what's right? If we fall into sin, whose fault is it? Did the Devil make you do it? If we fall, where can we go for forgiveness? Who provides us the victory over each temptation and ultimately over sin, death, and the Devil? When will we no longer have to worry about being tempted to sin?

## PASSAGES

These passages can be assigned as memory work or simply discussed in class as to how they fit the lesson. Discuss as time permits: Ephesians 6:10-18; 1 Corinthians 10:13

Lower
Matthew 26:41 - "Watch and pray, lest you enter into temptation. The spirit indeed is willing, but the flesh is weak."

Middle any of the above and...
1 Peter 5:8 - Be sober, be vigilant; because your adversary the devil walks about like a roaring lion, seeking whom he may devour.
Hebrews 4:15 - (Jesus) was in all points tempted as we are, yet without sin.

Upper any of the above and...
1 Corinthians 10:13 - No temptation has overtaken you except such as is common to man; but God is faithful, who will not allow you to be tempted beyond what you are able, but with the temptation will also make the way of escape, that you may be able to bear it.

## HYMN CHOICES

"I am Trusting Thee, Lord Jesus" (TLH 428 all, esp 1, 5-6)
"Rise, My Soul, to Watch and Pray" (TLH 446 all, esp 1, 5-6)
"A Mighty Fortress is Our God" (TLH 262 all)

## STORY

The Marriage at Cana - John 2:1-12

## TEACHER PRAYER

Dear Father in Heaven, through the miracle at the wedding at Cana help us to believe that He was not only a good man, but also the Son of God sent to be our Savior. Strengthen our faith in Him that we may turn to Him both for forgiveness and for whatever needs we may have. And having asked, help us to leave our needs in His powerful hands to meet them according to His will. You, O Lord, established the estate of marriage from the 6th day of Creation. Today marriages are so much under attack and so many homes lie shattered by thoughtless sin and selfishness. I pray that you would impress on us Your desire for a Christ centered home where Jesus Christ's blessing will rest, even as He blessed with His presence and glory that marriage at Cana. In Jesus Name we ask, Amen.

## VOCABULARY

*Manner of purification* - Jewish customs and religious ceremonies used large quantities of water for washing and cleaning. Guests would bathe their feet upon entering the house; people would wash before and after every meal, and various household objects would be cleansed. The water was stored in large pots.
*Master of the feast* - he was in charge of the servants and the arrangements for the feast. Wine and food were prepared under his supervision before being given to the guests.
*Manifested His glory* - revealed, or made known His divinity, that He was God as well as man.

## OUTER AIM

Jesus changed water into wine to show He is God.

## INNER AIM

Jesus' miracles strengthen our faith that He is God and will take care of all our needs.

## BACKGROUND

*Rupprecht Bible History References Vol.2, pp. 94-99)*
Although Jesus is God, in order to save us He took the body of a human being and lived under the laws of God. When He walked this earth those thirty-three years of His life, people saw Him primarily as a human being. Yet at times, Jesus let people see that He was also true God as He helped people with their problems and the effects of sin. This helped strengthen the faith of those who believed in Him as their Lord and Savior. It also further convicted those who rejected Jesus. (John 20:30-31; 10:37-38)

John 2:1
- A wedding was an especially joyous occasion for the Jews.
- The bride was led to the home of the groom.
- After the wedding, the feast would begin. This wedding feast might last for more than a day.
- Then the bridal couple went to the bridal chamber.
- This was the third day after John the Baptist sent Andrew and John to follow Jesus.
- This Cana is traditionally placed about 4 miles north east of Nazareth, Jesus' home town. See Rupprecht for connection of Galilee with Is 9:1-2.
- Jesus' mother Mary was there, but no mention is made of Joseph.

v. 2

▸ Jesus and His disciples attend the wedding.

▸ Five disciples had been called at this point: Andrew, Peter, John, Philip and Nathaniel (Bartholomew).

▸ From this many see Jesus' continued blessing on the estate of marriage and of celebrating weddings as special occasions.

▸ This event brings us to see that God favors marriage; the drink of choice may be alcoholic, but we know God doesn't approve of drunkenness.

v. 3

▸ Wine, often mixed with water, was used commonly throughout Palestine since much of the water was not good for drinking. And at a celebration it was also appropriate.

▸ Whether too many guests had come or the family had insufficient funds, the celebration (which lasted sometimes for days) had used up all the wine.

▸ Mary came to Jesus, requesting His special aid for the family when they ran out of wine.

▸ From Jesus' reply in the next verse, we sense that Jesus thought she was out of line with her expectations of Him.

v. 4

▸ Note that Jesus calls her only "woman" (like the modern term, "lady") and not "Mother." His mild rebuke lets her know that in matters of His work, she does not have authority over Him.

▸ (This passage condemns the false Catholic belief that Mary is "Co-redemptrix" or the "Queen of Heaven" or in some way equal to, or even greater than Jesus.)

▸ Jesus knew full well the situation and had in mind what He would do and when He would do it.

v. 5

▸ Mary accepted the rebuke of Jesus, yet showed her faith in Him with this request to the servants of the house.

▸ Her request implied the thought, "No matter how ridiculous it may seem, do it." Cf. 2 Kings 5:1-18

v. 6

▸ See vocabulary notes. Note the quantity: 120-130 gallons.

v. 7

▸ The servants thus far did what Jesus commanded, carrying water to the house to fill the jars to the brim.

v. 8

▸ Here the servants' faith was tested.

▸ Taking water to be used as wine to the master of the feast could get them into serious trouble.

▸ Despite that, they again obeyed Jesus and took the water to the Master of the feast. (see vocabulary notes.)

v. 9

▸ The man in charge of the feast suddenly found an abundant source of wine, whereas shortly before the wine had been gone.

▸ Only the servants knew where the wine had come from, the miracle performed by Jesus.

v. 10

▸ The wine that Jesus so graciously and miraculously provided not only was real wine but was better in quality than what had been previously served.

▸ This gift to His hosts served their needs and would be a gift they could keep on using for months or years.

v. 11

▸ This miracle was the first one that Jesus performed.

▸ Other traditions and writings speak of Jesus doing miracles in His youth, but this scripture contradicts them.

▸ He did this miracle a) to serve the needs of others and b) to reveal to people that He was the Christ, the Son of God, prophesied to be their Savior.

▸ We see that through this sign, Jesus' disciples believed in Him, as Jesus revealed the glory of His person, His purpose, and His work.

## STUDENT PRAYER

Dear God, Our Father in Heaven, help us to see through the awesome miracle He did that Jesus was not only a good man but also the Son of God come to earth to be our Savior. Teach us to turn to Jesus for our needs, knowing that in the way that is best for us, He will meet those needs, as He helped those people at Cana in their time of need. O Lord, bless our homes with your presence too and strengthen our trust in You for forgiveness of sins and all that we need. In Jesus' name we pray, Amen.

## PRESENTATION

Briefly review previous story as time allows. Make links to the new story when possible.
Tell the story: Teachers, be encouraged to tell the story in your own words while remaining faithful to the scriptural account.

Discuss the story: While reviewing the major events of the story, discuss the possible applications to the students' lives. Ask questions that make them think about the story and show that they understand the story.

## ACTIVITY

You may want to have the children glue page 4 on a separate sheet before doing this activity to make the vase more stable.

## APPLICATIONS

1. Jesus used a miracle to strengthen the faith of His people. God uses this story and the rest of God's Word to make our faith stronger as well. We cannot make genuine wine instantly from water, so what does this show us about Jesus?

2. Review why Jesus performed miracles. He did not do them to show-off, just to impress people with His power. He did not do them for selfish reasons. He did them to a) prove that He was the Son of God, true God and True Man in one person, and 2) to serve people in time of need. The miracles were signs that pointed to Jesus as the One who could make satisfaction for the sins of the world. Jesus' primary work was to die on the cross for the sins of the world, so the miracles were never intended to overshadow Jesus' purpose.

** Note: The discussion of whether God performs miracles today may be beyond the scope of the time given to your lesson. God still does miracles today though we may fail to recognize them as such. In our time of need, we leave it to God to provide whatever method of deliverance He considers best as we pray "Thy will be done." Because we have God's Word, we do not need to be shown miracles today to believe in God or Jesus as our Savior. (Luke 16;16-31; John 20:30-31; Romans 10:17)

## PASSAGES

These passages can be assigned as memory work or simply discussed in class as to how they fit the lesson. For possible discussion: Genesis 2:22-24 - God created the first marriage.

Lower
Psalms 50:15 - Call upon Me in the day of trouble; I will deliver you, and you shall glorify Me.

Middle any of the above and...
Genesis 2:24 - Therefore a man shall leave his father and mother and be joined to his wife, and they shall become one flesh.

Upper any of the above and...
John 20:30-31 - And truly Jesus did many other signs in the presence of His disciples, which are not written in this book; but these are written that you may believe that Jesus is the Christ, the Son of God, and that believing you may have life in His name.

## HYMN CHOICES

"Oh, Blest the House, Whate'er Befall" (TLH 625 all)
"Commit Whatever Grieves Thee" (TLH 520: 1,4, 5-9)
"The Lord My Shepherd Is" (TLH 426 :1-6)

## 9

## STORY

Peter's Catch of Fish and Jesus' Call of Apostles - Luke 5:1-11 & 6:12-16
(Also see: Matthew 4:18-22; 10:1-10, Mark 3:13-14)

## TEACHER PRAYER

Dear Lord Jesus, you have called me to be your teacher of the students entrusted to me. Help me to faithfully carry out my calling and let nothing distract me from serving You. Enable me to lay aside any doubts about my abilities but rather to trust You to provide the "catch" as I follow your command to throw the net of Your Word into the waters. Bless Your Word carried through me that my students will hear of Your great power and grace in sending Jesus and also sending those who tell others of Jesus so that in the end You may gather in an abundance of souls into heaven with You for all eternity. In You, Lord Jesus, I trust as I pray, Amen.

## VOCABULARY

*Multitude* - A large group of people. Many people came to hear and see Jesus at this point.
*Lake of Gennesaret* - also known as the Sea of Galilee, Sea of Tiberius (N.T.), or Sea of Chinnereth (O.T.). Located 60 miles NE of Jerusalem and 27 miles from the Mediterranean Sea. (see Rupprecht p 123) {see map}
*Forsook* - Left behind
*Simon the Zealot* - Zealots were a group of Jews who opposed the rule and authority of the Romans over the Jews. Sometimes they used violence for their cause. Jesus chose Simon, and delivered him from that bad company.
*Apostles* - people "sent out" - these were particular men whom Jesus would send out to preach the Gospel as eyewitnesses of Jesus' work and words. Their calling had a special authority needed in the early Church and their job was more specific than that of other believers who are called to spread the Word.

## OUTER AIM

Jesus called some fishermen to preach the Gospel.

## INNER AIM

Jesus enables those He calls to preach the Gospel.

## BACKGROUND

*(Rupprecht Bible History References Vol.2, pp. 122-130)*
This event happened after Jesus had been preaching for a year in Palestine (see Rupprecht p 122).Jesus had already called these men to faith (John 1:35-51, elsewhere), so they were believers. He then called them to apostleship - witnesses to the world of the crucified and risen Jesus. The emphasis is not on the miracle, or on these men and their faith. It is on Jesus and the power of His influence in their lives.
Luke 5:1
▸ Jesus had a large following of people by this time. They came to hear "the word of God."
v. 2
▸ Most fishing was done in the early morning or late evening. This was the middle of the day so they were washing their nets between shifts of fishing.
v. 3
▸ Jesus asked Simon (Peter) to take him out a little way from the land. This allowed Jesus a little space from the people and also made use of His location on the water to carry the sound farther to more people.

v. 4

▸ After Jesus had given the crowds enough to think about for a while, He commanded Peter to do a peculiar thing. Both the time of day and the location went against the usual rules of fishing. But Jesus said they would have a catch of fish.

v. 5

▸ Peter noted what also made the request peculiar, that after fishing the previous night, they had not caught anything. But Peter acted by faith at the command of Jesus.

v. 6

▸ The fishermen caught so many fish in their net that the net began breaking!

▸ This was a miracle because the catch was contrary to what anyone could have expected to happen.

v. 7

▸ The fishermen needed reinforcements, and even with two boats they had so many fish that the boats started to sink from the weight.

▸ This caused a strong message, preparing these men for what Jesus would ask of them next.

vs. 8-10a

▸ Peter, James, John, and those who saw the miracle recognized that only the power of God could have created such a huge catch of fish, despite.

▸ And in the presence of the holy God, all sinners (should) feel fear because of their sins and feel undeserving and thankful for even the smallest of blessings.

▸ Yet the sinner needs to turn to the Lord to receive forgiveness of sins through the Lord's grace in Jesus Christ.

v. 10b

▸ Jesus dispelled their fear with the command to "fear not," an echo of the angel's tidings to the shepherds.

▸ But Jesus continued with the promise to Peter, "from now on you will be fishers of men."

▸ Beyond the blessings of the catch of fish, God had a special calling for them. Jesus called them to be full-time apostles who would, by the power of the Word given to them, bring people into the kingdom of God, even as they had gathered the fish placed in the nets.

▸ They were not to fear that they did not have the power or abilities, for Jesus would gather in the souls of men as they faithfully followed His guidance.

v. 11

▸ With faith in what Jesus had said, these four men left behind the amazing catch of fish (which would have brought them great profit), their homes, and their trade and all else in order to take up the work to which Jesus had called them.

▸ Here is the powerful lesson of the miracle. By faith we are able to let go of all other blessings for the sake of Jesus and the particular callings He gives us. (Cf similar messages: Mark 8:34-38; Luke 9:57-62; 14:25-35)

Luke 6:12

▸ Jesus went to an isolated place and prayed. Especially before selecting the twelve particular men who were to serve as apostles, He knew He had to talk with his heavenly Father. And His prayer wasn't a quick, last minute prayer but He took the entire night to weigh the selection, even as He knew the shortcomings of those chosen.

v. 13

▸ Jesus had many disciples, people who believed in Him and followed Him to learn what He had to teach them. But from these many, He chose twelve whom He would send out with special authority as His chosen leaders to help carry the Gospel into the world.

vs. 14-16

▸ Scripture reveals more about some of these men, but we know that all of them were sinners in need of a Savior.

▸ They were called from a variety of common class trades, not highly educated, yet by God's grace enabled to serve in the special calling Jesus gave them.

▸ Although all of these men would show their sinful failings, it is only of Judas Iscariot, that we hear of a fatal sin.

▸ Jesus issued the call and gave the ability to serve in that calling, but the responsibility rested upon the person how faithfully he would carry out that work.

## STUDENT PRAYER

Dear Jesus in Heaven, Thank you for calling people to special tasks within Your Church to regularly teach us Your Word. Help us to appreciate them as your servants given for our good. We know that you have given each of us a calling for our lives, to serve You. Bless the work that we do in Your name that many people may be gathered into Your family as believers in You for their salvation. When we fail to serve You faithfully, provide those who will bring Your Word to us, calling for repentance and assuring us of Your forgiveness through Your death in our place, that in the end, we and many others may be gathered into heaven with You, in Whom we trust when we pray, Amen.

## PRESENTATION

Briefly review the previous story as time allows. Make links to the new story when possible.

Tell the story: Teachers, be encouraged to tell the story in your own words while remaining faithful to the scriptural account. When scripture records the story in more than one place, you may want to harmonize the accounts (including extra details found in each account.) Let the students know where they can find the additional details in the Bible. Point out details and commentary from teachers' notes. (i.e. Why Peter was so incredulous at Jesus' suggestion of fishing at that time and place.)

Discuss the story: While reviewing the major events of the story, discuss the possible applications to the students' lives. Ask questions that make them think about the story and show that they understand the story.

## APPLICATIONS

1. Jesus called Peter and these other men to be preachers and teachers of God's Word. He wanted them to concentrate on bringing the saving Gospel to people so God could gather them into His kingdom. That would be their full-time calling for life. Throughout history, God has continued to call certain individuals (both men and women) to full time service to Him as pastors and teachers. God provides the call, the gifts, and the results of the work. What a joy and privilege it is for a person to serve in this way for an entire lifetime, telling others of Jesus, their Savior. Every believer should consider carefully whether God has called him or her to serve Him as a public teacher or preacher.

2. If you personally are not led to become a full-time worker in the Church of God, you still have been called to preach and teach His Word. Every believer, no matter what his other roles in life may be, can share with others the comfort and assurance of the message of salvation in Christ. God gives the gifts and will bless the work that you do for Him.

3. Following Jesus can be both a test and a reinforcement of faith. The Lord gave a command Peter obeyed even though it was not a very reasonable or logical thing for him to do. Faith trusts God and takes Him at His Word, no matter what the cost. Discuss why Peter and the others left behind that great catch of fish and all that they had.

## PASSAGES

These passages can be assigned as memory work or simply discussed in class as to how they fit the lesson.

Lower
Matthew 6:33 - But seek first the kingdom of God and His righteousness, and all these things shall be added to you.

Middle any of the above and...

Matthew 16:24-25 - Then Jesus said to His disciples, "If anyone desires to come after Me, let him deny himself, and take up his cross, and follow Me. For whoever desires to save his life will lose it, but whoever loses his life for My sake will find it."
Philippians 1:6 - being confident of this very thing, that He who has begun a good work in you will complete it until the day of Jesus Christ;

Upper any of the above and...
Ephesians 4:8, 11-12 - Therefore He says: "When He ascended on high, He led captivity captive, and gave gifts to men." ... And He Himself gave some to be apostles, some prophets, some evangelists, and some pastors and teachers, for the equipping of the saints for the work of ministry, for the edifying of the body of Christ.

## HYMN CHOICES

"Blessed Jesus, at Thy Word" (TLH 16 all)
"All Depends on Our Possessing" (TLH 425: 1-3, 5-6)
"Thou Who the Night in Prayer Didst Spend" (TLH 493:1-4)

## 10

## STORY
Jesus and Nicodemus - John 3

## TEACHER PRAYER
Heavenly Father, I thank you the privilege of coming to Jesus, Who is a teacher come from God.  I thank you for the opportunity to learn more about Jesus so that I can better teach these children entrusted to my care.  I pray that the Holy Spirit would work mightily to create and sustain the faith of these children.  I thank you for the gift of baptism which is truly a washing of regeneration and renewal by the Holy Spirit. Amen.

## VOCABULARY
*Sanhedrin* - the seventy elders, religious and political leaders of the Jews

*Kingdom of God* - God's rule in our hearts through the Gospel

*born again* - being made a child of God by the Holy Spirit; it does not mean accepting Jesus as one's Savior

*regenerate* - to be born again or to renew

## OUTER AIM
Jesus Reveals the Nature of the Kingdom of God

## INNER AIM
Jesus Has Made Me a Part of His Kingdom By Water and the Spirit

## BACKGROUND
This event takes place at the beginning of Jesus' ministry.  John tells us that Jesus had turned the water into wine at Cana of Galilee and manifested His divine glory.   Jesus and His followers went to Jerusalem to celebrate the Passover, the remembrance of God's great salvation act of the Old Testament.  John's Gospel account centers around the three Passovers that Jesus celebrated in Jerusalem, the last one culminating in His death.  Jerusalem was not only the political capitol of Israel, it was also the religious center.  Here was Herod's temple and its additions to the temple built after Solomon's temple was destroyed.  Jesus got the attention of the people and the religious establishment when he drove the money-changers out of His Father's house (John 2:13-22).  The hopes and fears of many years began to stir as the Jews looked for that Messiah who would drive out the hated Romans and restore the kingdom to Israel.  Jerusalem was filled with the news of this strange person, Jesus.  "And many believed in His name when they saw the signs which He did" (John 2:23).  The actions and activities of Jesus attracted the attention of a leader of the Jews, Nicodemus, a member of the Sanhedrin.

## STUDENT PRAYER
Dear Jesus, come to us as You came to Nicodemus and reveal Yourself to us as the Promised Messiah.  Thank You for having made us God's children by baptism and the power of the Holy Spirit.  May we learn that God so loved us that we should not perish but have everlasting life.  Be with us this day and bless us in our study of Your Word.  Amen.

## PRESENTATION

Nicodemus, a Pharisee and ruler of Jews, came to Jesus by night. Jesus had already ruffled the feathers of the religious establishment by driving the money-changers out of the temple. This action struck the pocketbooks of those elders who had a share of the profits. It also exposed their greed and hypocrisy to the people. So Nicodemus came to Jesus secretly, at night so that he would not be identified with this strange teacher and His doctrine. Nicodemus recognized that Jesus was a rabbi, that is a teacher. From the signs Jesus performed, Nicodemus even recognized that Jesus was a teacher from God. However, Nicodemus did not understand who Jesus was or why He had come into the world.

Jesus took Nicodemus right to the heart of the matter by speaking to him about the Kingdom of God. What a difference in how this concept was understood! Nicodemus immediately thought in terms of an earthly kingdom that would be ushered in by the Messiah. Jesus was speaking about God's rule within you, a spiritual rule by the Gospel. To this end, Jesus sought to instruct Nicodemus. He stated that unless a person was born again, he could not see the kingdom of God. This made no sense to Nicodemus. With his concept of an earthly kingdom, he could not understand how a person could be born again and enter into God's kingdom. His first thought was that Jesus was somehow talking about a new physical birth-a fresh start.

Jesus was speaking of a *spiritual* kingdom and entrance being only through the Holy Spirit. It is still true that what is born of the flesh is and remains sinful flesh, while that which is born of the Spirit is spiritual. You must be born of water and the Spirit to gain entrance into the Kingdom of God. Jesus here refers to the water of baptism and the regenerative power of the Holy Spirit. It is sad that in modern decision theology, being born again means that you have accepted Jesus as your Savior and dedicate your life to Him. The emphasis in Jesus' words to Nicodemus is the change God works in sinners through water and the Spirit. The Holy Spirit is like the wind in that it works when and how it wants. All we see are the results of the Spirit's activities.

Jesus goes on to proclaim the Gospel to Nicodemus by taking him back to the brass snake in the wilderness during Israel's forty-year journey to the Promised Land. Jesus would be put upon a pole (the cross), and whoever looked to Him in faith would be saved from eternal death. "For God so loved the world that He gave His only begotten Son, that whoever believes in Him should not perish but have everlasting life." (John 3:16)

We hear no more of Nicodemus until the crucifixion of Jesus. John points out that Nicodemus stood under the cross and understood what Jesus was talking about that first secretive night. While Jesus' own disciples fled lest they be identified with Him, Nicodemus stepped forward and claimed the body of Jesus for burial. Nicodemus and Joseph of Arimathea confessed their faith before the world. Nicodemus was born again.

## APPLICATION

Jesus answers our questions with loving patience and leads us to learn more about the Kingdom of God as He led Nicodemus.

The Kingdom of God is not an earthly kingdom. Rather, it is His gracious rule in our hearts because of Jesus' love.

The Holy Spirit leads us to believe in Jesus. Luther's explanation of the third article confesses, "I believe that I cannot by my own reason or strength believe in Jesus Christ my Lord or come to Him, but the Holy Spirit has called me by the Gospel." Faith is a direct work of the Holy Spirit. This fact is a direct contradiction held by many today who emphasize that each individual must decide to accept Jesus as his Savior.

The Holy Spirit works through the means of grace, that is, the Gospel in Word and sacraments. Where the Word is preached and the sacraments are administered, the Holy Spirit creates the Church.

Jesus emphasizes the power of baptism by speaking of the "new birth" as coming by means of water and the Spirit.

Nicodemus was later led at time of Jesus' death to confess his faith and put his life on the line by claiming Jesus' body for burial.

## PASSAGES
**These passages can be assigned as memory work or simply discussed in class as to how they fit the lesson.**

(John 3:5) Jesus answered, "Most assuredly, I say to you, unless one is born of water and the Spirit, he cannot enter the kingdom of God.

(John 3:16) "For God so loved the world that He gave His only begotten Son, that whoever believes in Him should not perish but have everlasting life.

(Titus 3:4-7) But when the kindness and the love of God our Savior toward man appeared, {5} not by works of righteousness which we have done, but according to His mercy He saved us, through the washing of regeneration and renewing of the Holy Spirit, {6} whom He poured out on us abundantly through Jesus Christ our Savior, {7} that having been justified by His grace we should become heirs according to the hope of eternal life.

## HYMN CHOICES
God Loved the World So That He Gave - TLH #245
Come, Holy Spirit, Come - TLH #225:1,4,5
Holy Spirit, Hear Us - TLH #229:7
Let the Children Come to Me - Worship Supplement #753

## 11

## STORY
Jesus and the Samaritan Woman - John 4:1-43

## TEACHER PRAYER
Heavenly Father, I thank you for the grace and mercy you revealed in sending your Son Jesus to die for the sins of the world. Help me realize my own sinfulness and the miracle of your grace in bringing me to faith in Jesus. Enable me thereby to speak to these children of your accepting grace in terms that they can understand and live by. Bless this hour we spend studying Your word. Amen.

## VOCABULARY
*Samaritan* - a mixed race of people despised by the Jews

## OUTER AIM
Jesus came to seek and to save all sinners

## INNER AIM
Jesus came to seek and to save me

**BACKGROUND** Jesus told Nicodemus that "God so loved the world that He gave...." These were radical words for the Jews who thought of themselves as God's special people. The self-righteousness of the Pharisees was revealed in their attitude toward other people. They trusted in themselves that they were righteous. As a byproduct of this error, they despised others. At Jacob's well, Jesus revealed Himself as the Savior of the world and the Savior of all sinners.

## STUDENT PRAYER
Dear Jesus, help us to understand your perfect love for all people. We thank you that you came to seek and to save those who were lost. We ask that you would bless our study this morning so that we may understand your grace in our lives. Help us never to look down on or despise any other person. Thank you. Amen.

## PRESENTATION
A knowledge of the historical background is helpful for the understanding of this story. Samaria is located between Judea and Galilee. The Samaritans were Jews who had been left behind at the time of the Babylonian captivity. When the nation of Judah returned from the Babylonian captivity, the Samaritans were not allowed to participate in the rebuilding of the temple. (Neh. 2:10; 4-6) There were racial reasons for the Jews' hatred of the Samaritans (John 4:9); they were a racially mixed people. There were also religious reasons. Their religion was a mixture of the truth and falsehood. (They accepted the first five books of Moses and worshiped at Mt. Gerizim.) Finally there were political reasons for their hatred. Historically, the Samaritans had always been political enemies of the Jews.

It is against this background that Jesus reached out for the Samaritan woman who was an open sinner. Instead of going around Samaria as was normal for a Jew, Jesus chose to journey through it and thus came to the Well of Jacob near Sychar. Jesus' disciples proceeded into town leaving Jesus to minister to the needs of this woman.

In the truest sense, God sought out this woman in her need. She had not come looking. Jesus came giving. Jesus offered the woman "living water" promising that if she drank of it, she would never thirst. Jesus promised her a spiritual drink that would satisfy her deepest spiritual needs. Jesus had something wonderful to give to her. This water would become a well "springing up into everlasting life." (4:14)

Jesus brought this woman to the point of confessing that she needed a Savior. He revealed her evasive answer to His direction, "Go and get your husband." He told her that she was living with a man who was not her husband. He thus revealed to her that He was a prophet; indeed, the Messiah of whom the Samaritans also knew. (4:26) She revealed faith in Jesus although she did not yet realize the fullness of what that meant. Jesus revealed Himself to her as the promised Messiah.

The purpose of this account is seen in 4:34-38. Jesus saw the world as ripe for the harvest, the ingathering of souls. Already we have an indication of the worldwide nature of this harvest pictured in the Samaritan woman. This was an important part of Jesus' training of His disciples to be prepared to "go out and make disciples of all nations."

This woman brought many from her village to see Jesus. The good news had to be shared. Because of Jesus' words, many believed. Here we see a beautiful picture of our mission spirit and zeal as it should be today. We pray that the Lord would send forth laborers to gather in His harvest.

## APPLICATION
The obvious application is that Jesus seeks for sinners and individually ministers to their spiritual needs. There is no one excluded from the kingdom of God because of his or her race or color. But not so obvious is the truth that no one is outside of God's grace on account of his or her sinfulness. All of need to realize our personal sinfulness.

Jesus captures this woman's attention with the promise of "living water" of which she could drink and never thirst again. People have spiritual needs which are not being met today. They need to understand that material things can never satisfy man's deepest needs. The only answer is to be found in Jesus who is the "water of life" and the "bread of life."

It is important to discuss ways in which children can reach out to others. At the same time discuss barriers that exist today which might prevent our reaching out with the Gospel.

When the woman found salvation in Jesus, she wanted to share it with others. The people in this village believed, not just because of the woman's testimony, but because of the words of Jesus.

## PASSAGES
**These passages can be assigned as memory work or simply discussed in class as to how they fit the lesson.**
Luke 19:10 - "For the Son of man has come to seek and to save that which was lost."

John 4:14 - "But whoever drinks of the water that I shall give him will never thirst. But the water that I shall give him will become in him a fountain of water springing up into everlasting life."

Luke 10:2 - Then He said to them, "The harvest truly is great, but the laborers are few; therefore pray the Lord of the harvest to send out laborers into His harvest."

## HYMN CHOICES
Hark! the Voice of Jesus Crying - TLH #496
I Heard the Voice of Jesus Say - TLH #277

**12**

## STORY
Jesus Heals the Man at Bethesda - John 5:1-47

## TEACHER PRAYER
Heavenly Father, give me faith to believe that Jesus is able to heal my diseases because He is the Son of God and my Savior. Also give me the faith to accept those infirmities which reveal Your strength in my life. May the Holy Spirit, working through me, make Jesus real to these children. Bless my preparation in Your Word and my presentation of that Word. Amen.

## VOCABULARY
*Sabbath Day* - the 7th day (Saturday) on which Old Testament Israel was to do no work

*infirmities* - weaknesses, often used in connection with physical diseases

*Scriptures* - God's written Word

## OUTER AIM
Jesus Heals the Man and Reveals Himself as the Son of God

## INNER AIM
Jesus Heals Me and Reveals Himself to Me Through the Holy Scriptures

## BACKGROUND
John emphasizes the fact that Jesus revealed Himself as the Messiah and the Son of God. He takes us from Galilee back to Jerusalem. Here Jesus set forth His claim to the Jewish leaders that He was the promised Messiah through His miraculous healing of the man who had not walked for the past thirty-eight years.

## STUDENT PRAYER
Dear Jesus, You are able to help us when no one else can. You have revealed Yourself as Lord over sickness and disease. According to your will, help us when we are sick. You have revealed Yourself through the Bible. Help us learn more about You as we search the Scriptures for there we will find You. Amen.

## PRESENTATION
Jesus found Himself at Bethesda. Here was a pool enclosed by five porches near the sheep market and close to the "Sheep Gate." The pool was for healing. An angel moved the waters and the first person to enter the pool at that time would be healed. (Note that verse 4 in the King James is not in all the manuscripts.) Here Jesus found people in great need, i.e. the blind, the lame, the paralyzed.

Our attention is drawn to a man who had been an invalid for thirty-eight years. He had no friend to help him get into the waters, and yet he hoped for a cure. Jesus turned the man's attention away from the pool and centered it upon Himself (vs.7). Jesus cured the man, and he walked.

This healing took place on the Sabbath Day, the day of rest. It was not a violation of the Sabbath rest but a bringing of rest to this poor man. The Jews became angry at him because he was carrying his rolled-up mat on the Sabbath Day. This was to them a violation of the letter of the Sabbath law.

At this time, the man had no idea WHO had healed him. Jesus who had given him physical healing also gave him spiritual and inward healing. Jesus reminded him of a worse punishment than his physical sickness, i.e. eternal condemnation.

Jesus revealed Himself to the Jewish leaders as the Messiah and the Son of God (vs. 18). Their opposition to Jesus continued to grow as He revealed Himself to them as their Savior, the Son of God who alone gives life.

Note how Jesus tied Himself to the Old Testament scriptures. (vs. 36ff). If they would believe the Scriptures, they would believe in Jesus. However, the religious leaders believed neither Jesus nor the Scriptures.

## APPLICATION

Jesus healed this man by His divine power. Disease is a result of sin. Even those people Jesus healed eventually died. The final healing from disease will not take place until we are with Jesus in heaven.

Jesus heals us. However, He does not heal all diseases nor does He always do so with a miracle. Even sickness has a purpose in strengthening our faith and bringing us closer to Jesus.

The religious leaders rejected Jesus and even wanted to kill Him, not only because He healed on the Sabbath Day, but because He claimed to be the Son of God (John 5:18). People today also react strongly to Jesus' claim to be the Son of God.

Jesus is revealed in the Scriptures. The Old Testament testifies concerning Him. Jesus encourages us to search the Scriptures. We are not to casually read the Bible just on Sundays. We are to dig into the Bible daily and mine its depths. If you do not find Jesus in the Bible, you have missed the main message of the Scriptures. If someone does not believe the words of God in the Bible, he or she will not believe Jesus.

## PASSAGES
**These passages can be assigned as memory work or simply discussed in class as to how they fit the lesson.**

John 5:39 - "You search the Scriptures, for in them you think you have eternal life; and these are they which testify of Me.

2 Tim 3:15-16 - "And that from childhood you have known the Holy Scriptures, which are able to make you wise for salvation through faith which is in Christ Jesus. All Scripture is given by inspiration of God, and is profitable for doctrine, for reproof, for correction, for instruction in righteousness."

## HYMN CHOICES
God's Word Is Our Great Heritage - TLH #283
We Have a Sure Prophetic Word - TLH #290
What a Friend We Have in Jesus - TLH #457

## STORY
Jesus Heals the Paralyzed Man - Matthew 9:1-8; Mark 2:1-12

## TEACHER PRAYER
Dear Father in heaven, the world around us offers so many alternatives to You to deal with sin and sickness. Help us to learn that God alone has the real solutions to these problems. Help me to be Your spokesman to tell my students to look to You alone for complete forgiveness of sins through Jesus' blood and righteousness. Teach us to be persistent and not let obstacles keep us from bringing our needs to You for the best solution. Trusting in Jesus, I pray, Amen.

## VOCABULARY
*His own city* - Jesus used Capernaum as a base of operations at times. He had not received a good welcome in His hometown of Nazareth.
*Blaspheme* - claiming to be God when not truly God, or misusing the name of God in a false or sinful way, insulting God.
*Scribes* - originally men who copied the Scriptures by hand. But as their knowledge of the scriptures grew from their work, they were considered authorities of it and were regarded as "professors of theology" are today. They held high positions in the religious government of the Jews. (See Rupprecht pp. 47-48)
*Paralytic* (KJV) - a person who has no movement in some or all of the body.

## OUTER AIM
Jesus heals a paralyzed man.

## INNER AIM
Jesus has the power and authority to forgive sins.

## BACKGROUND
*(Rupprecht Bible History References Vol.2, pp. 137-142)*
There are many kinds of sicknesses today. Some of these are very serious. Everyone tries to find a cure for disease. The thing that is not understood is that sickness is a result of sin, of man's rebellion against his Creator-God. Because of this, it was necessary for Jesus to fulfill the prophecy of Isaiah (Is. 53 and Matthew 8:17), "He took up our diseases and carried our illnesses." In this episode, Jesus made the connection between sin and sickness and showed that He had power to heal both.

Mark 2:1
▸   Jesus traveled throughout Galilee and in the regions on both sides of the Sea of Galilee.
▸   According to Matthew 9:1, this event happened when Jesus returned to the west side of the Sea of Galilee, after serving on the east side for a time.
▸   News about Jesus' location rapidly traveled about because at this time He was very popular with the people. *Use map to find Sea of Galilee and Capernaum.

v. 2
▸   People quickly came to hear Jesus and be healed by Him.
▸   This time the crowd was so thick that people were crowded outside the house to hear Him.
▸   Jesus did not waste the opportunity to preach.

v. 3

▸ The friends of a paralyzed man brought him to Jesus.

v. 4

▸ In testimony to their faith, these people did not let the crowd discourage them from their goal.

▸ They went up outside stairs onto the flat roof. Roofs were made either of branches and mud or else clay tiles. (see Rupprecht pp. 138-139)

▸ So with some effort they were able to open up the roof above Jesus to lower the bed of the man down to Jesus.

▸ The bed was portable, perhaps a stretcher or cot-like bed.

v. 5

▸ Jesus, as both God and man, knows the thoughts and intents of the heart. Jesus knew what was most important to the sick man, but calling him "son," Jesus shows His love for the man, and indicates His saving relationship with this man through the forgiveness of sins..

▸ More than healing of any diseases or sickness, people need to have their sins forgiven. Matthew 9:2 adds, ".. be of good cheer, .." for the forgiveness of sins brings peace and joy to replace sorrow over sin.

(Many have had the misconception that a specific sickness is a direct cause of a particular sin. Although some sicknesses can be the consequences of sinful behavior, sickness is one of the results of all people being sinful. No matter how unusually good they and we are, we and they will continue to suffer ailments until the end of this sinful world.)

vs. 6-7

▸ On scribes, see vocabulary. The scribes became jealous enemies of Jesus and audited His public appearances in order to find fault with Him. They thought within themselves that only God had the authority to forgive sins but failed to believe that Jesus was God. So they thought Jesus was blaspheming by claiming to do something that only God had the power and authority to do.

▸ Ironically, they became the ones blaspheming because they denied Jesus had the power of God.

v. 8

▸ Even before they had a chance to criticize Jesus, Jesus knew what was in their hearts and answered their thoughts!

▸ In a demonstration that He was God, He asked them why they thought such things (and by implication, why they didn't believe He was God).

v. 9

▸ Jesus' asked a reasonable question: which impossible thing is easier for a man to do?

▸ Directly forgiving sins and healing a paralyzed man with only a spoken word are things only God is able to do.

vs. 10-11

▸ To show them that He, as God, had the power of God to do what only God could, Jesus commanded the paralyzed man to arise.

v. 12

▸ And immediately, without a long recovery period or months in therapy, the man who had been paralyzed got out of his bed, picked up his bed, and walked (maybe even ran) to his house. Amazing!

▸ That would be our reaction too if we had been there.

▸ And the people glorified God, saying "We never saw anything like this." Or as Matthew says, glorified God for giving such power to mankind. Note that the people realized the supremely astounding truth that God had indeed given the authority to forgive sins to <u>people</u> (note: plural "men," not just to a man, Jesus of Nazareth. This is a prelude to the giving of the Keys – John 20.

▸ This miracle highlighted for the scribes and the people that Jesus' power was God's.

▸ Yet not all would believe in Him even after this and other miracles.

## STUDENT PRAYER

Dear Lord, Jesus, You show us through Your Word today Your great power over sin and sicknesses. When our sins trouble us, draw us in faith to You for the forgiveness that You alone can give so that we may find peace and joy through sins forgiven. And when sickness comes upon us, give us a patient faith to continually come to You in faith. And when we are healed may Your name be glorified before those who doubt You. We pray, trusting in Your grace and mercy, Amen.

## PRESENTATION

Briefly review previous story as time allows. Make links to the new story when possible.

Tell the story: Teachers, be encouraged to tell the story in your own words while remaining faithful to the scriptural account. When scripture records the story in more than one place, harmonize the accounts (including extra details found in each account.) Let the students know where they can find the additional details in the Bible.

Discuss the story: While reviewing the major events of the story, discuss the possible applications to the students' lives. Ask questions that make them think about the story and show that they understand the story.

## APPLICATIONS

1.  Jesus knows and is able to take care of our greatest ailment: sin. He searches our hearts in order to bring comfort to those who need assurance of sins forgiven and to instruct those who need to learn more about Jesus. The sicknesses and needs of the body are not as dangerous and permanent as our spiritual condition. So Jesus meets our spiritual needs first.

2.  Jesus also is concerned about our physical needs. The world and its storms are restrained by His power so that they can do only what God allows. Sometimes, as the disciples and the paralyzed man discovered, God demonstrates His loving power so that people may end up glorifying Him. Usually God works in natural ways: adults work and earn money to buy us food, clothing and a home. Doctors are given skills and medicines to use to heal and repair us when we are sick or hurt. God gives people knowledge to predict storms and to protect themselves from them. We can plant gardens and crops where God grows food for us. But because these support systems are imperfect we are made to realize that He alone can help. When we are in need, we should look to Jesus alone in confidence and trust. 1 Peter 5:7

3.  Jesus proved He is true God by His power to forgive sins. In John 20:23 Jesus gives His Church the authority to forgive sins on His behalf. Every Christian has the power given them by Jesus to announce or withhold the forgiveness of sins. We can forgive the sins of the penitent sinner or the impenitent sinner is stuck with his sins as long as he doesn't repent.

## PASSAGES

These passages can be assigned as memory work or simply discussed in class as to how they fit the lesson.

Lower
1 Peter 5:7 - casting all your care upon Him, for He cares for you.
1 John 1:7 - ..the blood of Jesus Christ His Son cleanses us from all sin.

Middle any of the above and...

Matthew 11:28-29 - "Come to Me, all you who labor and are heavy laden, and I will give you rest. Take My yoke upon you and learn from Me, for I am gentle and lowly in heart, and you will find rest for your souls."

Upper any of the above and...
Romans 3:23-24 - for all have sinned and fall short of the glory of God, being justified freely by His grace through the redemption that is in Christ Jesus,

## HYMN CHOICES

"O Faithful God, Thanks be to Thee" (TLH #321 *can change tune*)
"When in the Hour of Utmost Need" (TLH #522)
"Alas, My God, My Sins are Great" (TLH #317 - 1, 4-6)

## STORY
Jesus Raises the Daughter of Jairus - Luke 8:40-56; Matthew 9:18-26; Mark 5:21-43

## TEACHER PRAYER
Dear Father in heaven, I know that death is not natural but a result of the sin that infects us all.  Many would teach that death is the normal way of evolution, but You created the world to live, not die. Help me to teach my students that You are the God of Life.  You through Your Spirit reverse spiritual death through faith in Jesus and reunite us with You as your beloved Children.  We also know that when physical death is finally ended on the last day, just as Jesus rose, we will be raised and You will keep all believers from eternal death and give to us instead eternal life with Jesus.  Send Your Spirit as I share Your Word that all who hear may have life in Jesus' name. Amen.

## VOCABULARY
*Synagogue* - The local church of the Jews.
*Thronged/ throng* -  people crowded around Him very closely.
*Talitha Cumi* -  Aramaean words, translated in the text, "Little girl, arise."  This was the language spoken by the people of Palestine at that time.
*Charged* -  Jesus urgently commanded them.

## OUTER AIM
Jesus shows His power over sickness and death.

## INNER AIM
Faith in Jesus gives us life.

## BACKGROUND
*(Rupprecht Bible History References Vol. 2, pp. 142-148)*
The gospel of Luke stresses Jesus' compassion as He helps people where He finds them and in their deepest needs.  This section stresses the power of faith in Jesus.  Jesus' power calls forth the response of faith.  May the Holy Spirit give us a faith like this.
Luke 8:40
▸    Jesus had left the region to preach and heal in the country of the Gaderenes.
▸    There His power scared the people so that they asked Him to leave.
▸    On His return to the west side of the Sea of Galilee, crowds of people again came to hear Him and be healed.
v. 41
▸    Jairus was a ruler or leader of the local synagogue.  See Rupprecht p 143-144 to learn more.
▸    He showed Jesus great respect by pleading at Jesus' feet.
v. 42
▸    Jairus' only daughter was at the point of death when Jairus sought out Jesus.
▸    In Jewish culture, daughters were considered of age, an adult woman, at the age of 12. (Rupprecht p 145)
▸    But Jesus was met with delays before He could answer the request.
v. 43
▸    God does not give cures for some sicknesses to doctors.
▸    This woman had spent all that she had before coming to Jesus.
▸    Then as now, people are willing to spend great sums to find a cure for diseases, though because of sin,

there will always be sickness to remind us of sin.

v. 44

▸ The woman's faith was such that she believed that even by simply touching Jesus' clothes she would be healed.  See also Matthew 9:21 & Mark 5:22.

▸ And, upon touching Jesus' garment, she was healed.

▸ Of course the fabric of Jesus' clothes was not powerful, but the healing power came from Jesus and went to her because of her faith in Him, not His clothes.

▸ Jewish law made her "unclean" and separated her from normal contact with people until the sickness should be cured.

v. 45

▸ Despite Jairus' daughter being at the point of dying, Jesus stopped to find out who had touched Him.

▸ Jesus knew what would happen with Jairus' daughter and also who had touched Him, but He stopped in order to encourage people's faith.

▸ Jesus' disciples thought Jesus' question strange considering how many people were closely crowded around, probably bumping into Him.

▸ Notice, no one would admit having touched Him.

v. 46

▸ Despite the disciples' confusion at Jesus' question, Jesus continued to ask for the person who touched Him and was healed.

v. 47

▸ With fear and trembling (see also Mark 5:33), the woman realized that Jesus knew what she had done and confessed her act of faith in front of the people.

v. 48

▸ With loving compassion, Jesus called her "daughter," stilled her fear, and assured her that her faith was well placed in Jesus.

▸ She should go in peace, knowing that He had cured her.

v. 49

▸ This intentional delay by Jesus had the result that the daughter of Jairus died.

▸ The servants brought the message with a discouragement to the faith of Jairus.

▸ They didn't know or believe that Jesus could be of any further help.

v. 50

▸ But Jesus called Jairus to continue to believe in Jesus' power despite the seeming finality of death.

▸ Jesus promised that she who was now dead would be made well.  What a difficult promise to believe.

v. 51

▸ Jesus kept the crowds and onlookers outside, bringing with Him only His three  closest disciples and the parents of the young girl.

▸ This would minimize the confusion and publicity for what was to come.

v. 52

▸ The Jewish custom at death in those days was to cry and weep loudly, even sometimes hiring mourners to show the great sorrow felt at the loss of a loved one (see Rupprecht p146-147).

▸ Jesus called for them to stop crying and believe that the girl's death wasn't final.

v. 53

▸ To human experience, death is final and not just sleeping.

▸ So they, not knowing or believing in Jesus and His power over death, laughed at His apparently foolish description of death.

v. 54

‣ Jesus sent the mourners away, keeping only the three disciples and the parents with Him.

‣ Then, Jesus took her by the hand, and commanded the girl to get up.

‣ Notice in Mark 5:41, Peter has remembered the exact words of Christ used.

‣ Peter was one of the eyewitnesses then. (Mark wrote down the Gospel as Peter had told it to him.)

v. 55

‣ Again, the response to Jesus' words was immediate and complete.

‣ Her spirit returned to her body.

‣ She got up immediately and even walked as Mark tells us.

‣ There was no long recovering of strength or nursing back to health from the edge of death. She was fully alive and healthy.

‣ Jesus with understanding, commanded them to bring her something to eat, which also implies that she was well.

v. 56

‣ Her parents, including her father who had waited until the last minute to seek help from Jesus, were totally astonished at this miracle.

‣ But Jesus strictly commanded them not to tell anyone what had happened.

‣ He didn't want people to come to Him only because of the great miracles that He did but rather to see Him as their Savior.

## STUDENT PRAYER

Dear Lord Jesus, we have learned that even death must bow to Your command for You are the God of Life. Help us, oh Lord, to call upon You for all our needs, however great or small they might seem. If, in Your wisdom, You delay Your help, teach us to be patient in faith, trusting that You will give us the help that we need. For we know that we must patiently live our lives in faith until you call us from this life to the eternal life you have won for us through Your own death and resurrection. We pray, patiently trusting in You, Lord Jesus. Amen.

## PRESENTATION

Briefly review previous story as time allows. Make links to the new story when possible.

Tell the story: Teachers, be encouraged to tell the story in your own words while remaining faithful to the scriptural account. When scripture records the story in more than one place, you may want to harmonize the accounts (including extra details found in each account). Let the students know where they can find the additional details in the Bible.

Discuss the story: While reviewing the major events of the story, discuss the possible applications to the students' lives. Ask questions that make them think about the story and show that they understand the story.

## APPLICATIONS

1. This is a good opportunity to talk about death. Death can be defined as "separation". The Bible describes three forms of death: 1)Spiritual death - separation of a person's soul from God by sin and unbelief. John 3 talks of this as Jesus tells Nicodemus that sinful people must be born again by the Spirit who creates and sustains faith in Jesus. See also Isaiah 59:2; 2) Physical death - separation of the soul

from the body until God reunites them on Judgement Day or in the few miracles God records in the Bible. From this story notice in verse 55 the girl's spirit returned to her body at Jesus' command and she was alive. And 3) Eternal death - the eternal separation of the unbelievers' body and soul from God for all eternity. Stress that sin brought death (Genesis 2:17; 3:1-19 Romans 5:12ff). It is not natural as the evolutionists claim. But, Jesus has the power over death through His death and resurrection as Paul tells us (1 Corinthians 15). So, even though for time we are separated from those who die, yet in eternity we will be reunited with those who believed on Jesus as their Savior from sin.

2.      This story also encourages us to patiently believe when we make requests to God. The woman's faith humbly looked to Jesus to heal what no other person was able to help her with. Jairus surely felt the clock ticking for his sick daughter as Jesus was delayed by the sick woman needing healing and encouragement in her faith. When the servant came and announced his daughter's death, that could have caused the death of Jairus' faith and hope. Yet, Jesus bolstered his faith with a renewed promise that death would not prevent Jesus from making her well. God with His words, comforts and encourages us to continue in faith even in what seems the most hopeless of situations. And, as He did for Jairus, God proves that such patient faith is not in vain, for with God all things are possible.

## PASSAGES
These passages can be assigned as memory work or simply discussed in class as to how they fit the lesson.

Lower
John 11:25 - Jesus said to her, "I am the resurrection and the life. He who believes in Me, though he may die, he shall live."

Middle any of the above and...
Hebrews 11:1 - Now faith is the substance of things hoped for, the evidence of things not seen.
Romans 5:12 - Therefore, just as through one man sin entered the world, and death through sin, and thus death spread to all men, because all sinned.

Upper any of the above and...
1 Corinthians 15:55-57 - O Death, where is your sting? O Hades, where is your victory? The sting of death is sin, and the strength of sin is the law. But thanks be to God, who gives us the victory through our Lord Jesus Christ.
1 Thessalonians 4:13-14 - But I do not want you to be ignorant, brethren, concerning those who have fallen asleep, lest you sorrow as others who have no hope. For if we believe that Jesus died and rose again, even so God will bring with Him those who sleep in Jesus.

## HYMN CHOICES
"Jesus Christ, My Sure Defense" (TLH 206)
"If Thou but Suffer God to Guide Thee" (TLH 518)
"Commit Whatever Grieves Thee" (TLH 520 1,6)

**15**

## STORY
The Centurion's Servant - Matthew 8:5-13; Luke 7:1-10

## TEACHER PRAYER
Dear Lord, You promise to hear those who call upon You in truth. In our times many have attacked Your Word as unreliable and not to be completely trusted. Yet, as we see Your hand working throughout history for the benefit of all nations, we know that Your Word is true and backed by Your ultimate power and authority. Strengthen the faith of those who hear this lesson that they may, as the Centurion did, trust with humble faith the power and reliability of Your Word. For the message of salvation in Jesus is in Your Word and needs to be trusted by all. You have promised that Your Word will never be destroyed, but also warned that it can depart from those who despise it. I pray that Your Word may truly be respected and believed by me and those with whom I share it that You may continue to bless us through that Word and our Lord and Savior, Jesus Christ. Amen

## VOCABULARY
*Centurion* - a Roman commander of about 100 men, this one commanded the garrison at Capernaum
*Gnashing* - grinding of teeth, normally in frustration or anger
*Gentile* - any person who is not of Jewish ancestry
*Israel* - a small country east of the Mediterranean Sea, the region in which Jesus conducted His ministry

## OUTER AIM
Jesus heals a Centurion's servant

## INNER AIM
God gives faith to trust in Him.

## BACKGROUND
*(Rupprecht Bible History References Vol.2, pp. 179-186)*
We walk by faith not by sight. If you can see something or have proof of its existence, you do not need faith. Faith comes into play in those spiritual areas which are not subject to scientific proof. (Hebrews 11:1) "Now faith is the substance of things hoped for, the evidence of things not seen." In this episode we have an example of genuine "faith."

Luke 7:1
- ▸   This event took place after Jesus had preached the "Sermon on the Mount."
- ▸   Again we find Him in Capernaum where He had been well received.
- ▸   Capernaum - (village of Nahum ) was on the western shore of the Sea of Galilee. (Matthew 4:13) It was in the "land of Gennesaret," [ (Matthew 14:34) comp. John 6:17,21,24 ] It was of sufficient size to be always called a "city," (Matthew 9:1; Mark 1:33) and had its own synagogue, in which our Lord frequently taught, (Mark 1:21; Luke 4:33,38; John 6:59) The only interest attaching to Capernaum is as the residence of our Lord and his apostles, the scene of so many miracles and "gracious words." It was when he returned thither that he is said to have been "in the house." (Mark 2:1) - Smith's Bible Dictionary

v. 2
- ▸   The local Centurion or Roman commander had a servant whom he loved dearly..

- The servant was sick (Matt: paralyzed and dreadfully tormented) and about to die.

v. 3
- The Centurion was Roman, a Gentile, a non-Jew, asking a favor of an important Jew, Jesus.
- So he sent some of the Jewish Elders to ask that Jesus go out of His way to heal his servant.

vs. 4-5
- The Jewish messengers respected the Roman commander, for he had treated the Jews well and even built a synagogue for them.
- They pleaded that Jesus would also respect the centurion for those reasons and honor his request.

v. 6
- Jesus for His own reasons consented to heal the servant (Matt 8:7) and went with the messengers towards the Centurion's house.
- But before arriving, the Centurion sent friends again to Jesus.
- The Centurion felt unworthy (knowing he was ceremonially unclean) of having Jesus come to his house and didn't want Jesus to expose Himself to the discomfort of becoming "contaminated" by contact with Gentiles.

v. 7
- So unworthy did the Centurion feel that he didn't feel respectable enough to come himself to Jesus.
- But he believed in Jesus' power to simply say the word, and his servant would be healed.

v. 8
- He understood authority, for he was a soldier accustomed to the "chain of command" system.
- When he was given or gave a command, that order was carried out without question.
- The Centurion trusted that Jesus held absolute authority over sickness in the same way. He knew that Jesus could heal the sickness by giving an order if Jesus would but wish to do so.

v. 9
- Even Jesus marveled that a Gentile would display such a faith in Jesus and His authority.
- So He pointed it out to the crowd around Him, emphasizing that He hadn't found such a faith among the Israelites.
- The centurion had showed his faith 1) in his love for his servant 2) in his humble feeling of unworthiness before Jesus and 3) his confidence in Jesus' power to heal with a simple command.

Matthew 8:11-12
- Jesus adds this warning: Many Gentiles from the ends of the earth will believe in Jesus and so enter heaven with the Forefathers of the Jews.
- But the Jews who reject their promised Messiah will be cast out of heaven into outer darkness, that is, Hell, where they will be tormented for their sins and unbelief.

Matthew 8:13 (Luke 7:10)
- Jesus' reply to the Centurion quantifies the miracle of healing by the faith shown. And indeed the servant was healed at Jesus' command, without His presence or a special sign.

## STUDENT PRAYER

Jesus Christ, My Savior, thank You for bringing Your word also to us and to people of every nation. Help us to trust Your Word with humble and courageous hearts that we may lay hold of all Your precious promises. For we know that You have the power and the Love to do all that You have promised. So, when we call upon You, we know that You will answer. With Jesus as our

Savior we know that we will be saved.  And when we pray, we know that Your answer will be what is best for all whom our prayer touches.  We come to You, Jesus, in whom we trust, Amen.

## PRESENTATION

Briefly review previous story as time allows.  Make links to the new story when possible.

Tell the story: Teachers, be encouraged to tell the story in your own words while remaining faithful to the scriptural account.  When scripture records the story in more than one place, you may want to harmonize the accounts (including extra details found in each account.)  Let the students know where they can find the additional details in the Bible.

Discuss the story: While reviewing the major events of the story, discuss the possible applications to the students' lives.  Ask questions that make them think about the story and show that they understand the story.

1.  Why did the soldier come to Jesus? *(His servant was very sick.)*
2.  What did the soldier believe Jesus could do? *(Heal the servant.)*
3.  The soldier was humble and had a strong faith. What did he believe Jesus could do? *(Heal the servant without coming into his house.)*
4.  How are you like the soldier? *(We believe Jesus will help and save us.)*

## APPLICATIONS

1.  The centurion trusted Jesus' Word, that it would accomplish whatever Jesus wanted it to.  That same powerful word of God created the world, keeps the stars in their courses, sends the seasons, and assures us of salvation in Jesus.  We should trust it as confidently and humbly as the Centurion did. We should not need any more proof God's Word is truth and profitable for life and salvation.  To deny part of the Word of God threatens all of it and ultimately destroys our assurance of salvation in Jesus Christ.
2.  An additional point to be made in connection with Jesus' powerful Word is that He can and did heal a deadly earthly disease by simply saying the word. What a comfort that can be to young and old alike when they or a family member or friend are afflicted with any disease of any severity. Our Lord can care for our well-being in any way He may choose.
3.  How thankful we can be that Jesus wants all people to be saved, not just one particular race or nation. We are a part of those who have "come from the east and the west" to sit at His table.  God's Word is able to create faith in the hearts of people from all nations. That is  why God sends us with His Word to all nations.

## PASSAGES

These passages can be assigned as memory work or simply discussed in class as to how they fit the lesson.

Lower
Hebrews 11:1 - Now faith is the substance of things hoped for, the evidence of things not seen.

<u>Middle</u> any of the above and...

Psalms 130:3-5 - If You, LORD, should mark iniquities, O Lord, who could stand? But there is forgiveness with You, That You may be feared. I wait for the LORD, my soul waits, And in His word I do hope.

Psalms 50:15 - Call upon Me in the day of trouble; I will deliver you, and you shall glorify Me."

<u>Upper</u> any of the above and...

Psalm 46 all.

Psalm 107:19-20 - Then they cried out to the LORD in their trouble, And He saved them out of their distresses. He sent His word and healed them, And delivered them from their destructions.

Isaiah 55:10-11 - "For as the rain comes down, and the snow from heaven, And do not return there, But water the earth, And make it bring forth and bud, That it may give seed to the sower And bread to the eater,  So shall My word be that goes forth from My mouth; It shall not return to Me void, But it shall accomplish what I please, And it shall prosper in the thing for which I sent it."

## HYMN CHOICES

"Lord, as Thou Wilt, Deal Thou With Me" (TLH 406)

"When in the Hour of Utmost Need" (TLH 522: 1-2, or all)

"My God, My Father, Make Me Strong" (TLH 424)

## STORY

The Young Man of Nain - Luke 7:11-17

## TEACHER PRAYER

Dear Jesus, I know that You have been given all power over things in heaven and on earth. I also remember how You instructed your disciples to feed Your lambs. Please grant me Your Spirit to rightly show the pupils entrusted into my care that You indeed have power over all things. Sins and short-comings and even the grave no longer hold any terrors for many of us because of Your gracious redemptive work. May I never forget to offer thanks. In Your saving name. Amen.

## VOCABULARY

*bier\coffin* - not a closed box, such as we have today, but rather an open platform. The body was usually covered with a black shroud, or cloth.

## OUTER AIM

Jesus raises the young man of Nain from the dead.

## INNER AIM

Jesus's Word of Life has the power over death.

## BACKGROUND

The raising from the dead of the young man at Nain is one of three such resurrection miracles of Jesus recorded in the Gospels. Luke is the only Evangelist to record this miracle. Matthew and Mark write of the raising of Jairus's daughter, and John tells the account of Jesus's raising of Lazarus. Each of these resurrection miracles of Jesus is in some ways similar to those performed by Old Testament prophets, but differ in one important way. Old Testament prophets carried out their work in the Lord's name and by His power, often exerting themselves while being used as God's instruments. Jesus's miracles occur immediately through the Almighty power of His Word. They demonstrate His power over death. A natural focal point of this Bible story is therefore the power of Jesus's Word.

Below are notes on each verse of the account:

V.11

▸ "The day after" refers to the short time following Jesus's healing of the centurion's servant recorded earlier in the chapter 7.

▸ Jesus was quite popular at this time in His ministry and was attracting large crowds wherever He went.

▸ The village of Nain is in southern Galilee, 5 miles southwest of Nazareth, 25 miles southwest of Capernaum.

▸ This town of Nain is not mentioned anywhere else in Scripture.

▸ Nain was built on the slope of a hill and most likely had only one gate.

V.12

▸ Cities in those days had gates for protection, to control what came in and what went out of a town.

▸ As Jesus entered the city with His large following of life, He met a large funeral procession of death.

▸ A dead man was being carried out of the city to be buried was the Jewish custom (to have a tomb inside the city was a defilement).

▸ Sepulcher graves hewn into the hillside have been found to the southeast of Nain.

▸ The fact that he was the only son of a widow makes the mourning all the more poignant.

▸ The Greek word used seems to suggest that this was not just the widow's only son, but her only child as well.

v.13
▸ Jesus felt "compassion" (pity, sympathy) for this widow and mother, in a distinctly human way.
▸ His instruction to her, "Do not weep," would indicate that she was visible crying over the loss of her child.
▸ We may often speak those words, "Don't cry," but Jesus spoke them as a remedy to remove the reason for her sorrow.
▸ Luke refers to Jesus as "Lord," one who has the authority to forgive sins and has the power over death itself.

V.14
▸ Jesus's words, "Young man, I say to you, 'Arise,'" indicate the age of the man as relatively young, perhaps only a teenager; someone you wouldn't expect to die.
▸ The Jews did not use closed coffins; the coffin was probably an open box, or perhaps something similar to a stretcher.
▸ This resurrection is similar to an Old Testament account of Elijah's raising a young man from the dead (I Kings 17:17-24).

V.15
▸ The "dead" man immediately began to do things only the living can do, sitting and speaking.
▸ Jesus gave the young man back to his mother out of love and concern for her. (Elijah in a similar manner presented the raised boy to his mother in the I Kings account.)

V.16
▸ The crowd was awestruck and praised God for such a miracle, but failed to see Jesus as the Messiah, thinking Him rather to be a great prophet, like those of the old Testament.
▸ He was perhaps called a "great" prophet by the people because He performed the miracle with words only.

V.17
▸ Word of this miracle spread quickly throughout the area, causing an even greater following for Jesus.

## STUDENT PRAYER

Dear Father in heaven, we thank You for sending Your Son, Jesus Christ, into the world to suffer and die for our sins. We know that You have given Jesus all power in heaven and on earth. Help us to remember that Jesus is able to keep all harm and danger away from us. Give us trusting hearts that cling to Jesus's promise to be with us always, especially in the hour of our death, after which we will wake to be with You forever. In Jesus's name. Amen.

## PRESENTATION

The story should be told in the words of the teacher using appropriate background information from the Background section. The Middle and Upper Levels could read the story from the student folder.

# Activity One - Draw a face that shows how the people in the story felt.

How do you think the mother felt about her son's death? (Sad)

How do you think the mother felt when Jesus made him alive? (Happy)

How did the crowd of people feel when Jesus made the young man alive? (Surprised)

## APPLICATIONS

1. Funerals are a necessary part of our lives in this sinful world. We do not attend funerals to honor the dead, nor just to remember the one who's died. We attend to show our support for the living relatives. We sympathize with each other and know we will miss the individual that has died - but we do not despair. For that loved one is now with the Lord and on the last day Jesus will restore him with all believers.

2. Emphasize how this young man was probably about their age. He died. We often think as young people that we will live forever, and may even take foolish risks with our lives. Young people do die, however. Are we ready to die? Live each day keeping in mind that it could be your last day. Confess your sins and be comforted by the forgiveness Christ daily provides through His Word.

3. It is important for us to remember the Lord's compassion. Jesus not only "feels sorry" for us, but He truly knows and understands our sorrows and troubles and wants to help us with them. "Come to Me, all you who labor and are heavy laden, and I will give you rest." (Matt. 11:28) The Lord Jesus is truly the only One who can take away our greatest problem, sin. It was through His sacrifice on the cross that Jesus defeated Satan, paid for our sins, and conquered death itself. Even when we must pass through the valley of the shadow of death we know Jesus will be there to guide us to His heavenly pastures.

4. Emphasize the power of Jesus's Word. It is the Word that brought us to faith in Baptism. We were raised from spiritual deadness by the life-giving Word - an even greater miracle than that which took place at Nain. It is the Word that forgives our sins in the Lord's Supper. It is the Word that keeps this world under God's protective care. It will be Jesus's word that will bring all things to an end. It is His word which will call us out of our graves unto life eternal. The Word overcomes Satan, condemns sin, cuts to the heart causing Godly sorrow and repentance. The Word helps us overcome temptations and sinful thoughts and desires (Matt.4). It is the Word which give us wisdom, strength, and guidance in this dark world (PS. 119:105).

## PASSAGES

These passages can be assigned as memory work* or simply discussed in class as to how they fit the lesson.

Lower
Whoever lives and believes in me shall never die. John 11:26
Because I live, you will live also. John 14:19*
Yea, though I walk through the valley of the shadow of death, I will fear no evil; for You are with me. Ps. 23:4*

Middle any of the above and...
All authority has been given to Me in heaven and on earth. Matt. 28:18*
The Lord is near to all who call upon Him to all who call upon Him in truth. Ps. 145:18
I kill and I make alive. Deut. 32:39

Upper any of the above and...
O Death, where is your sting? O hades, where is your victory? The sting of death is sin, and the strength of sin is the law. But thanks be to God, who gives us the victory through our Lord Jesus Christ. I Cor. 15:55-56
For I am persuaded that neither death nor life, nor angels nor principalities nor powers, not things present nor things to come, nor height nor depth, nor any other created thing, shall be able to separate us from the love of God which is in Christ Jesus our Lord. Rom. 8:38-39
I am the resurrection and the life. He who believes in Me, though he may die, he shall live. And whoever lives and believes in Me shall never die. John 11:25-26*

## HYMN CHOICES
"Christ the Lord is Risen Today" (TLH #193:1,4-6)
"Lord, It Belongs Not to My Care" (TLH #527:1-3,5)
"Who Knows When Death May Overtake Me" (TLH #598:1,6,8,9)

## 17

## STORY
The Parable of the Sower and the Seed - Matthew 13

## TEACHER PRAYER
Dear Holy Spirit, help me to bring the children in my care to pray daily, "Speak, Lord, for Thy servant heareth." Make me and the children aware of how important it is for us all to continuously use of Thy holy Word. Amen.

## VOCABULARY
*sower* - planter

*fowls* - birds

*scorched* - burned

*hundredfold* - each seed produced a hundred seeds

*waxed gross* - grown hard

*wicked one* - Satan-also called the enemy

*tares* - weeds-unwanted plants

## OUTER AIM
Show how the Savior uses a familiar scene from spring planting to reveal why His Word experiences different growth patterns.

## INNER AIM
Lead the children to pray that the Lord through His Word would make their hearts good ground for the seed of His Word.

## BACKGROUND
*Rupprecht Bible History References, Vol. 2,* pp. 151 ff.

Draw on the children's knowledge of gardening. In Jesus' day the farmer (sower) scattered the seed by hand and it fell on many different kinds of soil-stony, shallow, deep, or on the path itself. Jesus builds on the known, the familiar to teach spiritual truths. In this parable, He reveals to the disciples the difference between themselves and the many others in Israel.

vs. 10-17 Why teach (explain) to the disciples and hide from the scribes and Pharisees? Isaiah already gave the answer. The unbelievers have hardened their hearts against God's Word, will not listen; so the Lord turns away from them and hides knowledge from them.

vs. 19 by the wayside-seed never took root, for it fell on hardened soil.

vs. 20 stony ground-good beginnings, as the soil warmed quickly, but there was no depth.

vs. 22 thorns-external cares and trouble choked the tender plant.

vs. 24 good ground-not natural to sinful mankind; it is ground prepared and created by the Holy Spirit through the Word itself; prepared and sustained by the Word until the time of harvest.

**STUDENT PRAYER**    TLH #284 1 and 6

Father of Mercies, in Thy Word What endless glories shine;
Forever be Thy name adorned For these celestial lines.
Divine Instructor, gracious Lord, Be Thou forever near;
Teach me to love Thy sacred Word and view my Savior here.

## PRESENTATION

Briefly review previous story as time allows.  Make links to the new story when possible.  Tell the story:
Teachers, be encouraged to tell the story in your own words while remaining faithful to the scriptural account.
When scripture records the story in more than one place, you may want to harmonize the accounts (including
extra details found in each account).  Let the students know where they can find the additional details in the
Bible.

Discuss the story:  While reviewing the major events of the story, discuss the possible applications to the
students' lives.  Ask questions that make them think about the story and show that they understand it.

## APPLICATION

How dependent we humans are on the Word of God!  That fact should lead us again and again into that Word.
Our daily prayer should be, "Through Your Word, O Lord, create and maintain my faith so that I bring forth
fruit abundantly until the day of eternal harvest."

## PASSAGES
**These passages can be assigned as memory work or simply discussed in class as to
how they fit the lesson.**

**Lower**
Romans 10:17 - So then faith comes by hearing, and hearing by the Word of God.
I Sam. 3:9 - Speak, Lord; for Your servant hears.

**Middle**
Romans 10:17 - So then faith comes by hearing, and hearing by the Word of God.
I Sam. 3:9 - Speak, Lord; for Your servant hears.
John 8:31-32 - If you abide in My Word, you are My disciples indeed.

**Upper**
Romans 10:17 - So then faith comes by hearing, and hearing by the Word of God.
I Sam. 3:9 - Speak, Lord; for Your servant hears.
John 8:31-32 - If you abide in My Word, you are My disciples indeed.
Psalm 119:105 - Your Word is a lamp to my feet, and a light to my path.

## HYMN CHOICES
How Precious Is the Book Divine - TLH #285 vs. 1 and 6
God's Word is our Great Heritage - TLH #283

## 18

## STORY
Jesus Feeds the Five Thousand - Matthew 14:13-21, Mark 6:34-44; Luke 9:10-17; John 6:1-16

## TEACHER PRAYER
Dear Heavenly Father, You have richly blessed our land so that our bodily needs appear to be easily provided. Yet so often we take these blessings for granted and forget that You provide them and not we ourselves. Prevent our pride from failing to turn to You if we think we lack for any material need. Help me to show my students through my life as well as by this lesson, that we can trust in You to provide for us, even if we don't see how You will do it. But also may we learn to think not only of our bodily needs but also of our spiritual needs. In Your Word You have provided food for our faith so that we trust in Jesus. For You have sent Jesus as our substitute to take the punishment of our sins upon Himself so that we are forgiven and can live in eternity with You. Though our eyes may not see, may we trust in Thee, to whom we pray, for everything today, Amen.

## VOCABULARY
*Denarii* - a silver coin worth roughly a quarter in today's money. (see Rupprecht figures for 1947)

## OUTER AIM
Jesus showed his love and mercy to more than 5000 people by feeding them both body and soul.

## INNER AIM
God provides for our physical and spiritual needs.

## BACKGROUND
*(Rupprecht Bible History References Vol. 2, pp. 193-200)*
Jesus had sent out His disciples to preach in Judea and they had returned with news of all that they had done. Also Jesus heard that John the Baptizer had been beheaded by Herod.. After these things, Jesus tried to be alone with His disciples to rest. Jesus had crossed to the northeast side of the Sea of Galilee. (Rupprecht p. 194) This miracle is the only event of Jesus' ministry, other than His suffering and death, which is recorded by all four evangelists. The feeding of the 5,000 proved to be a watershed in Jesus' ministry. When He would not be their "bread-king," the majority of the people no longer followed Him.
Mark 6:30-32 (Luke 9:10)
- ‣ Jesus attempted to give His disciples and Himself a much needed break in these hectic times of His ministry.
- ‣ Mark tells us that they didn't even have a chance to eat (v.31) because of all the activity.
vs. 33-34
- ‣ But the people heard where Jesus and the disciples were going and arrived on foot even before they had gotten there.
- ‣ Jesus, despite the physical need to rest "was moved with compassion for them because they were like sheep not having a shepherd." Jesus saw their great need for spiritual guidance since they weren't getting it elsewhere.
- ‣ So He again began to teach them about the kingdom of God (Luke) and to heal their diseases.
John 6:2
- ‣ The miracles (signs) had the purpose of identifying Jesus as the promised Messiah; however, they had the effect of becoming more important than the person to whom they pointed. The people came to Jesus to satisfy their own physical needs.

v. 3
- Jesus had tried to find an isolated spot to rest. It also gave Him a vantage point from which to see the large crowds gathered to see and hear Him.

v. 4
- This detail places the time of the event in the second year of Jesus' public ministry.
- A year later He would be crucified.

v. 5
- The other evangelists show that Jesus taught late into the day.
- The disciples urged Jesus to send the crowds away to find food and lodging for the night.
- In this verse we see Jesus' reply directed toward Phillip but also to the other disciples. He wanted them to consider ways to feed the people.

v. 6
- Jesus questioned Phillip and eventually the other disciples to get them to see how their thoughts were directed not toward faith in God, but to human means.

v. 7
- Phillip's answer shows that he could see only the money that they might have been able to gather among themselves.
- But he felt that with so many (perhaps over 20,000 people) they couldn't buy enough bread.

vs. 8-9
- Andrew's answer, although helpful, was also limited by human thinking.
- He had looked beyond the money, to other people, but still hadn't seen Jesus' ability.
- So, he too thought they couldn't perform the task the Lord gave them.

v. 10
- So Jesus set out to show them what they should have realized themselves. He could provide.
- The other gospels note that they had the people sit in ranks of 50 men. This allowed them to see how many people there were. Notice also the count is only of the men, not of women and children who were also there (Matthew).

v. 11
- Jesus took what was available, prayed in thanksgiving for what was provided, and had the disciples distribute the bread and the fish. And they had enough to feed all those people, as much as the people wanted to eat!
- The before meal prayer of thanksgiving and blessing is a good example to follow.

v. 12
- When everyone was full (not just the edges of their hunger satisfied, but full) Jesus told His disciples to gather what remained so that it wouldn't be wasted. (Note Jesus' concern that we don't waste what He provides.)

v. 13
- The quantities of leftovers impressively demonstrated Jesus' ability to provide more than enough food for the people.

v. 14
- The people too recognized the miracle that had taken place.
- They thought that He could very well be the Prophet that Moses had prophesied would come (Deuteronomy. 18:15, see also John 7:40f).

v. 15

- ▸ But Jesus knew that many of the people began to think of Him as only a provider of physical food and bodily needs, not as their Savior.
- ▸ See what happened the following day: John 6:22-71, especially 66.

## STUDENT PRAYER

Dear Lord Jesus, we so easily fail to appreciate the food and clothing and other rich blessings that You provide to keep our bodies alive. Give us wisdom to use those blessings with thankfulness and without wastefulness. Help us to trust in You to continue to meet those needs even if we can't see how You will do it. But, also lift our eyes beyond our bodily needs to trust in You for our greater needs, those of our souls. Lead us often to repent of our sins and to trust in You for forgiveness. Don't let us take that forgiveness lightly but rather help us to appreciate that You purchased our forgiveness with Your own life by dying on the cross for our sakes. For then we will also give thanks for our Salvation as we pray in faith to You. Amen.

## PRESENTATION

Briefly review previous story as time allows. Make links to the new story when possible.

Tell the story: Teachers, be encouraged to tell the story in your own words while remaining faithful to the scriptural account. When scripture records the story in more than one place, you may want to harmonize the accounts (including extra details found in each account). Let the students know where they can find the additional details in the Bible.

Discuss the story: While reviewing the major events of the story, discuss the possible applications to the students' lives. Ask questions that make them think about the story and show that they understand the story.

## ACTIVITY ONE - WHO REMEMBERS THE STORY?

Teacher, read the following questions and answers to the class <u>one set at a time</u>, and have the students circle the letter of the right answer. Alternatively, read all the answers, then have the pupils raise their hands for the correct answer as you read the answers a second time. After each question, give the right answer. Do this as a <u>game</u>, rather than as a quiz. This also provides review/reteach opportunities.

## ACTIVITY TWO - ART WORK - Teacher, have the students draw pictures <u>illustrating the following themes</u> (You may wish to prepare in advance a few "outline" pictures for coloring in, in case some pupils balk at drawing their own): Note that #4 is not a theme.

## APPLICATIONS

1. We need to learn what the disciples learned from Jesus. Our sinful pride tries to make us believe the we can and must provide for our bodies by ourselves. The Lord says that it is He who provides. (Psalm 145:15-16; Matthew 6:31-34) God gives us food, clothing, goods and home. He usually does this through natural means, giving parents the strength and ability to work. He gives us doctors and nurses

and medicine and hospitals to help us when we are sick. We must learn to trust in Him to provide sufficient earthly blessings for our daily needs. Although we need to be good stewards with what He gives us, we must NOT trust in the blessings themselves. What are some ways that we can show God that we appreciate what He has given to us? (Pray before and after meals and use His gifts without wasting them)

2. Jesus also, and more importantly, provides for our souls. He was disappointed that the people began to think of Him only for their bodily needs. He had come to be their Savior, to suffer and die for them as their substitute so that their sins would be forgiven and they would have eternal life. Although we can trust in God for our bodily needs, we also need to trust Him daily for our spiritual needs. In faith, we can show we appreciate His work as our Savior by praying daily and often for His forgiveness of our sins and not "wasting" His forgiveness by sinning against Him.

3. Jesus gave His disciples a test or difficulty for their faith in order to strengthen their faith. He used the lack of physical solutions to help them grow spiritually. They learned to trust more confidently in Jesus, rather than to look only to themselves or to what their senses could perceive. (Proverbs 3:5-6).

## PASSAGES

These passages can be assigned as memory work or simply discussed in class as to how they fit the lesson. Explain the meaning of this Scripture ("the miracles performed by Jesus prove that He is truly the Son of God, and our Savior from sin"), and spend five minutes helping the children to memorize it.

Lower
Psalms 145:15-16 - The eyes of all look expectantly to You, and You give them their food in due season. You open Your hand and satisfy the desire of every living thing.

Middle any of the above and...
Proverbs 3:5-6 - Trust in the LORD with all your heart, And lean not on your own understanding; in all your ways acknowledge Him, and He shall direct your paths.

Upper any of the above and...
Matthew 6:31-33 - Therefore do not worry, saying, 'What shall we eat?' or 'What shall we drink?' or 'What shall we wear?' For after all these things the Gentiles seek. For your heavenly Father knows that you need all these things. But seek first the kingdom of God and His righteousness, and all these things shall be added to you.

## HYMN CHOICES

"Praise God, From Whom all Blessings Flow" (TLH #644)
"The Lord's My Shepherd, I'll not Want" (TLH #436)
"All Depends on Our Possessing" (TLH #425:1-3,5)

## 19

## STORY

Jesus Walks on the Sea - Matthew 14:22-33; Mark 6:45-52; John 6:15-21

## TEACHER PRAYER

Dear heavenly Father, our reason and our senses, the world and doubting friends, suggest many reasons to doubt Your Word and Promises. By Your Spirit, strengthen my faith and the faith of those whom I am about to teach about Your amazing power and will to help in time of need. Help us to walk confidently with faith in You over the troubled waters of life that we may come to You safely in the end. And if doubts threaten us, rescue us from them that we may firmly believe in Jesus our Savior who alone is able to deliver us from every evil of body and soul. In His name we pray, Amen.

## VOCABULARY

*Bethsaida* -  this town was on the northwest side of the Sea of Galilee, a few miles north of Capernaum (see Rupprecht p. 194, 201).

*Fourth watch of the night* -  using the Roman method of keeping time, this would be between three a.m. and six a.m.

*Ghost* -  also in those times people were afraid of ghosts and spirits.

*Boisterous* -  noisy and very turbulent or exuberant; of wind, flowing strongly and in various directions.

## OUTER AIM

Jesus walked on water to help His disciples.

## INNER AIM

Believe in Jesus without a doubt.

## BACKGROUND

*(Rupprecht Bible History References Vol.2, pp. 200-204)*

This story follows immediately after Jesus fed the 5,000+ with 5 loaves and 2 fish. It reminds us that people, even with great proofs for their faith, might still doubt and need God to continue to strengthen their faith. God wants us to believe in Him without doubting, for He alone can truly be trusted. Doubts are a sin against the 1st commandment because they reveal a lack of trust in God and instead, show trust in something else, whether it is our senses or someone other than God.

Matthew 14:22

▸ After Jesus had miraculously fed the thousands of people, they wanted to make Him their earthly king who would provide them with all their needs (John 6:15).

▸ To try to prevent that, Jesus sent everyone away.

▸ He sent the disciples by boat to the other side of the Sea of Galilee. In a boat, they wouldn't be coerced by the crowds who wanted to make Jesus a "Bread-King."

▸ Jesus sent the crowds away.

▸ A note on the destination: Mark 6:45 names their destination as Bethsaida while John 6:17 says they went toward Capernaum. The Bethsaida on the northwest side of the sea is a few miles north of Capernaum and the home of some of the disciples. The disciples could have been trying to visit their homes that night and then, the following day, plan to meet Jesus at Capernaum where He would be preaching next (John 6:24).

Matthew 14:23

▸ Jesus had much to pray about as He saw the people looking at Him, not as their Savior, but as their "bread king."

- He spent many hours alone in prayer on a mountain talking with His Father. He prayed into the evening, long after sunset.

v. 24

- The Sea of Galilee is about 40 miles across. On a good day, it wouldn't have taken the disciples a very long time to cross.
- A storm came up and the wind was against them. As their boat was tossed by the waves, they strained hard at the oars (Mark 6:48); in the hours of fighting the storm, they had gone only three to four miles (John 6:19).
- Jesus, on the land, saw the disciples caught in the storm. Jesus may or may not have needed to use His omniscience (all knowing ability) to see the disciples, depending on conditions which we don't know. We know only that He saw them. Mark 6:48.

v. 25

- Jesus waited until after three a.m. to come to His disciples. Then he did it in a miraculous way. He walked on the stormy water itself.
- As the Creator of all and divine Ruler over the laws of nature, He could command the water to support His human body.
- Mark tells us that He would have passed them by as a further test of their faith.

v. 26

- The disciples' reacted with fear and superstition. They thought that Jesus was a ghost and they cried out in fear as their reason grappled with what their senses told them.

v. 27

- Immediately Jesus speaks words of comfort, "Be of good cheer; it is I, do not be afraid." Literally: "Be courageous; I myself am, don't be afraid." The comforting voice of the Lord speaks through the storm to encourage them not to fear, for He is with them.

v. 28

- Peter responded with a bold request. "Lord, if it is You, command me to come to you upon the water." This might also be saying that Peter wouldn't believe unless He had proof. The others took Jesus at His Word.

v. 29

- Jesus' simple word of command calls Peter to trust Jesus to allow Him to walk safely across the violent sea.
- With a storm raging around him, Peter courageously stepped out of the boat and began to walk across the shifting sea toward Jesus.

v. 30

- Ah, but Peter took his eyes off the Lord and was overwhelmed by his reason and senses and questioned what his Lord had shown was possible.
- The strong wind blew making the waves rough. How could he, a mere human being, walk on water? In his fear and doubting, he began to sink as the grip of his faith relaxed its hold on the Lord's promise.
- Yet, he cried out to the Lord to save him as he began sinking.

v. 31

- Immediately, Jesus' hand caught Peter before he could drown.
- Jesus chided him, "O you of little faith, why did you doubt?"
- Peter, bold at first, didn't remain strong in faith when put to the test. Peter's doubts had let him down, but the Lord would not have abandoned him if Peter had continued to trust in Jesus.

v. 32
- ► This was a night of miracles: not only did Jesus and Peter walk on stormy water, but as soon as Jesus and Peter entered the boat, the storm stilled and, as John says, immediately the boat reached the other shore.
- ► Not coincidence, but these miracles occurred as Jesus' continued to display His love and power to the disciples.

v. 33
- ► The disciples reacted with overwhelming amazement and wonder.
- ► As Mark says (6:52), their hearts had been hardened or dull, and they hadn't grasped the lesson from Jesus' feeding the thousands with the loaves. They didn't grasp that Jesus was God who could be trusted to take care of them. But these amazing miracles brought the message home to them (see Mark 8:17). Now, in faith, they welcomed and worshiped Jesus saying, "Truthfully, You are the Son of God."

## STUDENT PRAYER

Dear Heavenly Father, Your Word calls us to believe in Your promises. Your Word gives us many examples of Your power to do the humanly impossible in order to help those who trust in You. Strengthen our faith in You and Your Son Jesus Christ our Savior, that we may firmly believe without doubting anything that You have told us and promised us. When we are afraid, remind us of Your protection; when You ask us to do difficult things, give us courage to step forward without doubts. And if doubts distract our faith, rescue us when we call for Your help. We pray with trust in You who spared not Your own Son but delivered Him up to be our Savior, knowing that You alone can be trusted in every need, Amen.

## PRESENTATION

Briefly review the previous story as time allows. Make links to the new story when possible.

Tell the story: Teachers, be encouraged to tell the story in your own words while remaining faithful to the scriptural account. When scripture records the story in more than one place, you may want to harmonize the accounts (including extra details found in each account). Let the students know where they can find the additional details in the Bible.

Discuss the story: While reviewing the major events of the story, discuss the possible applications to the students' lives. Ask questions that make them think about the story and show that they understand the story.

> **For the activity, you will need to have supplies ready. See the student lesson for those materials.**

## APPLICATIONS

1. Jesus knew that the disciples' faith needed to be strengthened, for they did not see how much they could trust in Him to take care of them in times of trouble. He allowed them to experience the storm in order to show them that He was able to protect them. They learned that Jesus could do the humanly impossible to help them, such as walking on the stormy sea and stilling the sea at will. They also saw from Peter's example what happens when doubts overcome faith. Yet, they also saw that the Lord was quick to rescue Peter when he called for help as his doubts let him down. As their faith grasped these truths, they responded in worship of Jesus as the Son of God. Jesus wants us to have a strong, unwavering trust in Him as well. From this story and others and the promises of God's Word, we learn that we too can trust in

God confidently , despite the doubts that our senses, our reason, or other people will suggest against such faith. If we divert our eyes from God and His promises, we will sink. But if we start to sink, we know that Jesus' rescuing hand will bring us to safety. God is faithful to those who trust in Him.

2. Fear, worry, and doubt can replace faith. Faith is a firm trust and confidence in God and His Word. Why are fear, worry, and doubt sins against the first commandment? Why can't we always trust our senses, our reason, or sometimes, other people in matters of faith and life? (Sin prevents us from seeing how God can work in spite of how the situation may seem to us.) How do we know that we can trust in God even when our faith is being tested (Romans 8:31-39)? Discuss how Psalm 46 is an encouraging declaration of faith. See also James 1:6.

3. Jesus is able to protect His people from every danger. Consider examples from the Bible of how God protects His people from danger. Talk over with the children how God is able to take care of His dear children.

## PASSAGES
These passages can be assigned as memory work or simply discussed in class as to how they fit the lesson.

<u>Lower</u>
Psalms 50:15 - Call upon Me in the day of trouble; I will deliver you, and you shall glorify Me.

<u>Middle</u> any of the above and...
Psalm 46:1-3 - God is our refuge and strength, a very present help in trouble. Therefore we will not fear, even though the earth be removed, and though the mountains be carried into the midst of the sea; though its waters roar and be troubled, though the mountains shake with its swelling.

<u>Upper</u> any of the above and...
Romans 8:31-32 - What then shall we say to these things? If God is for us, who can be against us? He who did not spare His own Son, but delivered Him up for us all, how shall He not with Him also freely give us all things?
Romans 8:38-39 - For I am persuaded that neither death nor life, nor angels nor principalities nor powers, nor things present nor things to come, nor height nor depth, nor any other created thing, shall be able to separate us from the love of God which is in Christ Jesus our Lord.

## HYMN CHOICES
"Oh, For a Faith That Will Not Shrink" (TLH 396 1, 3, 6)
"If God Himself Be For Me" (TLH 528 1-3, choose more)
"Abide, O Dearest Jesus" (TLH 53)

## 20

## STORY
The Woman of Canaan - Matthew 15:21-28; Mark 7:24-30

## TEACHER PRAYER
Lord, Jesus Christ, help us to look to You for all our needs, especially our utmost needs for the forgiveness of sins, faith, Your Word, life, and salvation. Help us through Your Word to humble ourselves so that we plainly and clearly see the need for these gifts and for complete dependence on You at all times. Although You may test our faith severely as You did in the case of the woman in this lesson, grant that the test strengthens our faith. Do not let us weaken or lose our faith over such tests. In Your name we ask this. Amen.

## VOCABULARY
*Tyre and Sidon* - Two ancient cities that for a time were powerful cities. They were both located on the eastern edge of the Mediterranean Sea about 21 miles apart. *Find these cities on the map. (see Rupprecht p. 205-206)

*Canaan* - a general term for the geographical region of Palestine. Here, it's used to show the woman was not Jewish. (Regarding Canaan, Young's Concordance of the Bible has a good, though dated summary. Compare also the following: Syro-Phoenician used in Mark 7:27)

*Syro-Phoenician* - a person from the Roman territory that combined Syria with Phoenicia. Phoenicia was a narrow strip of land along the Mediterranean coast that had at one time been a great shipping power (similar boundaries to modern-day Lebanon). Syria was the region east of Phoenicia (similar to today's Syria).

*Demon-possessed* - In Jesus' time the devil and the devil's fallen angels were allowed the power to take limited physical control of people's bodies. (see Rupprecht pp133-134) While it gave the devil the ability to show his anger against Christ, it also gave Christ the opportunity to show His ultimate power over the devil and the demons. It emphasized for the people the great spiritual conflict being played out between the devil and God.

## OUTER AIM
A Gentile woman persevered in seeking help from Jesus.

## INNER AIM
Our faith looks expectantly to God for all of our needs.

## BACKGROUND
*(Rupprecht Bible History References Vol.2, pp. 205-210)*
Jesus had recently performed many amazing miracles in Galilee and preached powerful messages in Capernaum. In this story He tries again to take a break from His work by going north from Galilee to a region not as populated by the Jewish people.
Matt. 15:21
- Jesus went from the region of Gennesaret (Galilee) to the region of Tyre and Sidon. He may not have gone into those cities themselves but to the countryside and villages around them.

v. 22
- Mark informs us this woman was a Syro-Phoenician, a Greek. "Greek" as used here and other places in the New Testament, often means a non-Jew, a Gentile, a heathen,. She was Greek or Hellenistic in outlook or culture, not in national origin. See vocabulary above.

- The woman's words, "O, Lord, Son of David," indicates she looked upon Jesus as the promised Jewish Messiah. She believed Him to be her Savior who possessed divine power for forgiveness and healing. She asks that her demon-possessed daughter be healed.

v. 23
- Jesus, knowing exactly what He would do and what would happen, seemingly ignores her.
- The disciples are perturbed by her and wish to be rid of her somehow.

v. 24
- Jesus, knowing that she lived surrounded by unbelievers, seeks to strengthen her faith by testing it.
- Jesus lets her know that His first priority was the lost sheep of Israel, meaning the Jewish people of Israel who needed to be gathered through repentance and faith into Jesus' sheepfold (kingdom).

v. 25
- She does not let the seeming brush-off, the rejection, disturb her in the least. It made her more persistent and worshipful.
- She begs Jesus for help.

v. 26
- Yet Jesus' severest test of her faith is shown.
- He implies she is a dog and not worthy to receive the full meal on the master's table.
- The meal pictures the Gospel that was to be for the "children" (cf. Mt 3:9; Rom. 9; Gal 3:7), not the dogs or the heathen.
- The Jews of that time often referred to heathens as dogs.

v. 27
- Her reply makes her faith shine all the more brilliantly, because all she asks for is the crumbs from the Gospel table, not the whole meal.
- Such was her faith that she knew God's mercy was so great that even a small portion would be sufficient for her needs.

v. 28
- Jesus expresses amazement at her faith, hoping that others would look to imitate her great faith and perseverance.
- He grants her the "crumbs" for which she asked by healing her daughter.
- Mark tells us that she found her daughter lying peacefully on the bed and completely healed.

## STUDENT PRAYER

Dear God, you have shown us in this story that even though You may severely test our faith in You, surely You desire us to keep our faith. Help us always to strongly and faithfully trust and hope in You to the end, so that by faith in Your saving work, we may enter Your everlasting home and be with You forever. Amen.

## PRESENTATION

Briefly review the previous story as time allows. Make links to the new story when possible.

Tell the story: Teachers, be encouraged to tell the story in your own words while remaining faithful to the scriptural account. When scripture records the story in more than one place, you may want to harmonize the accounts (including extra details found in each account). Let the students know where they can find the additional details in the Bible.

Discuss the story: While reviewing the major events of the story, discuss the possible applications to the students' lives. Ask questions that make them think about the story and show that they understand the story.

**ACTIVITY TWO** - Help the students memorize the passage and reference. Then have them cut out the boxes and glue them to paper to make a get-well card for someone who is sick. You will need to fold the extra sheet of paper appropriately to make a card.

## APPLICATIONS

1. Many times we may and should go to the Lord in times of need and trouble or problems. He tells us to call upon Him in the day of trouble and He will deliver us. We should also see how God may be working on us to show how persistent we can be. Will we be like the woman who did not accept what seemed to be a "no" after her second request? We also need to realize that God does not always answer our prayers in the way we expect Him to.

2. We should realize that we too are "dogs," undeserving of God's mercy because of our many and daily sins. We also are the non-Jews, the Gentiles to whom God also "scattered the crumbs", that is, reached out to after many of the Jews rejected their birthright and Savior. We are made "children" only through Jesus Christ. For Jesus redeemed us, forgives us our sins, and calls us by the Holy Spirit with the Word to believe in Jesus as our Savior. Because of our many sins, even as Christians, each day we need to come many times seeking God's merciful forgiveness and healing and to be reassured of our place as God's children.

3. In this life we should expect the Lord to allow tests of our faith. He permits these trials to strengthen our faith and make heaven appear all the more dear to us. (James 1:2-3,12f; 1 Peter 1:3-7) These trials lead us to long for the assurance of forgiveness and heaven. We know that after the troubles, God will send us times of joy, both now with the peace of forgiveness and in eternal life without tears.

4. Temptation should urge us to have greater reliance upon God instead of relying on ourselves, the world's ideas, or others. (James 1:12ff) Our help is in the Lord.

## PASSAGES

These passages can be assigned as memory work or simply discussed in class as to how they fit the lesson.

Lower
Psalms 50:15 - "Call upon Me in the day of trouble; I will deliver you, and you shall glorify Me."
1 Peter 5:6-7 - Therefore humble yourselves under the mighty hand of God, that He may exalt you in due time, casting all your care upon Him, for He cares for you.
Matthew 11:28 - "Come to Me, all you who labor and are heavy laden, and I will give you rest.

Middle any of the above and...
Matthew 11:28-30 - "Come to Me, all you who labor and are heavy laden, and I will give you rest. Take My yoke upon you and learn from Me, for I am gentle and lowly in heart, and you will find rest for your souls. For My yoke is easy and My burden is light."
Lamentations 3:22-23 - Through the Lord's mercies we are not consumed, because His compassions fail not. They are new every morning: great is Thy faithfulness.

Upper any of the above and...

1 Corinthians 10:12-13 - Therefore, let him who thinks he stands take heed lest he fall. No temptation has overtaken you except such as is common to man; but God is faithful, who will not allow you to be tempted beyond what you are able, but with the temptation will also make the way of escape, that you may be able to bear it.

Romans 8:28 - And we know that all things work together for good to those who love God, to those who are the called according to His purpose.

## HYMN CHOICES

"What a Friend We Have in Jesus." (TLH 457 all)

"I am Trusting Thee, Lord Jesus" (TLH 428 all)

"Rise to Arms, With Prayer Employ You" (TLH 444 all)

"Rise, My Soul, to Watch and Pray" (TLH 446 all)

## 21

## STORY

The Transfiguration  - Matthew 17:1-9; Mark 9:2-10; Luke 9:28-36

## TEACHER PRAYER

Dear Father in Heaven, this lesson reminds us again of Your amazing love toward us, that Your beloved Son, would humble Himself, even to the death on the cross, in order to save us sinners from what we deserve.  We thank and praise You and Jesus Your Son for this amazing act of love for us.  Jesus endured the shame of the cross with the goal of our redemption in His sight.  Set before our eyes, His cross and the certainty of heaven which it gives us so that, when we face those tough tests of faith, or walk through the valley of the shadow of death, we will know Your love and the goal You have in mind for us.  For our times are safely in Your hands, so we must trust in Thee. Amen.

## VOCABULARY

*Transfigure* -  change appearance
*Tabernacles* -  special temporary shelters made of branches or tents used for worship such as in the Jewish Feast of the Tabernacles.
*Rabbi* - "teacher" and used as a title or form of address.
*Decease* -  in Greek, literally "departure."  His death would soon take place and, after His resurrection,
Jesus would leave them.
*Scribes* - originally simply men who copied the scriptures by hand.  But as their knowledge of the Scriptures grew from their work, they were considered authorities of it and would be regarded  as Professors of Theology today.  They held high positions in the religious government of the Jews. (See Rupprecht pp. 47-48)

## OUTER AIM

Jesus shows the disciples He is the true God.

## INNER AIM

Jesus shows us He is our God and our Savior.

## BACKGROUND

*(Rupprecht Bible History References Vol.2, pp. 221-225)*
During His ministry, Jesus took upon Himself the form of a servant (Phil. 2:4-6) and humbled Himself and became obedient unto death.  But at this one point in Jesus' ministry, God revealed the glory that rightfully belonged to Jesus.  This reveals a striking contrast for us and the three disciples who would also see Jesus at the most humiliating point in His work from the Garden of Gethsemane to
His death on the cross.
Matthew 17:1
▸    Six days before, Peter had confessed that He believed that Jesus is "the Christ, the Son of the living God."  (Note: Luke reports eight  days, perhaps by including the day of Peter's confession and the day of the Transfiguration.)
▸    After that, Jesus began to explain to His disciples that He must soon suffer and die in Jerusalem. (Mt 16:21)
▸    Jesus often chose these three particular disciples to be witnesses of special events in His ministry.

▸    This time they went up on a mountain to watch Jesus while He prayed, as Luke tells us.

v. 2
- ▸ While praying (Luke), Jesus' appearance was altered to reveal His holiness and glory as God.
- ▸ The disciples and thus the Gospel writers struggled to describe it for human eyes.
- ▸ His face shone as the sun, and His clothes were white and glistening, as snow, whiter than any launderer on earth can achieve, white as light itself.

v. 3
- ▸ Moses, wrote the first five books of the Old Testament, including the transmission of God's Law for His people.
- ▸ Elijah powerfully represented all the prophets of the Old Testament.
- ▸ So, these two men symbolized the entire Old Testament. Moses had been buried by God (Deut 34:6) and then resurrected afterwards, and Elijah had been carried by God into heaven (2 Kings 2:10-11).

Luke 9:30-31
- ▸ The two men also appeared in the glory of their resurrected bodies Phil 3:21 (see Rupprecht p.223).
- ▸ They talked with Jesus about the events surrounding His death or departure which would be completed in Jerusalem. (Please see: 1 Peter 1:10-12)
- ▸ The Old Testament has many passages that speak of Jesus' suffering, death, and resurrection.

v. 32
- ▸ This eyewitness' testimony (1 Peter 1:16-18ff) describes not only the event but also what the disciples experienced. They were at first sleepy, as in Gethsemane, but woke up when they saw Jesus in His glory talking with the two men who, they realized, were Moses and Elijah.

Matthew 17: 5
- ▸ God the Father in effect, replied to Peter's babbling. as a bright cloud came and overshadowed them so that they entered it (Luke).
- ▸ The voice of God the Father came from the cloud, "This is My Beloved Son, in whom I am well pleased. Hear Him!"
- ▸ What a testimony: a) Jesus is God's Son, b) God's beloved Son, c) Who has pleased the Father with His entire life and ministry to this point (and beyond John 10:17-18).
- ▸ And also a command: a)Hear the Prophet of whom Moses had spoken (Deut 18:15) and the b) Messenger of the covenant (Mal 3:1b), the Lord about to enter His temple to establish the covenant of grace.

v. 6
- ▸ The actual voice of God the Father caused the three disciples to fall down on their faces in worship, honor, and fear.
- ▸ Seeing the awesome glory of Jesus and then hearing God the Father speak overwhelmed these sinful mortals.

v. 7
- ▸ Yet Jesus took away their fear with his comforting touch and His command not to be afraid.

v. 8
- ▸ Recovering, they saw only Jesus, appearing once again in His human form with His glory hidden.

v. 9
- ▸ This was to be a private event, meant only for those three disciples until after Jesus had risen from the dead. Until then, they alone could draw strength from it.
- ▸ Jesus' command for silence may have been to help prevent Satan from misusing their telling of it to interfere in Christ's work.
- ▸ After Jesus had risen from the dead, John and Peter (and probably James too) told of that special piece of heaven that they witnessed. (John 1:14, 1 Peter 1:16-18)

- The disciples still had questions and didn't understand about Jesus' resurrection until after it happened Mark 9:10f. (Cf John 20:8 and the Emmaus disciples Luke 24:13-27)
- The purposes: The transfiguration and the conversation took place both for Jesus' sake and for the disciples' sakes.
- For Jesus: the revelation of His glory reminded Jesus, the man of the glory, that would be His when He had successfully completed His work. The prophets' words may have reminded Him of the prophecies describing, not only His suffering and death, but also the results that would come from them. (Hebrews 12:2)
- For the disciples: They saw that Jesus was indeed God, just as they had come to believe Him to be. Soon they would witness from "front-row seats" the coming horrible conclusion of Jesus' work and this memorable glimpse of heaven would strengthen them. Eventually, they would also understand how the events that would shortly take place were according to God's plan as described in the Old Testament. But the disciples weren't to talk of these things until after Jesus' death and resurrection had completed the picture of Jesus' victory.

## STUDENT PRAYER

Dear Lord Jesus, our imaginations try to grasp in a limited way what You must look like in all Your glory. We know that as sinners we would be terrified of Your holiness and how we have failed to be holy. But we also know Your great love, for You laid aside Your glory to come to this earth as a human being and give Your holy life as payment for our sins. By faith, we glimpsed Your great love for us as we see You preparing for that expensive sacrifice for us. As You prepared and strengthened Your disciples to face the difficult months ahead, so strengthen our faith before and as we face the many tests in our lives so that our Faith in You doesn't waver. Keep the image of Your Love and the heavenly goal You have won for us before our eyes. As You have nourished us in faith, in the end we will see Your glory without the fear of our sins and may worship You for all eternity. We pray trusting in Your name, and in all You have revealed to us. Amen.

## PRESENTATION

Briefly review the previous story as time allows. Make links to the new story when possible.

Tell the story: Teachers, be encouraged to tell the story in your own words while remaining faithful to the scriptural account. When scripture records the story in more than one place, you may want to harmonize the accounts (including extra details found in each account). Let the students know where they can find the additional details in the Bible.

Discuss the story: While reviewing the major events of the story, discuss the possible applications to the students' lives. Ask questions that make them think about the story and show that they understand the story.

## ACTIVITY

Try this ahead of time so you know the correct size for the cloud. You may want to make copies of clouds of the correct size.
-Cut a large cloud shape out of a piece of paper.
-Tape it to the picture so you can show how the cloud dropped down to cover Jesus and the disciples. One piece of tape at the top works well.
-Have the children retell the story, using the picture and cloud.

## APPLICATIONS

1. We need to take with us into life this lesson's picture of Jesus. He is not simply a human being who could do great things and taught important truths, He is God Himself with all the glory and holiness and awesomeness that God possesses. Yet, (Phil 2:5-8) for our sakes, He humbled Himself and became obedient to the point of death, even the death of the cross. He knew exactly what He MUST suffer until and including the cross, yet He went forward, for us! John 15:13 "Greater love has no one than this, than to lay down one's life for his friends." If we can begin to understand what this really means for us, we will have done well. To do this, discuss why Jesus, who here shows He is God, had to lay aside His glory and had to suffer and die for us.

2. The three disciples witnessed Jesus' glory, the glorified Moses and Elijah, and heard God's powerful testimony. God strategically prepared them before they witnessed the terrifying events of Jesus' fall from popularity, betrayal, arrest, trials, sufferings, crucifixion, death, and burial. Those would be trying days for the disciples as they struggled to believe in Jesus as the Christ, the Promised One who would save His people. At this point Jesus was very popular, but from here on out His enemies would be allowed to take Him to do what they wanted with Him. God will also give us opportunities to strengthen our faith by hearing His Word and learning of His gracious plans to carry us through the difficult times of life until we reach eternity. If we use those times to strengthen our faith, we will be prepared also when we face the really difficult challenges to our faith. Discuss in what ways God prepares us with glimpses of His glory and heaven before those times when it's difficult to see the final goal ahead.

## PASSAGES

These passages can be assigned as memory work or simply discussed in class as to how they fit the lesson.

Lower

John 15:13 - Greater love has no one than this, than to lay down one's life for his friends.

Matthew 17:5 - Suddenly a voice came out of the cloud, saying, "This is My beloved Son, in whom I am well pleased. Hear Him!"

Middle any of the above and...

John 1:14 - And the Word became flesh and dwelt among us, and we beheld His glory, the glory as of the only begotten of the Father, full of grace and truth.

John 10:17-18 - Therefore My Father loves Me, because I lay down My life that I may take it again. No one takes it from Me, but I lay it down of Myself. I have power to lay it down, and I have power to take it again.

Upper any of the above and...

Matthew 16:15-16 - He said to them, "But who do you say that I am?" Simon Peter answered and said, "You are the Christ, the Son of the living God."

Philippians 2:5-8 - Let this mind be in you which was also in Christ Jesus, who, being in the form of God, did not consider it robbery to be equal with God, but made Himself of no reputation, taking the form of a bondservant, and coming in the likeness of men. And being found in appearance as a man, He humbled Himself and became obedient to the point of death, even the death of the cross.

Hebrews 12:1-2 - Therefore we also, since we are surrounded by so great a cloud of witnesses, let us lay aside every weight, and the sin which so easily ensnares us, and let us run with endurance the race that is set before us, looking unto Jesus, the author and finisher of our faith, who for the joy that was set before Him endured the cross, despising the shame, and has sat down at the right hand of the throne of God.

## HYMN CHOICES

"Tis Good, Lord, to be Here" (TLH 135 all, esp 6)

"Come Unto Me, Ye Weary" (TLH 276)

"O Savior, Precious Savior" (TLH 352 all)

"Jesus and Shall It Ever Be," (TLH 346 all)

## 22

## STORY

The Parable of the Unforgiving Servant - Matthew 18

## TEACHER PRAYER

Dear Lord Jesus, teach us to use Your Word to bring sinners to repentance that heaven's door may be opened to them. Let me reflect Thy gracious forgiveness to all who live with me in this sinful world. Amen.

## VOCABULARY

*take account* - examine in detail
*talent* - a very large sum of money-10,000 talents equals millions of dollars
*compassion* - have and show mercy

## OUTER AIM

The Lord reveals a most forgiving heart in contrast to the hardness of human nature.

## INNER AIM

Teach the children to pray the Fifth Petition with Christian understanding and deep concern for those who sin against them.

## BACKGROUND

*Rupprecht Bible History References*, *Vol. 2,* pp. 225 ff.

In the verses preceding this Parable of the Unforgiving Servant, the Savior had been speaking to the disciples about their forgiving and retaining sins (the use of the Ministry of the Keys). Peter quickly came with the question, "Lord, how oft shall my brother sin against me, and I forgive him? Till seven times?" In response to that very human question-how often-Jesus tells the Parable of the Unforgiving Servant.

vs. 22  Seventy times seven:  an unlimited number

vs. 23  take account:  see how servants had met their responsibilities

vs. 24  began to reckon:  began to look into or examine in detail

vs. 25  a servant whose debt was far beyond what he could ever pay

vs. 26  the servant was unaware of his inability to pay

vs. 27  the king forgave

vs. 28  100 pence:  how small in comparison to 10,000 talents

vs. 33-35  contrast between merciful king and demanding servant.

## STUDENT PRAYER     TLH #412 v. 1

May we Thy precepts, Lord, fulfill
And do on earth our Father's will  As angels do above;
Still walk in Christ, the living Way,
With all Thy children and obey The Law of Christian love.

## PRESENTATION

Briefly review previous story as time allows.  Make links to the new story when possible.  Tell the story:
Teachers, be encouraged to tell the story in your own words while remaining faithful to the scriptural account.
When scripture records the story in more than one place, you may want to harmonize the accounts, including
extra details found in each account.  Let the students know where they can find the additional details in the
Bible.

Discuss the story:  While reviewing the major events of the story, discuss the possible applications to the
students' lives.  Ask questions that make them think about the story and show that they understand the story.

## APPLICATION

- Reflect on the unbounded daily love that our God has shown us by forgiving us our countless sins without
  any merit or worthiness in us. "Forgive us our trespasses . . ." (Fifth Petition.)
- Reflect on the mercy and grace of the Lord in forgiving the sins of those who sin against us, not only seven
  times but seventy times seven. "As we forgive those who trespass against us." (Fifth Petition.)

## PASSAGES
## These passages can be assigned as memory work or simply discussed in class as to
##    how they fit the lesson.

**Lower**

Luke 23:34 -  "Father, forgive them; for they do not know what they do."

**Middle**

Luke 23:34 -  "Father, forgive them; for they do not know what they do."
Matt 5:44 - "Love your enemies, bless those that curse you, do good to those that hate you, and pray for those
    who spitefully use you, and persecute you."

**Upper**

Luke 23:34 -  "Father, forgive them; for they do not know what they do."
Matt 5:44 - "Love your enemies, bless those that curse you, do good to those that hate you, and pray for those
    who spitefully use you, and persecute you."

John 20:23 - "If you forgive the sins of any, they are forgiven them; if you retain the sins of any, they are
    retained." (Ministry of the Keys)

## HYMN CHOICES

Forgive Our Sins, Lord, We Implore - TLH #458 v. 6
Yea, As I Live, Jehovah Saith - TLH 331 vs 1 and 3

## 23

## STORY

The Parable of the Pharisee and the Publican - Luke 18:9-14

## TEACHER PRAYER

Dear Father in heaven, help me to make clear to the children the need to turn their eyes and thoughts ever away from their deeds and works to the life, death and resurrection of their Savior, Jesus Christ. May they ever pray, "Lord, be merciful to me a sinner," so that in Jesus' life and death they stand justified before Thee. Amen.

## VOCABULARY

*extortioners* - those who use their position of power to take money or goods from others

*fast* - to go without food

*tithe* - to give a tenth or portion of one's goods

*smote* - strike

*justified* - to be declared just or righteous

*exalteth* - build up in honor

*abased* - humbled, brought down

## OUTER AIM

To show the difference between those who trust in themselves and those who look to the Savior.

## INNER AIM

To lead the children to despair of their own works and to rely completely on Jesus for salvation.

## BACKGROUND *Rupprecht Bible History References, Vol. 2,* pp. 276 ff.

The Pharisees and the Publicans were very much a part of the scene when Jesus lived on earth. The Pharisees were highly respected by the populace and the Publicans were greatly despised. The Old Testament laws were the object of the Pharisees' teachings. They stressed outward obedience to these laws. They made a great show of keeping them. It was taught by them that the fulfilling of the Law would open heaven's doors for them. This stress on works is very much a part of the religious scene in our day also. It is very much a part of human thinking-to get something, I have to give something. We find it taught in the lodges, scouting, and even in many of the organized Christian church bodies. Salvation by works is proclaimed boldly and openly. This parable should shed God's light on all who attempt to get to heaven by their works.

vs. 9-10  Pharisee - promulgator of salvation by one's works

Publican - a tax collector for the Roman government. They were despised for serving the Roman government as well as for collecting more than they should have. They were looked upon as being thieves.

vs. 11  a prayer exalting one's own deeds

vs. 12  fast twice a week-more than was required

tithes of all–tithing was required on only certain items

vs. 13  publican does not boast–knows himself to be a sinner, with eyes cast down, and striking his breast in humility, he pleads for mercy. . . "just as I am without one plea but that Thy blood was shed for me . ."

vs. 14  Jesus looks at the two and makes it clear that the publican was declared just, righteous, by God "went down to his house justified."  While the pharisee was turned away.

## STUDENT PRAYER   - TLH 388 vs. 1 and 5
Just as I am, without one plea But that Thy blood was shed for me
And that Thou bidd'st me come to Thee, O Lamb of God I come, I come

Just as I am, Thou wilt receive, Wilt welcome, pardon, cleanse, relieve,
Because Thy promise I believe, O Lamb of God, I come, I come.

## PRESENTATION
Briefly review previous story as time allows.  Make links to the new story when possible.  Tell the story: Teachers, be encouraged to tell the story in your own words while remaining faithful to the scriptural account. When scripture records the story in more than one place, you may want to harmonize the accounts (including extra details found in each account).  Let the students know where they can find the additional details in the Bible.

Discuss the story:  While reviewing the major events of the story, discuss the possible applications to the students' lives.  Ask questions that help make them think about the story and show that they understand the story.

## APPLICATION
*   When coming into God's presence in prayer, don't boast of your deeds.
*   When coming into God's presence in prayer, make Jesus your claim to glory, "In the cross of Christ I glory ..."
*   Beware of teachers and organizations that would lead you to exalt yourself.

## PASSAGES
**These passages can be assigned as memory work or simply discussed in class as to how they fit the lesson.**

Lower
Psalm 51:9 - "Hide Your face from my sins, and blot out all my iniquities."

Psalm 50:15 - "Call upon Me in the day of trouble; I will deliver you, and you shall glorify Me."

Middle
Psalm 51:9 - "Hide Your face from my sins, and blot out all my iniquities."

Psalm 50:15 - "Call upon Me in the day of trouble; I will deliver you, and you shall glorify Me."

Psalm 51:17 - "The sacrifices of God are a broken spirit, a broken and a contrite heart–These, O God, You will not despise."

Upper

Psalm 51:9 - "Hide Your face from my sins, and blot out all my iniquities."

Psalm 50:15 - "Call upon Me in the day of trouble; I will deliver you, and you shall glorify Me."

Psalm 51:17 - "The sacrifices of God are a broken spirit, a broken and a contrite heart–These, O God, You will not despise."

Luke 14:11 - "For whoever exalts himself shall be abased, and he who humbles himself will be exalted."

Romans 3:23-24 - "for all have sinned and fall short of the glory of God, being justified freely by His grace through the redemption that is in Christ Jesus."

## HYMN CHOICES
My Hope is Built on Nothing Less - TLH #370
Jesus, Thy Blood and Righteousness - TLH #371
Just as I Am, without One Plea - TLH #388

## 24

## STORY

Jesus Teaches with Children - Matthew 18:1-6, 10; Mark 10:13-16; Luke 9:46-48) and Blesses Them - Matthew 19:13-15; Mark 10:13-16; Luke 18:15-17

## TEACHER PRAYER

Dear Father in Heaven, help me to remember again the lessons that Your Son Jesus taught through children. Show me again how to be humble and trusting in my faith before You all the days of my life. And as I set out to teach the "little ones" in my care, help me to remember how very important they are to You. Do not let anything I say or do mislead them into sin, or worse, into doubting or unbelief. As you have assured us it would be so when the children are brought to You, bless them in their precious faith that they may trust You for Salvation and all else that they need. I depend on You for all my needs as I come to You in prayer. Amen.

## VOCABULARY

*Converted* - "turned", spiritually, turned from being a child of Satan to a child of God.
*Receive the Kingdom of heaven or God* - the Holy Spirit places faith in the heart, making a person a member of God's kingdom.

## OUTER AIM

Jesus taught His disciples to be child-like in faith.

## INNER AIM

A child-like faith looks to Jesus for all things.

## BACKGROUND

*(Rupprecht Bible History References Vol. 2, pp. 239-244)*

On two separate occasions, Jesus brought His disciples down to earth with lessons about children. A number of times the disciples argued about who was or would be greatest of them. Sometimes they asked Jesus if they could sit as rulers on thrones with Jesus. Other times they wanted to imitate the rich and powerful. Visions of an earthly kingdom danced in their heads. But Jesus used a lesson with little children to teach them about greatness. Another time, Jesus' disciples did not want to bother Him with children. Sometimes children don't seem to be important to some people. They say things like, "He's just a child." But Jesus lets us know that children are very important to Him and can teach us something important about believing.

**The first lesson: against pride**

Luke 9:46

▸    These events happened shortly after the Transfiguration when Jesus had separated three of the disciples from the others to witness that event.

▸    Perhaps out of envy, Jesus' disciples started to argue as to who was greatest among them.

Matthew 18:1

▸    They finally came to Jesus and voiced their question.

Luke 9:47

▸    Jesus, knew exactly what they were thinking and decided they needed a lesson in greatness. So He took a little child and set him before them.

Matthew 18:3

▸    Jesus wanted them to really think about what He had to say.

- Although the disciples confessed to believe in Jesus, their hearts still needed to be turned from their vain ambition and pride to the genuine humility of little children.
- Pride doesn't allow faith to confess how bad one's sins make one and how deserving a person is of punishment. Pride won't plead for mercy only on Christ's merits without any worthiness within. Pride would rather say, "I'm not as bad as other people. I've done a lot of good and deserve to be rewarded for it."
- You won't get anywhere in the kingdom of heaven where Christ rules with His Gospel if you have such pride.

Matthew 18:4
- A person whose faith and life is genuinely as humble as that of a little child will be lifted up before God in the kingdom of heaven.

Luke 9:48
- The proud are likely to despise the humble and the "little ones," namely children or people who are new to the Christian faith.
- But Jesus says that accepting them is the same as accepting Him and also God the Father.
- For in God's eyes, their humble faith in Him makes them great.

Matthew 18:6
- Then Jesus contrasts receiving them with causing them to sin.
- If in pride you turn away one of these little ones, or mislead them to sin in any way, you have done very serious harm.
- It would be better to lose your physical life, than to cause someone to lose his or her spiritual life by your misguiding them.

Matthew 18:10
- Jesus further warns, watch out how you treat these "little ones."
- Don't despise them for God has assigned angels to watch over them and report directly to Him all that happens with them. You don't want God to hear from them that you have looked down on or mistreated them, do you?

**The second lesson: be innocently trusting of God**

Mark 10:13
- Some parents, usually assumed to be their mothers, brought little children, Luke says infants, to Jesus for Him to bless them.
- According to the Jewish custom, parents often brought children to the rabbis and priests to be blessed.
- But the disciples rebuked them and tried to turn them away. Perhaps the disciples thought that these very small children and infants wouldn't be able to understand a blessing from Jesus. Or they didn't want to wear Jesus out after His long day of preaching.

v. 14
- Jesus became very angry, very indignant with his disciples when He saw them doing that.
- He told them to let the little children come to Him and don't forbid them.
- Why? Because infants also can and do believe, and their faith, which is dependent, without doubting, but simply accepting Jesus at His Word, exemplifies what all believers' faith should be like.
- From this we know also that infants and little children can be baptized, receiving from baptism the blessings of faith and forgiveness.
- It is wrong to prevent in any way children from receiving spiritual blessings from the Lord.

v. 15

▸ Jesus speaks very seriously to them. Without a faith like that of a little child, no person can have the Gospel rule their heart.

v. 16

▸ As further evidence of their importance, Jesus did gather them up in His arms, and personally gave them a blessing.

▸ Nothing implies their need for physical healing so we will assume that Jesus gave them spiritual blessings. For indeed, as infants they can believe and receive spiritual blessings.

## STUDENT PRAYER

Dear Lord Jesus, in the lesson today You are telling me how precious I am to You. You assure me that Your angels are watching over me. And that I too can receive the great blessings of forgiveness and Salvation that You have purchased for me. I ask Your blessing upon me today also. Help me to be and remain humble and trusting in You, now and as I grow older. Do not let me think that I don't need You for everything that is good for me. Let me never forget how important the "little ones" of life are to You. Thank You, oh Lord, for giving also to me all these many blessings and more besides. I trust in You, My Lord. Amen.

## PRESENTATION

Briefly review the previous story as time allows. Make links to the new story when possible.

Tell the story: Teachers, be encouraged to tell the story in your own words while remaining faithful to the scriptural account. When scripture records the story in more than one place, you may want to harmonize the accounts (including extra details found in each account). Let the students know where they can find the additional details in the Bible.

Discuss the story: While reviewing the major events of the story, discuss the possible applications to the students' lives. Ask questions that make them think about the story and show that they understand the story.

## APPLICATIONS

1. These are important lessons that we can learn from little children. a) Jesus wants humility in us, not being proud and demanding the best positions. For "God resists the proud but gives grace to the humble." See Jam. 4:6-7; Luke 18:9-14. Discuss when children are humble and not proud. When does pride get in the way of faith? b) Jesus also wants our faith to be like that of infants. They trust completely without doubting and depend completely on others to provide their needs and care for them. So we need to do with our trust in God. We need to trust God completely when He speaks and guides us. We realize that we are entirely dependent upon Him for all our needs, both physical and spiritual. When people get older they begin to think that they can meet their own needs without Jesus or only depend on Him for certain things, but think they can do the rest on their own. This is foolishness, for in Him we live and move and have our being (Acts 17:28). Grace is a gift of God, not of works (Eph 2:8).

2. These lessons teach how important children are to God. God has even directed special angels to watch over the "little ones" of all ages. He wants to protect them and nurture them in their faith. When children have parents and families who recognize that and teach them about Jesus, God is blessing them indeed. Certainly it is important that children, even infants, be brought to be baptized and be nurtured with the Word. The latter story is used in the Baptismal Liturgy as testimony that Baptism indeed brings the

blessings of faith and forgiveness to infants and children as well. Discuss how the children can know that God loves them too, no matter what their age. Let them know they can pray to God, learn from Him, and be blessed by Jesus too.

## PASSAGES

These passages can be assigned as memory work or simply discussed in class as to how they fit the lesson.

<u>Lower</u>
Mark 10:14 - Jesus said, "Let the little children come to Me, and do not forbid them; for of such is the kingdom of God."
Psalms 119:105 - Your word is a lamp to my feet and a light to my path.

<u>Middle</u> any of the above and...
James 4:6-7 - But He gives more grace. Therefore He says: "God resists the proud, but gives grace to the humble." Therefore, submit to God. Resist the devil and he will flee from you.

Proverbs 3:5-6 - Trust in the LORD with all your heart, and lean not on your own understanding; in all your ways acknowledge Him, and He shall direct your paths.

<u>Upper</u> any of the above and...
2 Timothy 3:15 - And that from childhood you have known the Holy Scriptures, which are able to make you wise for salvation through faith which is in Christ Jesus.

2 Timothy 3:16-17 - All Scripture is given by inspiration of God, and is profitable for doctrine, for reproof, for correction, for instruction in righteousness, that the man of God may be complete, thoroughly equipped for every good work.

Psalms 19:7 - The law of the LORD is perfect, converting the soul; The testimony of the LORD is sure, making wise the simple;

Psalms 19:8-10 - The statutes of the LORD are right, rejoicing the heart; the commandment of the LORD is pure, enlightening the eyes; the fear of the LORD is clean, enduring forever; the judgments of the LORD are true and righteous altogether. More to be desired are they than gold, yea, than much fine gold; sweeter also than honey and the honeycomb.

Psalms 19:12-14 - Who can understand his errors? Cleanse me from secret faults. Keep back Your servant also from presumptuous sins; let them not have dominion over me. Then I shall be blameless, and I shall be innocent of great transgression. Let the words of my mouth and the meditation of my heart be acceptable in Your sight, O LORD, my strength and my Redeemer.

## HYMN CHOICES

"Dear Father, Who Has Made Us All" (TLH #299)
"Dearest Jesus, We are Here" (TLH #300)
"Gracious Savior, Gentle Shepherd" (TLH #627)
"Shepherd of Tender Youth" (TLH #628)

## 25

## STORY

The Good Samaritan - Luke 10:25-37

## TEACHER PRAYER

Dear Lord, this parable also speaks to me about loving my neighbor. You have shown to me such great love by sending Jesus to be my Savior from sin. You saw my need and performed all that was needed to meet my needs. Help me to have a thankful heart that seeks to love You and my neighbor with such a great love as You have shown to me. Help me to recognize my neighbor in my students, in the people who live around me, in the people of my country and anyone who lives in this world. Keep me from being prejudiced against anyone in any way. Guard my tongue, guide my hands, and kindle my heart to do whatever will meet the needs of those around me. This I ask, trusting in Jesus who has done so much for me. Amen.

## VOCABULARY

*Lawyer* - the same as a scribe; someone who studied the Law of God enough for people to consider him an expert in it.

*Wanting to justify himself* - the lawyer wanted to show off how much he knew and how well he had kept the law.

*Jerusalem to Jericho* - the second is 15 miles northeast of the first and 1,575 feet lower.

*Levite* - a member of the tribe of Levi who served in the temple, probably as a teacher.

*Samaritan* - a person who lived in Samaria, the region between Judea and Galilee. These people were descendants of a mix of Jews and heathens. Their religious beliefs, though they contained some of the Scripture, also mixed in heathen beliefs. The Jews despised them, holding a deep prejudice against them.

## OUTER AIM

Jesus showed how a man was a neighbor to a stranger.

## INNER AIM

God's love prompts us to love all men as neighbors.

## BACKGROUND

*(Rupprecht Bible History References Vol.2, pp. 230-236)*

A parable is an earthly story with a spiritual meaning. Because it is easier to learn from examples and concrete illustrations, Jesus used events and pictures from daily life to make His point. This parable is a practical one illustrating, "Who is my neighbor?"

Luke 10:25

▸ The leaders of the Jewish people were often trying to trap Jesus in what He said, rather than actually trying to learn from Him. This is another of those occasions.

▸ The question contradicts itself, because an inheritance is not usually earned, but rather a gift. But Jesus overlooks that issue because He wanted to help this lawyer grow, not embarrass him.

v. 26

▸ Jesus, knowing the man considered himself an expert on the law of God, asked him to answer the question.

v. 27

▸ The Lawyer quotes from the Scriptures: Lev. 19:18 and, with a little enhancement, Deut. 6:5.

v. 28
▸ Jesus agreed that by following the Law of God exactly, a person can live just as Lev. 18:5 says.
▸ But Jesus hoped that the man would realize that no one can keep the Law perfectly.

v. 29
▸ But the lawyer then wanted to justify asking the first question.
▸ Perhaps he hoped that either Jesus would answer wrongly or that he himself would be shown to be a true keeper of the law. So he asked, "Who is my neighbor?"

v. 30
▸ Jesus answers with a parable, a story to illustrate a moral or religious message.
▸ Concrete examples teach better than abstract thoughts or phrases.
▸ Jesus describes someone in serious need. Because of the location, the man likely was a Jew whom the thieves robbed and left wounded for dead, though Scripture doesn't say.

v. 31
▸ By coincidence, yet God works in all things (Acts 15:18), though this is a story, a priest came along the road.
▸ A priest was definitely a teacher and servant of God's Word. He surely should have known how to do the right thing before God and man.
▸ But, whether in fear of the robbers or just being selfish, the priest went to the opposite side of the road in order to go around the dying man. No sign of mercy there.

v. 32
▸ In the same way, a Levite, also a servant and teacher of the Law of God, should have done better, but also, avoided any contact with the dying man.

v. 33
▸ A Samaritan man was traveling there and came to the place where the man was.
▸ Samaritans were despised by the Jews as people not having true and pure religion, as being heathens and unworthy of respect.
▸ This man, unlearned though he was in the law of God, had genuine compassion on the man.
▸ He didn't just have pity, utter an "Oh my, that's too bad," and walk on.

v. 34
▸ He went to the man where he was and helped him in his need.
▸ Using the medicine of his day, he patched the wounds and brought him to safety where he could take care of the man himself.

v. 35
▸ And even though he had to continue his journey, the Samaritan paid money for their night's stay as well as how ever long it took the man to recover. He made sure that the wounded man would be taken care of well.

v. 36
▸ Then Jesus asked the lawyer his own question. Which of the three treated the wounded man as his neighbor?

v. 37
▸ The Lawyer, unwilling even to say the word "Samaritan," described him as the one who showed mercy.
▸ Jesus then replied in effect, if you consider yourself an expert of the law, then don't be just a reader and teacher of the law, you also need to perform the mercy behind the law.
▸ Law without mercy is a cruel, loveless taskmaster.

## STUDENT PRAYER

Dear Lord, this parable also speaks to me about loving my neighbor. You have shown to me such great love by sending Jesus to be my Savior from sin. You saw my need and performed all that was needed to meet my needs. Help me to have a thankful heart that seeks to love You and my neighbor with such a great love as You have shown to me. Help me to recognize my neighbor in my teacher, in my family, in the people who live around me, in the people of my country and anyone who lives in this world. Keep me from being prejudiced against anyone in any way. Guard my tongue, guide my hands, and kindle my heart to do whatever will meet the needs of any and all of my neighbors. For I know that You will enable me to do all that You set before me. This I ask, trusting in Jesus who has done so much for me. Amen.

## PRESENTATION

Briefly review the previous story as time allows. Make links to the new story when possible.

Tell the story: Teachers, be encouraged to tell the story in your own words while remaining faithful to the scriptural account. When scripture records the story in more than one place, you may want to harmonize the accounts (including extra details found in each account). Let the students know where they can find the additional details in the Bible.

Discuss the story: While reviewing the major events of the story, discuss the possible applications to the students' lives. Ask questions that make them think about the story and show that they understand the story.

## APPLICATIONS

1. Who then is our neighbor? Our neighbor is anyone who we see has a need. God created and died for all people and all people have the same great need for a Savior. (Gal 3:28. Matt. 28:19) Discuss prejudice for that is what the Jews felt towards Samaritans. Against whom do people today practice prejudice? Think both locally and in other countries. Not only other races, but Christians throughout the world also face prejudice and persecution.

2. In thanksgiving for how Jesus willingly came to our aid by giving up His life into death for us, we want to love our neighbors as ourselves, as God asked. Love goes beyond fine words when we are talking to others. It also takes action to help those we love. And since our neighbor is anyone that we see with a need, we never lack opportunity to show our thankfulness to God through loving actions towards our neighbor. Discuss some ways that God gives us opportunities to love our neighbors. Some states have passed "Good Samaritan" laws, encouraging people to help others.

3. The Lawyer believed that he was good enough at keeping the law that he could earn eternal life. He wanted to show that off to others by having Jesus acknowledge it. But Jesus showed him that keeping the law goes beyond just following the letter of the law. It extended also to having a heart ready to love, no matter who received that love. Show from Luther's explanation to the 5th commandment and others how this is true. As we see that we cannot keep the Law of God perfectly, how then do we hope to inherit eternal life?

## PASSAGES

These passages can be assigned as memory work or simply discussed in class as to how they fit the lesson.

Lower
Luke 10:27 - So he answered and said, "'You shall love the LORD your God with all your heart, with all your soul, with all your strength, and with all your mind, and your neighbor as yourself."

Middle any of the above and...
Galatians 3:28 - There is neither Jew nor Greek, there is neither slave nor free, there is neither male nor female; for you are all one in Christ Jesus.
John 15:5 - "I am the vine, you are the branches. He who abides in Me, and I in him, bears much fruit; for without Me you can do nothing."

Upper any of the above and...
Ephesians 2:8-10 - For by grace you have been saved through faith, and that not of yourselves; it is the gift of God, not of works, lest anyone should boast. For we are His workmanship, created in Christ Jesus for good works, which God prepared beforehand that we should walk in them.
Matthew 9:13 - But go and learn what this means:"I desire mercy and not sacrifice." For I did not come to call the righteous, but sinners, to repentance.

## HYMN CHOICES

"That Man a Godly Life Might Live" (TLH 287 1,6,11-12)
"O Holy Spirit, Enter In" (TLH 235 1-3,6-8)
"I Gave my Life for Thee" (TLH 405)
"Soldiers of the Cross, Arise" (TLH 501)

## 26

## STORY
Mary and Martha - Luke 10, 38-42

## TEACHER PRAYER
Dear Lord Jesus, grant that the door to my heart may always be open to welcome You to dwell there. Open my lips to make You known in all Your graciousness to the children in my care so that You may come and dwell in their hearts. Amen.

## VOCABULARY

## OUTER AIM
Jesus welcomed into the home of Martha and Mary

## INNER AIM

**BACKGROUND** *Rupprecht Bible History References, Vol. 2,* pp. 236 ff.

Jesus and His disciples were on the way from Perea (land east of the Jordan river) to Jerusalem to celebrate the Feast of the Dedication of the Temple. This festival had its beginnings some 160 years before the birth of Christ. It was also called the Festival of Lights. It is still observed by the Jews today. It is called Hanukkah. As they journeyed, the disciples, and perhaps Lazarus, with them went on to Jerusalem; Jesus stayed behind in Bethany at the home of Martha and Mary. This was a home that the Lord entered often and to which He enjoyed going.

Everything in life is a matter of priorities. People who can't prioritize their time will often find that although they have been running around all day, the things that need to get done are not done. People who can't prioritize their finances will constantly find themselves in debt or other financial troubles.

But the biggest problem that we all have is that we tend to prioritize the earthly over the spiritual. It is easy to think that eating and cleaning are more important than prayer and God's word, but Jesus teaches otherwise.

In our sinfulness we often think that our service to God is what is most important. Jesus teaches us that he cares far more about serving us than about us serving him.

**Mark 10:45   45 "For even the Son of Man did not come to be served, but to serve, and to give His life a ransom for many."**

Our whole lives we are taught it is more blessed to give than to receive. And that is true when we are talking about one another. But it is not true when we are talking about Jesus. Jesus has something to give us that is far more important than anything we could give him.

The teachers notes for today's lesson have a good suggestion for introducing the story. Bring three objects, a life preserver, an apple, some money. If you are on a sinking ship, which is most important? Because of our sin we are on a sinking ship. This earth is headed for judgement. The only thing that can save us is Jesus' forgiveness. Just like the life preserver the most important thing for us is Jesus' blessings in word and sacrament.

**A certain village** - Bethany, only a couple miles from Jerusalem, Jesus on more than one occasion stayed there when he had reason to visit Jerusalem. This takes place 3-4 months before Jesus' death.

He is on his way to Jerusalem to celebrate the festival of dedication. The festival of dedication is well known to most of us even today, but is usually known by a different name, Hannukah or the festival of lights. This was a celebration of the rededication of the temple after it was defiled by Antiochus IV Epiphanes. That would put our story in mid-December.

**Martha** - Martha had two siblings, Mary and Lazarus. Martha is probably the eldest and it sounds like the house belongs to her. In Aramaic Martha actually means mistress, as in mistress of the house. Out of love for Jesus, she regularly welcomes him into her home and provides for him. What a wonderful testament to her faith and love for Jesus, although as we are going to see she takes it a little too far. **"Lord, do You not care that my sister has left me to serve alone? Therefore, tell her to help me."**

How often do we think that we are right and that the Lord, if he were here, would back us up. Very often couples will come to me for counseling, each convinced that they are right and the other is wrong. In reality they aren't coming to hear God's word, they are coming so that I can back them up and tell their spouse they are wrong. The problem is that because of our sinful nature our priorities are wrong, and so hard for us to see that. We put being right first. It is more important to be forgiving than to be right. The one who is first to forgive is the one who wins the argument. We put cleanliness and tasks first. It is more important to have a loving attitude than to have a clean house. We put money first. It is better to be broke and happily married, than to be rich and be divorced. Above all else we ought to put the word of God first.

Martha's words may actually emphasize her love of Jesus, and in a good way her jealousy of Mary. Perhaps we she was motivated because she too wanted to sit and listen to Jesus, but felt like she had to finish the tasks first. Perhaps she wanted Mary to help her so she could get done and they could sit together at Jesus' feet. Jesus however reminds Martha and us not to allow earthly tasks to keep us from sitting at his feet. Simply put the housework down and come sit at my feet.

Jesus' words also show his love for Martha and for us. He doesn't need the food and service that Martha was offering. He doesn't care about our service to him nearly as much as he cares about his service to us. He would much rather serve us than that we serve him. So many churches get this backwards, they care more about serving God rather than receiving Jesus' service.

**Luke 10:41-42   41 And Jesus answered and said to her, "Martha, Martha, you are worried and troubled about many things.  42 "But one thing is needed, and Mary has chosen that good part, which will not be taken away from her.**

What a privilege it is to sit at the feet of Jesus. How often have you had questions about God and thought wouldn't it be nice to ask Jesus, Or been told we'll find out when we get to heaven. Mary and Martha had the opportunity to sit at the feet of Jesus and listen and ask questions. But Martha thought it more important to clean up and serve the food. It is easy to judge other people and think they should do this or they should do that. But life is always a matter of priorities. You always have to choose.

Martha thought that cooking and cleaning should come first.  Jesus disagreed. Mary had her priorities straight, to receive Jesus' gifts comes first. Getting our priorities straight not only brings us closer to God but releases us from the cares and worries of this world. Jesus promises that when we seek him first he will take care of all the rest.

**Matthew 6:33 But seek first the kingdom of God and His righteousness, and all these things shall be added to you.**

There is nothing more important than going to Jesus to receive from him the blessing and gifts that he offers. What a privilege to set down our daily tasks and sit with Mary at Jesus' feet.

*Mary and Martha- Lesson 26*

**Titus 2:11-13** For the grace of God has appeared, bringing salvation for all people, training us to renounce ungodliness and worldly passions, and to live self-controlled, upright, and godly lives in the present age, waiting for our blessed hope, the appearing of the glory of our great God and Savior Jesus Christ.

## STUDENT PRAYER  TLH #286, v. 1 and 6

How precious is the Book Divine, by inspiration given; Bright as a lamp its doctrines shine to guide our souls to heaven.

This lamp through all the tedious night, of life shall guide our way Till we behold the clearer light  Of an eternal day.

## PRESENTATION

Briefly review previous story as time allows. Make links to the new story when possible. Tell the story: Teachers, be encouraged to tell the story in your own words while remaining faithful to the scriptural account. When scripture records the story in more than one place, you may want to harmonize the accounts (including extra details found in each account).  Let the students know where they can find the additional details in the Bible.

Discuss the story:  While reviewing the major events of the story, discuss the possible applications to the students' lives.  Ask questions that make them think about the story and show that they understand the story.

## APPLICATION

As Jesus blessed the family in Bethany, so you will want Him to:
- bless your heart and home with His presence
- bless your heart and home with His instruction
- bless your heart and home with His correction

## PASSAGES
**These passages can be assigned as memory work or simply discussed in class as to how they fit the lesson.**

Lower
Luke 11:28 - "blessed are those who hear the Word of God, and keep it." Samuel
3:9 - "Speak, Lord; for Your servant hears."

Middle
Luke 11:28 - "blessed are those who hear the Word of God, and keep it." Samuel
3:9 - "Speak, Lord; for Your servant hears."
Luke 19:5 - "today I must stay at your house."

Upper
Luke 11:28 - "blessed are those who hear the Word of God, and keep it." Samuel
3:9 - "Speak, Lord; for Your servant hears."
Luke 19:5 - "today I must stay at your house."
Luke 24:29 - "Abide with us, for it is toward evening, and the day is far spent.  And He went in to stay with them."

## HYMN CHOICES
The Lord My Pasture Shall Prepare - TLH 368, vs. 1-4 The
Savior Calls; Let Every Ear - TLH 281, vs. 1-5

*Mary and Martha- Lesson 26*                                            *93*

## STORY

The Prodigal Son – Luke 15:11-32

## TEACHER PRAYER

Dear Lord Jesus, You came to earth to save sinners, of which I am the chief. In this lesson You teach me of your great love for me in forgiving all of my sins. I know that all of my sins – those that I regard as small and those that I regard as great – all are forgiven because of what You have done. Please give me the wisdom and ability to teach this truth to my students, that they may always turn to You and know Your loving forgiveness, no matter what sin they have committed. Amen.

## VOCABULARY

*Prodigal* – recklessly wasteful. A "prodigal" is one who spends lavishly and foolishly.
*Famine* – a time when there is not enough food to eat.
*Fatted calf* – a calf kept by itself, fed well, and preserved for special occasions.

## OUTER AIM

Jesus tells the parable of a foolish son who was lost and then found.

## INNER AIM

God shows His love for sinners by forgiving our sins.

## BACKGROUND

In Chapter 15 of Luke's Gospel, Jesus emphasizes the fact that God continues to love and seek after those who wander from the fold. This entire chapter demonstrates the depths of God's love and patience with sinful mankind. The Parable of the Prodigal Son was directed toward the Pharisees and scribes, who not only refused to attempt to regain those who had strayed from the fold of Israel, they would not even be seen with them. Their condemnation of anyone who would so associate himself is what prompted Jesus to speak the words of our parable. Since this is a parable, we are again to look for one central truth. This parable stresses the unconditional character of God's love and forgiveness.
v.11-12

- Note the love (and lack of selfishness) demonstrated by the "Father."
- By definition an inheritance belongs to an heir only after the benefactor dies.
- The young son had no claim to "his portion" while the father was still alive; still the father gives it freely.
- So we read that "he divided to them *his* livelihood."

v. 13

- The young son falls almost immediately into the same trap that snares so many young people who are given great wealth at a young age.
- Work is a blessing for many reasons. It occupies our time and energy in worthwhile endeavors, and it teaches us the value of what we receive.
- Emphasize to the student that having a great deal of money to spend and time to spend it – especially at a young age – may seem like something to be desired. It is in fact, a great temptation that almost no one can master.

v. 14-16

- Mercifully the money ran out.
- The young man no doubt regarded this inevitable consequence of his lavish lifestyle as a curse. It was in fact a great blessing from his God.
- It was not until the god, "money," was gone that the man "came to himself."

v. 17-19

- The son's contrition here is real. He "came to himself" in that he realized that he had sinned greatly in what he had done.

- He did not return to his father expecting anything but to work as one of his servants.
- He had forfeited his right to be called a son.
- He recognized that his father was under no obligation to give him anything.

v. 20-24

- The key to this parable lies in these verses. The father owed the son nothing, but forgave him freely and gladly reinstated him as a son.
- Note that the father reinstated the son before the son's confession.
- The son did not earn his father's forgiveness. It was freely given.
- The robe was a symbol of authority, proof that the son was again regarded as a son.
- The ring signifies the complete nature of the father's forgiveness. Many regard it as the ancient equivalent of a credit card. A father who did not fully forgive would never have entrusted his son with more "buying power."
- The sandals also indicated reinstatement, since servants usually went barefoot.
- The joy was based not so much on proximity as it was on condition; that is, they rejoiced not so much that the son was living at home again, but that he had been brought back to life from spiritual death.

v. 25-32

- The terrible condition of the youngest son's heart was obvious when he was living a wild, extravagant life of sin.
- The state of the older son's heart, though concealed, was just as bad.
- The older brother is a picture of the Scribes and Pharisees, to whom this parable was addressed.
- Note how the older brother refused to go in and rejoice that his brother had come to his senses and returned.
- He would not even acknowledge him as a brother, but referred to him as "this son of yours."
- The father demonstrates his love for both sons, for God is not willing that any should perish.

## STUDENT PRAYER

Dear Jesus, in this parable You have shown me how much I am loved by my Father in heaven. I did not deserve His love, yet He gave it freely because of Your death on the cross. Help me to remember at all times that no matter what I have done wrong, God the Father has freely forgiven me all my sins. Please give me now a spirit that is not jealous of this love and forgiveness, but one that makes me eager to share it with my neighbors, friends, and family. In Jesus' name I ask this. Amen.

## PRESENTATION

The account is short enough to read to the students, or to be read by them. If you are able, consider telling the story in your own words, using the written account as your guide.

## APPLICATIONS

1. God our heavenly Father loves all sinners like the father in our parable loved his sons. We have many faults, God loves us in spite of them – unconditionally. Guide the student to see himself in the prodigal son, for we too have been wasteful and lazy. We too have insisted on going our own way rather than God's way.

2. Work is a blessing. This is sometimes a difficult concept for children to understand, yet it would be well worth our time to have the children try to list some of these blessings on their own. Illustrate their correct ideas with examples from the story. (Greed of the young son, lack of appreciation for the value of money, laziness, seeking after worldly pleasures to the harm of his soul, too much free time led to sin, etc.)

3. Work at making the student realize the terrible nature of the sins of the prodigal son. God does not categorize sins as to "bad" and "not so bad," but we do. Help the child to see that the sins of the young son are among those we would categorize as very bad, demonstrating how God freely forgave them. We want our students to understand that our merciful God does not stop loving and forgiving us when we fall into even the most shameful sins.

4. This is an excellent opportunity to teach the children about true repentance. True repentance is not feeling sorry because you got caught. It is not even simply feeling sorry that you did something wrong. Godly repentance means that we are not only sorry for what we have done, it also includes believing that God the Father has forgiven our sin for Jesus' sake. A truly repentant sinner realizes that he cannot "make it up to God." God does not forgive us *because* we are sorry. He forgives us because of what Jesus has done for us.

5. Show the child what terrible things sin can do to us. What happens when we lie? Hurt someone? Curse someone? How do we feel? How do others feel about us?

## PASSAGES
These passages can be assigned as memory work or simply discussed in class as to how they fit the lesson.

Lower
Psalms 103:12 - As far as the east is from the west, so far has He removed our transgressions from us. 1 John 4:19 - We love Him because He first loved us.
John 15:9 - "As the Father loved Me, I also have loved you; abide in My love."

Middle any of the above and...
Luke 15:7 - "I say to you that likewise there will be more joy in heaven over one sinner who repents than over ninety-nine just persons who need no repentance.
1 Timothy 2:3b-4 - God our Savior… desires all men to be saved and to come to the knowledge of the truth.
1 John 1:9 - If we confess our sins, He is faithful and just to forgive us our sins and to cleanse us from all unrighteousness.

Upper any of the above and...
1 John 3:1 - Behold what manner of love the Father has bestowed on us, that we should be called children of God! Therefore the world does not know us, because it did not know Him.
Psalms 103:2-5 - Bless the LORD, O my soul, and forget not all His benefits: Who forgives all your iniquities, Who heals all your diseases, Who redeems your life from destruction, Who crowns you with lovingkindness and tender mercies, Who satisfies your mouth with good things, so that your youth is renewed like the eagle's.
Ephesians 2:4-5 - But God, who is rich in mercy, because of His great love with which He loved us, even when we were dead in trespasses, made us alive together with Christ (by grace you have been saved).

## HYMN CHOICES
"Redeemed, Restored, Forgiven" (TLH 32:1-2)
"From Depths of Woe I Cry to Thee" (TLH 329:1-3)
"O Thou that Hear'st when Sinners Cry" (TLH 325:1-4)
"The Man Is Ever Blessed" (TLH 414:1-3)

## STORY
The Rich Man and Poor Lazarus (The Poor Rich Man and Lazarus) - Luke 16:19-31

## TEACHER PRAYER
Dear Lord Jesus, You want me to recognize at all times the power and the effectiveness of Your Word, the very hand that sustains me. You want me to know that it is only through Your Word that anything good on earth can be accomplished; only through Your Word that any man can be brought to saving faith. Through the power of Your Word, enable me to teach these truths to my students, that they too may develop a deep and sincere reverence for Your precious, saving Truth. Your Word is truth. Amen.

## VOCABULARY
*Fared sumptuously* – a life full of luxuries and earthly riches.
*Bosom* – the front part of the chest, where something very dear is cradled or held.
*Hades* – literally "the underworld" or "the place of the dead," here used as another name for Hell.

## OUTER AIM
Jesus tells us a parable about true riches.

## INNER AIM
Jesus teaches us about the power of His Word, which alone can convert and save sinners.

## BACKGROUND
The Gospel of Luke, especially chapters 10-20, is rich in parables. A parable is a story from which we are to learn one central thought or truth. Though the central truth of this particular parable certainly applies to all of us, it was originally directed at the Pharisees "who were lovers of money…" (Luke 16:14) Earthly wealth neither saves nor condemns. It is not an indication of how God feels about the individual sinner. God looks at the heart, and the only thing that can change the heart is the Word of God. This is the central message of this parable: "If they do not hear Moses and the prophets, neither will they be persuaded though one rise from the dead." (Luke 16:21)

v. 19-21

- Jesus' description of the characters in the parable.
- To the Pharisees, earthly wealth and prosperity were indications of God's approval.
- Hard times and physical afflictions were proof of God's disapproval.
- Even Jesus' own disciples believed this for a time (John 9:1-2).
- Jesus looks at the inside: "You are those who justify yourselves before men, but God knows your hearts.
- For what is highly esteemed among men is an abomination in the sight of God." (Luke 16:15 – which immediately precedes this parable.)

v. 22
- In the parable Lazarus died and went to Heaven.
- The rich man died and went to hell.
- Note that poverty on earth did not save Lazarus, nor did wealth damn the rich man.
- Lazarus was saved by faith; the rich man was condemned because of his unbelief.

v. 23-24
- Hell is a real place, with real pain lasting an eternity.
- It is neither a myth nor a mere symbol for nonexistence.
- Note the utter misery of hell if even a drop of water on his tongue would give the sufferer comfort.

- The picture of Lazarus resting in Abraham's bosom draws a sharp contrast with the agony of the unbeliever in hell.
- Note also that even in hell this unbeliever still views Lazarus as his slave.

v. 25-26
- There is simple irony in these words, not cause and effect.
- The one who suffered on earth now receives comfort; the one who enjoyed all of the comforts is now tormented.
- Note that Abraham here only points to this irony. He does not make it the cause of a man's state in eternity.
- Since we are to glean only one central truth from a parable, we are not to create doctrine from other aspects of the story.
- Therefore we are not to imagine that the souls in hell will forever be bothering the saints in heaven, or that there is a physical gulf fixed between heaven and hell that we can see across.

v. 27-31
- Convinced that he can gain nothing from Lazarus for himself, the thoughts of the selfish man now turn to his five brothers.
- He believes that if Lazarus would rise from the dead his brothers would believe. (The implication is that God could have done more to save him.)
- The man's request seems reasonable to our human minds, but not when we consider that faith is not a rational decision made by the mind of man, but a working in the heart by the Holy Spirit through the Means of Grace – the gospel, in word and sacrament.
- This truth was proved beyond any doubt when Jesus himself rose from the dead, and still the Jews refused to believe in him.
- Here in v. 31 is the key to this parable.
- The Word of God is the only power that can bring a man to faith. "Moses and the prophets" refers to the Old Testament, which was the only part of the Bible available in Jesus' day.

## STUDENT PRAYER
Dear Father in heaven, we can never thank You enough for giving us Your Word, the Bible. From this parable of the Rich Man and Poor Lazarus, told to us by Your Son, we know that Your Word is the only power that can create saving faith in our hearts, and without faith we can't be saved. Help us to treasure Your Word all our lives, since Your Word has not only brought us to faith, it also is the hand that guards this faith in our hearts. Help us also to share Your Word with others, so that they may come to know You as their Savior. We ask this in Jesus' name. Amen.

## PRESENTATION
The story appears only in Luke, and is short enough that it can be read in its entirety by the teacher or by the Middle and Upper students. As always, telling the story in your own words can help the concentration and retention of the student.

## APPLICATIONS
1. When things go wrong or we have problems in our lives, it is tempting to try to blame someone else. "Yes, I stole some of the apples from Mr. Johnson's tree – but he should have put a fence around his yard if he didn't want me to take them." The Rich Man wanted to make it God's fault that he went to Hell. It was the man's rejection of God's Word, not his wealth, which condemned him. Jesus tells us the only thing that can turn an unbeliever into a believer is the Word of God. How thankful we ought to be that we have that Word of God and can read it every day!

2. It is a good thing that we don't have to rely on signs today before we will believe. Magicians today can create illusions that are truly baffling – making people, animals, even huge objects like airplanes just "disappear." We know that these are only tricks, but what if we had to rely on our eyes before we would believe something. What would we believe?

3. Why is it so foolish to live for the things of this world? How long do they last when compared with eternity? That is why we believe that the most important and most precious thing on earth is the Word of God. We ought to treasure it.

## PASSAGES
These passages can be assigned as memory work or simply discussed in class as to how they fit the lesson.

Lower
Psalms 119:105 - Your word is a lamp to my feet and a light to my path.
Luke 16:15a - God knows your hearts.
John 10:35 - The Scripture cannot be broken.

Middle any of the above and...
Luke 4:4 - But Jesus answered him, saying, It is written, "Man shall not live by bread alone, but by every word of God."
Luke 16:15b - For what is highly esteemed among men is an abomination in the sight of God.
Isaiah 55:11 - So shall My word be that goes forth from My mouth; it shall not return to Me void, but it shall accomplish what I please, and it shall prosper in the thing for which I sent it.

Upper any of the above and...
2 Timothy 3:15 - F rom childhood you have known the Holy Scriptures, which are able to make you wise for salvation through faith which is in Christ Jesus.
2 Timothy 3:16 - All Scripture is given by inspiration of God, and is profitable for doctrine, for reproof, for correction, for instruction in righteousness.
Hebrews 4:12 - For the word of God is living and powerful, and sharper than any two-edged sword, piercing even to the division of soul and spirit, and of joints and marrow, and is a discerner of the thoughts and intents of the heart.

## HYMN CHOICES
"Lord, Open Thou My Heart To Hear" (TLH #5:1-2)
"Preserve Thy Word, O Savior" (TLH #264:1,5)
"O Lord Look Down From Heaven Behold" (TLH #260:1, 4-5)
"O Jesus King of Glory" (TLH #130:3, 5-6)

## 29

### STORY
Lazarus Raised from the Dead  - John 11:1-54

### TEACHER PRAYER
Dear Lord Jesus, sin has brought death to this world.  Death has brought tears as we are separated from those we love.  Yet, as You have said in this lesson, You are the Resurrection and the Life.  You alone have power over death.  And, because of Your death for our sakes and Your own resurrection we know that we too will rise from death to life with You. And so, death is but a sleep from which You can and will awaken us.  Help me, O Lord, to share this comforting truth with the students in my care. They too will face death, that of loved ones and of themselves, and need Your reassurance that those who believe in You as their Savior will be reunited in heaven where there will be no more death or tears or sorrow.  I pray with faith in You, the Lord of Life. Amen.

### VOCABULARY
*Bethany* - a town two miles east of Jerusalem

*Anoint* - pour on oil as a special honor or to mark a person for a particular office.  Scented oil was also applied at the time of burial to help the body smell better.  See notes on verse.

*Love and Loved* - the original Greek language used five different words to describe what English includes in one.  In verses 3 and 36 the Greek word phileo describes a brotherly love or the strong affection between good friends.  In verse 5, the Greek word agapao (the verb form of agape) describes a committed love of understanding and purpose.  Agape love seeks to understand what is best for the person loved and commits to accomplishing it.  Christ's agapao love gave Himself for us by His death.

*Graveclothes* - In Jesus' time, bodies were wrapped up in strips of cloth with scented spices and perfumes mingled in and before being placed in tombs.  That is different from today when people are buried in normal clothing and placed in a casket which is usually buried.

*Pharisees* - This sect or faction of the Jews attempted to very strictly keep the Law of God and of the traditions passed down.  Jesus condemned many of them as hypocrites who acted holier than others but did not show mercy or believe in Jesus.  They generally held high positions in the Jewish church government.

*Expedient* - (Webster): "marked by a concern with what is advantageous without regard for fairness or rightness."

Prophesy - to serve as a mouthpiece for God (or another), many times in telling of future events.

### OUTER AIM
Jesus resurrects a man who has been dead for days.

### INNER AIM
Jesus, God's Son, has power over death.

### BACKGROUND
*(Rupprecht Bible History References Vol.2, pp. 281-290)*
This miracle was a turning point in Jesus' ministry.  When Jesus raised Lazarus from the dead, His doom was sealed.  The Jewish leaders could no longer ignore Jesus and hope that His following would go away.  They were afraid that as soon as people heard that Jesus had raised Lazarus from the dead, His following would become even larger.  (cf. John 11:47-54)  It was after this that the Jewish leaders felt it was necessary to get rid of Jesus.

John 11:1

▸ Sickness strikes in every family. Mary and Martha and Lazarus were well known in the Christian church and through other events in Scripture. (cf Luke 10:38-42; John 12:1-11).

v. 2

▸ This event demonstrates faith that was strengthened by the events of this lesson and should be included in your studies. It's recorded in John 12:1-8 and Matthew 26:6-13, (esp 13).

v. 3

▸ See vocabulary notes on "love." In faith, these good friends of Jesus let Him know their situation, trusting He would respond without saying how He should respond.

▸ This is a good way to approach God in a difficult situation. We will find that their expectations didn't guess the Lord's greater plans.

▸ Jesus may have been on the eastern side of the Jordan, outside of Judea, at this time (John 10:40; 11:7).

v. 4

▸ Jesus knew already what He would do in response to the request.

▸ His words offered comfort and encouraged faith while not specifically revealing His plans.

▸ Whatever Jesus did was to the glory of God, (1 Cor 10:31).

v. 5

▸ See vocabulary note on love. They were not only good friends to Jesus, He thought of their needs and would meet those needs.

v. 6

▸ This seems like a strange, uncaring reaction after having been told His good friend was very sick.

▸ This delay served to emphasize God's glory later and also tested the faith of the two sisters. Jesus knew what to do.

v. 7

▸ After delaying, Jesus announced it was time to go to Judea where Bethany was located.

v. 8

▸ The disciples, not understanding Jesus' plan concerning Lazarus or God's greater plan of salvation through Jesus, voiced their concern over the growing hostility of the Jews.

▸ The last two times Jesus visited Jerusalem the Jews had tried to stone Him to death. See John 8:59 and 10:31.

vs. 9-10

▸ This metaphor tells the disciples that Jesus isn't in any danger yet, because it isn't the appointed time for Him to die. He can continue to work without serious trouble for now.

▸ Jesus used the metaphor of hours for the timing of life in other places. (John 2:4; 12:23; 16:21; 17:1; Mark 16:41).

▸ While the Lord grants life, work can be done; in death, no work can be done. (cf. Last paragraph of the General Prayer, TLH p. 13)

v. 11

▸ After letting that sink in, He revealed the purpose of their journey.

▸ He knew Lazarus was dead but gives this accurate picture of death.

▸ For the believer who will rise again from death, death essentially is a sleep. (See Application 1 for description of death.)

vs 14-15

▸ Jesus clarifies for the disciples in their misunderstanding.

▸ Then He reveals more as He explains that He had purposely stayed away so that they would believe something more about Him.

▸ So even though Lazarus is dead, Jesus wants them to come and see Lazarus and received benefit for their faith.

v. 16

▸ Thomas shows his skeptical side, not understanding or believing Jesus' assurance that there was no danger yet.

v. 17

▸ Lazarus had been dead four days by this time. Some commentators feel that he died on the day Jesus received the message of his illness by allowing one day for the messenger, two days delay, and one day for Jesus to travel to Bethany. Though possible, calculation is not certain as travel time can not be accurately measured from the information we have.

v. 18

▸ Jesus' enemies were in Jerusalem, the major city of the country where the most people could hear of what would soon happen.

▸ This detail adds reality, suspense, and helpful information for calculating the speed of news, (v 46).

v. 19

▸ Mary and Martha were well known and respected. So a large crowd had come to comfort them in their loss.

v. 20

▸ Martha anxiously hurried to hear Jesus' comforting words for only He can give true comfort at such times.

▸ Mary remained behind, perhaps to give Martha a chance to speak with Jesus privately or she was simply absorbed by mourning.

v. 21

▸ This thought was probably on many believers' minds at this time (cf Mary  v. 32).

▸ They knew that Jesus was able to heal the sick, for by this time He had healed many people.

v. 22

▸ Perhaps Jesus' earlier reply (v. 4) had given her hope but she expressed her trust that Jesus could still do something about Lazarus' death.

▸ She isn't sure what is possible, but her faith in Jesus is evident. Nevertheless, her words imply she doesn't yet see that Jesus is actually God, but that only He can ask anything of God freely.

v. 23

▸ Jesus begins to create a newer faith and hope for her with this general statement.

v. 24

▸ Martha declared her belief in the final resurrection. The Old Testament also teaches this belief: (Ps 17:5, Deut 32:39; Dan 12:2; Is 26:19; Job 19:25ff; Hos 6:2; 13:14; Heb 11:10). But she didn't yet (dare?) believe that Jesus had the power to raise Lazarus from the dead after four days.

vs. 25-26

▸ This wonderful assurance declares Jesus' ability to raise all believers from the dead.

▸ Through faith, Jesus gives life to replace the hopelessness of death; for when a believer dies, Jesus will raise him or her to eternal life.

v. 27

▸ Martha doesn't then fully understand what Jesus is telling her but she humbly confesses her trust in His words by confessing her faith that Jesus is the Promised One, the Son of God sent into the world for her.

v. 28

▸ Then Martha leaves and secretly tells Mary that Jesus, the Teacher, wants to talk to her.

▸ Her choice of titles for Jesus perhaps was meant to encourage Mary to sit at Jesus' feet again to learn and find comfort from Him (Luke 10:38-42).

v. 29

▸ When she heard that Jesus wanted to speak to her, Mary quickly went to Him.

v. 30

▸ Jesus purposely remained out of town to have a chance to meet with Martha and Mary privately, before the town heard He was there and would crowd around Him.

v. 31

▸ But privacy was interrupted by custom, for the mourners felt it important to stay with Mary to comfort her in this time of loss. So they followed her.

v. 32

▸ When Mary found Jesus, she fell at His feet in sorrow and respect.

▸ With her words revealed at what point her faith was frustrated.

v. 33

▸ Sin causes great sorrow especially in its result, namely death.

▸ Jesus groaned in righteous anger as He saw the tears that sin had brought to the world He had created for life and joy.

▸ He fully empathized with Mary and those who felt the sorrow of death among them. (Heb 4:15, Is 53:3).

v. 34

▸ He asked to see the tomb where death held temporary sway.

v. 35

▸ This shortest verse in the Bible delivers a long sermon on the humanness of our Lord and Savior Jesus Christ.

▸ It assures us that we have in Him the perfect High Priest (Heb 4:15) and Savior who can meet us where we are and take the burden of our sins upon Himself to the cross and bring the oil of joy to replace our mourning.

▸ The Greek contrasts Jesus' quiet, yet sincere mourning and the loud, customary wailing of the general mourners.

v. 36

▸ Those who saw Jesus' weeping saw Jesus' love, though restricted it to His friend Lazarus.

v. 37

▸ Others mocked His tears, implying that if Jesus had indeed loved Lazarus, He certainly would have used the power to prevent Lazarus from dying in the first place.

v. 38

▸ Jesus, frustrated with the limited faith of the crowd, arrived at the tomb.

▸ To help the students visualize the story in their minds, point out the difference between the tombs of Jesus' day as here described and the graves of today.

v. 39

▸ Martha, still not fully grasping by faith what Jesus could or intended to do, attempted to discourage Jesus' seemingly insensitive order.

▸ She was right, a body four days dead would stink in those conditions.

v. 40

▸ Jesus reminded her of His previous assurances about the resurrection and added that she would be privileged to witness the truth behind those statements.

▸ In so doing, He called her again to increase her faith in Him.

vs. 41-42

▸ When the people then obeyed Jesus' command, He directed their attention to Heaven with His prayer of thanksgiving  spoken out loud for their benefit.

▸ The people needed to understand that Jesus' actions were not for self-glorification, but done according to God the Father's larger plan for His Son.

▸ As the effects of His current actions flowed into the whirlpool of events surrounding His death and resurrection, the people might then believe in Him as their Savior as God the Father intended Him to be.

v. 43

▸ Loudly, for the benefit of the crowd, though it would have been just as effective as a still, small voice, the Word of God's Son instilled life and action into the body that had been dead for four days.

v. 44

▸ See vocabulary notes on graveclothes.

▸ As the detail of the eyewitness account testifies, when God's Word resurrected Him, Lazarus wasn't a spirit or a ghost but the actual living body of Lazarus, restrained by the cloths that had bound him at his death.

▸ So that the people would realize this, Jesus commanded them to loose him and let Lazarus move freely.

▸ Jesus performed this greatest, most powerful of miracles of His life on earth to reveal to the people then and throughout history that He is indeed the Lord of Life with the power to reverse death and break the power of sin.

▸ For those who were there and those who by faith see this miracle through God's inspired Words, this lesson gives the assurance to follow Jesus, the Lord and Giver of Life, to death itself and beyond.

v. 45

▸ For many who saw it, this miracle had God's intended result.  They believed Jesus.

v. 46

▸ But others, in the hardness of their hearts rejected this clear message and went to Jesus' enemies with the news of what Jesus had done.  See vocabulary on the Pharisees.

vs. 47-48

▸ This amazing event and others worried Jesus' enemies so that they called a meeting to decide once and for all how to handle the perceived threat to their position as leaders of the people.

▸ They obviously hadn't obeyed Jesus' sermon to them recorded in John 10:25-38.

vs. 48-52

▸ In his arrogance, Caiaphas ironically condemned his fellow conspirators for not knowing what needed to be done, (Rom 1:22).

▸ And so, by the direction of the Holy Spirit, Caiaphas presented one of the more powerful summaries of the Gospel to them as the plot to destroy Jesus.

▸ John's inspired commentary shows how different Caiaphas' meaning was from how the Holy Spirit intended those words.

▸ For it was expedient, that is necessary and efficient though not fair, that Jesus must die in order to prevent the whole nation, in fact the whole family of God, from perishing.

v. 53

▸ And so, without knowing it, they chose to become pawns on the side of evil but still would accomplish God's plan of good.

v. 54

▸ So that the timing of God's plan would be accomplished, Jesus withdrew with His disciples from His enemies until His hour should come (John 12:23; 17:1).

## STUDENT PRAYER

Dear Lord Jesus, Through this lesson You call us to believe that You are the Lord of life with power over even death itself. Because of sin within us we fear death. But You suffered death for us and the punishment of sin that we fear in death. You have taken away the sting of death and replaced it with the assurance that those who believe in You will rise from death to Live again, with You, forever. Help us to view death through the eyes of faith in You and Your promises of a joyful resurrection. Although we may mourn the loss of our loved ones and the separation that death brings, may we also have the joyful hope of faith that You will awaken us to be with You and be reunited with our loved ones who have believed in You. We ask this, trusting in You as our Lord of Life and Savior. Amen.

## PRESENTATION

Briefly review the previous story as time allows. Make links to the new story when possible.

Tell the story: Teachers, be encouraged to tell the story in your own words while remaining faithful to the scriptural account. When scripture records the story in more than one place, you may want to harmonize the accounts (including extra details found in each account). Let the students know where they can find the additional details in the Bible.

Discuss the story: While reviewing the major events of the story, discuss the possible applications to the students' lives. Ask questions that make them think about the story and show that they understand the story.

## APPLICATIONS

1. This might be a good opportunity to talk about death. Why do we die? Sin brought death (Genesis 2:17; 3:1-19 Romans 5:12ff). It is not natural, as the evolutionists claim. God created the world "Good" without death and tears. What is death? Death can be defined as "separation." The Bible describes three forms of death: 1) Spiritual death: separation of a person's soul from God by sin and unbelief. John 3 talks of this as Jesus tells Nicodemus that sinful people must be born again by the Spirit who creates and sustains faith in Jesus. 2) Physical death: separation of the soul from the body until God reunites them on Judgement Day or as related in the few miracles God records in the Bible. See Ecc. 12:7 along with Gen. 3:19. In Luke 8:55 the girl's spirit returned to her body at Jesus' command and she was alive. 3) Eternal death: the eternal separation of the unbelievers' body and soul from God for all eternity in Hell. What does this lesson teach us about death? Jesus, the Lord of Life has the power over death (John 5:21-29). And through Jesus' death and resurrection, we are assured that believers will be raised and be given eternal life (1 Corinthians 15). We no longer need to fear death (as the sinful nature within us naturally does) but see it as a door to heaven to be with Jesus. Is it okay to cry when people die? We mourn that sin caused our temporary loss, but we also rejoice when a believer dies. Even though for time we are separated from those who die, yet in eternity we will be reunited with those who believed on Jesus as their Savior from sin and death.

2. Compared with those who believed on Jesus, Jesus' enemies reacted quite differently to the miracle Jesus performed. They refused to believe in Jesus despite the more and more proofs there were to believe in Him. Eventually they began plotting Jesus' death. Some enemies of Jesus won't be converted to faith in Jesus. Yet, despite their evil schemes, God turned their plans to good, even having the High Priest summarize the truth of the Gospel. Likewise, God turns the horror of death into a passageway to life for the believer. How is this comforting to us (Rom. 8:28)? (If students want to know why some believe and others don't, here is your answer. Scripture teaches if someone doesn't believe, it is his or her fault; and if someone does believe, it is none of his or her doing but God's grace alone at work. More than that, we cannot say without giving man credit for salvation or condemning God for man's damnation.)

3. (Upper levels) Jesus described death as a sleep from which Jesus could awaken people. The Bible teaches us what death is (see above) and also that all will rise from death (John 5:24-29, esp. 29). After all are raised from the dead, God will judge them on the basis of faith in Jesus as their Savior. Believers will inherit eternal life (John 11:25-26) but those who do not believe will be condemned to Hell. Those who believe will have shown it in their lives, but unbelievers will have shown their unbelief by their lives as well (Matt. 25:31-46). Use 1 Corinthians 15 (esp. 12-19) to compare the Christian hope of the resurrection to alternative views of death. Some religions teach that when a person dies, there is no life after death. Others believe in reincarnation, that people return to this life in a different form to try to do better than before and eventually achieve the highest level of good called "nirvana."

## PASSAGES

These passages can be assigned as memory work or simply discussed in class as to how they fit the lesson.

<u>Lower</u>
John 11:25 - Jesus said to her, "I am the resurrection and the life. He who believes in Me, though he may die, he shall live."
Hebrews 11:1 - Now, faith is the substance of things hoped for, the evidence of things not seen.

<u>Middle</u> any of the above and...
Job 19:25-27 - For I know that my Redeemer lives, and He shall stand at last on the earth; and after my skin is destroyed, this I know, that in my flesh I shall see God, whom I shall see for myself, and my eyes shall behold, and not another. How my heart yearns within me!
Romans 5:12 - Therefore, just as through one man sin entered the world, and death through sin, and thus death spread to all men, because all sinned.

<u>Upper</u> any of the above and...
1 Corinthians 15:55-57 - "O Death, where is your sting? O Hades, where is your victory?" The sting of death is sin, and the strength of sin is the law. But thanks be to God, who gives us the victory through our Lord Jesus Christ.
1 Thessalonians 4:13-14 - But I do not want you to be ignorant, brethren, concerning those who have fallen asleep, lest you sorrow as others who have no hope. For if we believe that Jesus died and rose again, even so God will bring with Him those who sleep in Jesus.

## HYMN CHOICES

"I Know That My Redeemer Lives" (TLH 200 1,3,5-8)
"Jesus Lives, The Victory's Won" (TLH 201 1,2,5)
"When My Last Hour is Close at Hand" (TLH 594 all or 4-5)

## 30

## STORY
Palm Sunday - Matthew - 21:1-11, Mark 11:1-11, Luke 19:28-40, John 12:12-19

## TEACHER PRAYER
Dear Heavenly Father, I am mindful how Your Son, our Savior, came in great humility to suffer and die for my sins, so I come to You now in great humility, asking You to guide me as I teach Your lambs Your Word. Unless Your mighty hand directs me I know that I cannot lead these children aright. I pray therefore that You would give me full measure of Your Holy Spirit that He may work through the Word in the hearts of Your little lambs. It is indeed a joy and a privilege to bring Your holy Word to Your children, knowing that You will accomplish great things in them through that Word. Thank You, dear Father. Amen.

## VOCABULARY
*Bethphage* – (BETH-fa-gee) A small town on the road from Jerusalem to Jericho (east of Jerusalem). No trace of the city remains today.

*"The Prophet"* – A phrase used often in the New Testament which can refer to any Old Testament prophet. Here it is a reference to the Prophet Zechariah.

*Zion* – The name of the southwestern hill of Jerusalem where David built a fortress and his own house. Zion later was used to refer to Jerusalem and its inhabitants, and still later to signify all of God's people (the Christian Church).

*Hosanna* – Means "Save!" "Save, I pray" or "Save now." It is a Hebrew or Aramaic expression that came to be used as an exclamation of praise or honor.

## OUTER AIM
Lower - Jesus rode into Jerusalem on a donkey.
Upper - Jesus entered Jerusalem in humility.

## INNER AIM
Lower - Jesus is our Savior, and we will worship Him.
Upper - Jesus, the Son of God, came as a humble servant to save all mankind.

## BACKGROUND
*(Rupprecht Bible History References Vol. 2, pp. 299-309)*
This account is used both in Advent and in Lent. In Advent it is used to point ahead to Jesus' Second Coming, and in Lent as the beginning of Holy Week. All four Gospels record the account, which tells us something of its importance. We find here a fulfillment of two Old Testament prophesies: Psalm 24:7-10 and Zechariah 9:9. (Consider reading these prophecies at the beginning of the lesson, asking the students to see if they can tell how they were fulfilled as the events of Palm Sunday progressed.)

v. 1-3
- ▶ Jesus traveled to Jerusalem knowing full well that He would die there. (Matthew 16:21) This is further evidence that neither Satan nor humans could take Jesus' life from Him, but He could lay it down willingly. (John 10:18)
- ▶ Jesus here demonstrated that, although He set aside the *full* use of his divine powers, He was still true God, able by His divine power to know of the donkey and know that the owners would allow his disciples to take it.

v. 4-6

- No matter how seemingly insignificant, Jesus did not leave even one prophecy unfulfilled. HereHefulfilled what was earlier spoken by the Prophet Zechariah.
- The choice of a donkey rather than a nobler mode of transportation is significant.
- When Jesus came the first time He came as our humble Savior.
- He came not to be served but to serve and to give His life as a ransom for many. (Mat. 20:28)
- The next time He comes will not be in humility but in power and great glory.
- With the shouts of praise from the people we are given a brief glimpse of that future glory.
- See the definition above for "Zion." "Daughter of Zion" probably referred specifically to the inhabitants of Jerusalem, but in a symbolic, spiritual way the words apply to all believers of all time, for Jesus rode into Jerusalem to save each one of us.
- v. 7-8
- These cut palm branches give the day its name.
- The spreading of palm branches and garments on the road was a greeting reserved for the arrival of conquering heroes, especially kings.
- What a strange procession we see here, as many of those who worshiped Jesus as king on Palm Sunday were probably among those later calling for his crucifixion.
- The scribes and Pharisees had hoped that Jesus would come to Jerusalem to celebrate the Passover, but they hadn't counted on this kind of reception by the people.
- They were powerless to stop it. Had the people not cried out, the very stones would have. (Luke 19:40)

v. 9

- Imagine the scene as "a very great multitude" sang out the praises of their King!
- Yet this is as nothing compared to the celebration of all the faithful on the Last Day, when Jesus returns in pure, unrestrained power and glory.
- Like the word *hallelujah*, *hosanna* came to represent more than just its literal meaning in the minds of the people.
- It came to be used as an expression of joy; "praise the Lord!" It had clear implications to the Promised Messiah, who alone could save.
- *"Hosanna in the highest"* was roughly equivalent to "May our shout of praise resound also in heaven."
- So also we sing "All Glory Be to God on High!" (TLH 237)

v. 10-11

- The commotion stirred the entire city to ask what was happening and what it meant.
- Since Jesus entered during the Passover, there were many more Jews in Jerusalem than usual.
- One census during the reign of Emperor Nero reckoned the number of Jews in Jerusalem during the Passover at 2,700,000.

## STUDENT PRAYER

Dear Jesus, on Palm Sunday You demonstrated to me just what kind of Savior-King You are. Although as true God You possessed all the power of heaven and earth, You set aside the full use of that power and became my humble servant-Savior. Thank You for coming to earth to take away my sins. Because You humbled Yourself and willingly went to Jerusalem to die for my sins, now I never have to fear death or hell. Please give me the same kind of humble, loving spirit that You had while on earth. I look forward to the day when You return again with all Your divine power clearly seen by all. Please keep me safe until that day, and please come quickly. Amen.

## PRESENTATION

A harmony of the four Gospel accounts of this story has been prepared. This can be read in class, or the teacher can tell the story, or both.

## ACTIVITY TWO

Photocopy the palm leaf on page 4 onto green paper (or have the students color the leaf provided) and cut out one for each student (or have them cut out the leaves). Have the children lay the leaves on the floor pretending Jesus is coming. They can say:

Hosanna! Hosanna! All the people sing.
Hosanna! Hosanna! For Christ the Lord is King.

## APPLICATIONS

1. Note the self-discipline and the determination of Jesus to walk the path to the cross. He went to Jerusalem knowing that thereHewould have to pay for the sins of the world – a punishment that made physical crucifixion seem easy. Discuss with your students how they would feel and what they would do if they could see into the future and could know ahead of time when and how they would die. (if they had even one guilty sin they had not given over to God for His forgiveness)

2. Discuss the difference between stealing and borrowing. When does borrowing become stealing? Did Jesus tell his disciples to steal the donkey? Answer: Jesus is special in thatHecan read hearts. He also knew that someone would give the disciples permission to borrow the donkey. Jesus, who could read hearts, would have known that the owner wouldn't object to lending his animal. We cannot read hearts; therefore we will want to always ask permission before we borrow something. In this case it was a great honor to supply the Son of God with the donkey.

3. When the Jews received Jesus as their king, they shouted the word, "*Hosanna!*" This word, as noted above, means "*Save now*." The people saw Jesus as a Savior, but most of them thought ofHimas some sort of earthly savior – a "bread king." When they shouted "*Hosanna,*" they might well have been thinking of Jesus as a king that would deliver them from Roman oppression. What Bible words or phrases do we use today without really thinking about what they mean? (Answer: Hallelujah, Praise the Lord, sanctification, justification, atonement, Thy kingdom come, etc.) We want to always strive for the meaning in Bible terms and truths.

4. What does it mean that Jesus is our king? (Answer: ThatHerules over us, not by force but with the faith and love worked in our hearts by the Holy Spirit. When we pray "Thy kingdom come" in the Lord's Prayer, we are praying that Jesus would establish and strengthen his rulership in our hearts.)

5. Palm Sunday can be seen as the day on which the Jews picked Jesus to be their king. This happened on the 10th of Nisan. It is no mere coincidence that this was the day on which the Jews annually selected their Passover lamb, which was then sacrificed five days later (after sunset on Thursday and therefore technically regarded as Friday by the Jews). Jesus was the Passover Lamb of God, sacrificed on Good Friday for the sins of the world.

## PASSAGES

If time permits it would be beneficial to take time to explain and apply the following passages to the events of Palm Sunday. You are encouraged to choose one for memory work.

Lower
Matthew 21:5 - "Behold, Your King is coming to you, lowly, and sitting on a donkey."
Matthew 21:9 - "Hosanna to the Son of David! 'Blessed is He who comes in the name of the LORD!' Hosanna in the highest!"
1 Peter 5:5 - "God resists the proud, but gives grace to the humble."

Middle any of the above and...
Matthew 24:30 - All the tribes of the earth will mourn, and they will see the Son of Man coming on the clouds of heaven with power and great glory.

Matthew 26:64 - I say to you, hereafter you will see the Son of Man sitting at the right hand of the Power, and coming on the clouds of heaven.

Upper any of the above and...
Hebrews 12:2 - Look unto Jesus, the author and finisher of our faith, who for the joy that was set before Him endured the cross, despising the shame, and has sat down at the right hand of the throne of God.
Psalms 24:9-10 - Lift up your heads, O you gates! Lift up, you everlasting doors! And the King of glory shall come in. Who is this King of glory? The LORD of hosts, He is the King of glory.


## HYMN CHOICES

"All Glory, Laud, and Honor" (TLH #160:1, 3-4)
"Ride On, Ride On, in Majesty" (TLH #162:1, 4-5)
"Great God What Do I See and Hear?" (TLH #604:1,4)

## 31

**STORY**
The Parable of the Ten Virgins – Matthew 25:1-13

**TEACHER PRAYER**
Lord Jesus Christ, you have made me wise unto salvation through faith in Your holy Word. Bless my efforts that I may be the instrument through whom the Holy Spirit gives the children in my classroom Your precious saving Word so that they will always be ready for the unknown hour of Your return.  In Your saving name,  Amen.

**VOCABULARY**
*Parable* – An earthly story with a heavenly meaning.  A teaching device Jesus used often.
*Lamps of oil* – This can symbolize for us of the whole work of God the Holy Spirit – that through God's Word He calls, gathers, enlightens, sanctifies, and keeps us in the one true faith. (Luther's explanation to the 3rd Article of the Apostle's Creed)
*Bridegroom* – Jesus Christ
*Wise Virgins* – Believers who faithfully persevered in God's Word.
*Foolish Virgins* –  Those who started out as believers, but who did not continue in God's Word and, as a result, fell from faith and were rejected by the Lord.

**OUTER AIM**
Keep on watching and being ready for the unknown time of Christ's Day of Judgment.

**INNER AIM**
God's Word will keep us steadfast and ready for Christ's Day of Judgment.

**BACKGROUND**
In context, chapters 24 and 25 of the Gospel of Matthew deal with the coming of Christ's Day of Judgment.  We recite in the Apostle's Creed…"…He will come to judge…"  There are two events – the coming and the judging.  Chapter 24 of Matthew deals mostly with the coming of Christ, while the 25th chapter deals mostly with the judging.  This parable of the Ten Virgins deals with both, but with an emphasis on the Day of Judgment and the results of persevering in the faith or not.  Being mindful that parables contain one main point, and we should not make doctrines out of the details, we also recognize that many of our Lutheran forefathers allegorized this parable according to the whole analogy of Scripture. For instance – the "lamp" is every Christian being a light in the world, the "oil" is faith, or the Word of God, etc.  While we don't want to make too much of the details of a parable, we also recognize applicable Bible truths that prepare us by faith for the great Day of Judgment by our Savior.

**STUDENT PRAYER**
Lord Jesus Christ, thank you for giving us faith to believe in the forgiveness of sins You have earned for us.  Lord, keep our faith steadfast in Your Word so that we keep on watching for Your second coming, and so that on Judgment Day we will be welcomed by You into heaven for the eternal celebration You have prepared for all believers.  Amen.

**PRESENTATION**
The Lord's second coming could happen at any time.  He could very well come in our lifetime – our "time of grace."  Also, our time of grace is in God's hands and so we may die before Judgment Day comes.  Hebrews 9:27 says, "It is appointed unto men once to die, but after this the Judgment."  So, when our time of grace is over – as you close your eyes in death, the next thing you know you'll be opening your eyes on Judgment Day.  Either way, we want God's assurance that Jesus not only is "the Author of our faith" but that He is

also "the Finisher of our faith." (Heb. 12:12)   In this parable, Jesus used the ten virgins to show the results of faithful perseverance to His Word verses unfaithful.  Jesus is speaking to all believers and warning the foolish to "wise-up."  The contrast can be compared to

**Vs. 1  *"Then the kingdom of heaven shall be likened to ten virgins who took their lamps and went out to meet the bridegroom."***
Some have equated the wise and foolish virgins as believers and unbelievers.  But the "kingdom of heaven" is Christ's ongoing ruling activity in our hearts and the hearts of all believers.  Jesus is here preaching to His own – they are all believers at the beginning.

**Vs.2-5  *"Now five of them were wise, and five were foolish.  Those who were foolish took their lamps and took no oil with them, but the wise took oil in their vessels with their lamps. But while the bridegroom was delayed, they all slumbered and slept."***
Using the whole analogy of Scripture, Martin Luther comments: "When the Kingdom is preached, these are the results:  Some receive it with all their heart and are serious about , believe the Word, make the most strenuous efforts to practice good works, let their lamps shine before the world; for they are well provided with lamps and oil, that is, with faith and love: these are represented by the wise virgins.  Then there are some that also accept the Gospel, but are sleepy, are not serious about it, think they can succeed with their works, are secure, and believe it can be paid for with works;  those are indicated in the foolish virgins.  In Scripture those are called foolish that do not obey the Word of God, but follow their own mind, will not be taught, accept no opinion but their own.  But it will happen to them at last as it here happened to the foolish virgins.  These two kinds of people are in this Kingdom, namely, where the Word of God is preached and there should be exercise of faith:  some follow, some do not follow…" (Luther, 11, 1925.2407)
Also note, the foolish virgins did not *forget* to bring oil, they took no oil with them.  Sleeping is something in which both foolish and wise are involved.  One commentator says that this could imply that, although being warned to be watchful and ready, "there is danger at all times that a false sense of security lulls the spiritual senses to sleep." (Kretzmann p. 139)  When the time comes, all are taken by surprise.

**Vs.6-10  *"And at midnight a cry was heard: `Behold, the bridegroom is coming; go out to meet him!' Then all those virgins arose and trimmed their lamps.  And the foolish said to the wise, `Give us some of you oil, for our lamps are going out.' But the wise answered, saying, `No, lest there should not be enough for us and you; but go rather to those who sell, and buy for yourselves.' And while they went to buy, the bridegroom came, and those who were ready went in with him to the wedding; and the door was shut."***
The midnight cry came to the wise virgins only unexpectedly, but to the foolish virgins also unpreparedly.  When asked, the wise virgins refused to share their oil with the foolish virgins.  When Judgment Day arrives, there will be no "borrowing" from others what is needed for entrance into heaven.
Luther: "Remember, then, in this Gospel that the lamps without oil signify a mere external thing and a bodily exercise without faith in the heart; but the lamps with oil are the internal riches, also the external works with true faith."
Conversion is to be coupled with faithful perseverance.  All this is given by God through the Means of Grace – the Gospel as it is found in the Word and Sacraments.

**Vs.11-13** *"Afterward the other virgins came also, saying, `Lord, Lord, open to us!' But he answered and said, `Assuredly, I say to you, I do not know you.' Watch therefore, for you know neither the day nor the hour in which the Son of Man is coming."*

The bridegroom in the parable took in only those virgins who were prepared to meet him. By the parable, Jesus taught that Christians should have faith and so be prepared to meet Him at all times. With faith we are prepared at all times. Those who lack faith, will have the doors of heaven closed to them. Matthew 7:21-23. Those that watch will receive the LORD and His grace. Those that are secure will find Him a merciless Judge.

## APPLICATION

Those who teach this lesson should be very careful not to moralize. Make sure that your children leave the Sunday School room knowing that God has prepared them through faith by the Gospel for His great Day of Judgment. Jesus is the Author and Finisher of our faith. That message encourages us to live lives committed steadfastly to Christ by faith.

Our parents, pastors, and teachers faithfully taught us the Word of God in all its truth and purity. "From childhood you have known the Holy Scriptures, which are able to make you wise for salvation through faith which is in Christ Jesus." 2 Timothy 3:15. The Holy Spirit will continue to use His Means of Grace to strengthen us to "fight the good fight" of our Christian lives, that we may finally "lay hold on eternal life." 1 Timothy 6:12.

If we are to be watchful at all times, then we should talk about distractions and ways to prevent them. What hinders us from things spiritual?

How does Jesus recognize us? John 10:11ff. John 8:47, "He who is of God, hears God's Word.

## PASSAGES
**These passages can be assigned as memory work or simply discussed in class as to how they fit the lesson.**

Matt. 24:42 - Therefore, keep watch, because you do knot know on what day your Lord will come.

Matt. 24:44 - So you also must be ready, because the Son of Man will come at an hour when you do not expect Him.

Matt 26:41 - Watch and pray that you enter not into temptation. The spirit is indeed willing, but the flesh is weak

Matt 7: 21 - Not everyone who says to me Lord, Lord, will enter the kingdom of heaven, but only he who does the will of my Father who is in heaven.

## HYMN CHOICES
Great God, What Do I See and Hear! - TLH #604
The World Is Very Evil - TLH #605
Wake, Awake, For Night Is Flying - TLH #609
And Will The Judgment Descend - TLH #610

## 32

## STORY

The Ten Lepers - Luke 17:11-19

## TEACHER PRAYER

Dear Father in Heaven, Jesus revealed Himself as the Promised Messiah by healing the deaf, the blind, and the lepers. I ask that Jesus' healing touch would be revealed in my life. More than this, I ask that I may see and believe that Jesus is the Christ, the Messiah. Then only can I teach these children whom You have entrusted to my care, that Jesus is their Savior. Amen.

## VOCABULARY

*leprosy* - a skin disease that often resulted in fingers and toes falling from the body
*Samaritan* - the people who lived between Galilee and Judah who were hated by the Jews

## OUTER AIM

Jesus Heals the Lepers

## INNER AIM

I Give Thanks Because Jesus Healed Me From the Leprosy of Sin

## BACKGROUND

Jesus began His final journey to Jerusalem. Matthew and Mark tell us that during this last journey great multitudes followed Jesus, and that He healed them and taught them. Jesus' journey took Him along the borders of Samaria and Galilee. Luke alone records the account of the healing of the ten lepers. This journey set the stage for Jesus' suffering and death in Jerusalem.

## STUDENT PRAYER

Heavenly Father, I am covered with the leprosy of sin. I am unclean in Your sight because of my personal sinfulness. May Jesus cleanse me from the leprosy of sin with His holy blood. I thank You for Your healing power in my life. Amen

## PRESENTATION

At the outset of His journey as Jesus entered a certain village, He met ten lepers. One of them was a Samaritan. Jewish law required these lepers to remain outside the village and far from contact with Jesus or any other person. Leprosy was considered a mortal disease. Lepers were commanded not to make contact with any other people or even to bear the appearance of mourners. When a leper came into contact with another person, he was to cry out, "Unclean! Unclean!" Rabbinic law declared that only a descendant of Aaron could proclaim a leper clean or unclean. In the Old Testament physical defects such as leprosy were seen as a representation of a spiritual uncleanness.

These ten lepers begged Jesus to heal them out of mercy. Without a touch or even a command to be healed, Jesus told them to go and show themselves to the priest as healed. And in their desperate state, the lepers obeyed Christ's command even before they had actually experienced healing. So great was their faith in this Messiah! And as they went, they were healed, all ten of them.

Of the ten equally recipient of this healing, nine Jews continued on their way to the priest to be pronounced healed and whole. Who could blame them? Only one of the ten, a Samaritan, returned to Jesus and with a loud voice glorified God. The grateful Samaritan, of all people, hurried back and with a loud voice of thanksgiving praised God. He fell at the feet of Him to Whom he gave thanks. This Samaritan received more than new bodily life and health; he found spiritual life and healing. He gave thanksgiving to Jesus for his healing and life.

Why did the nine Jews not return? It probably was the same thing that doomed the nation of Israel. They were more interested in the things of men than the things of God. They were obsessed with the world. The most important thing to them was their physical healing. Like Old Testament Israel, the many blessings of God led to a failure to acknowledge the true gifts of God. They, like so many in their day did not see the spiritual import of Jesus' miracles.

So Christ spoke to the Samaritan, "Arise, go your way. Your faith has made you whole." Only the Samaritan was totally whole. He found in Jesus the forgiveness of sins and gave thanks to Jesus.

## APPLICATION

Most of the people of Jesus' day were interested in Jesus only in terms of what they could get from Him. They followed Jesus eagerly to see or experience a miracle of healing. They were more interested in what was in it for them. If your pastor had the true gift of healing, the church would be full of people looking for relief from their diseases. If you could get rich following Jesus, people would be willing to pay lots of money to learn the secret.

People do not realize that there is a fundamental uncleanness that has to be taken care of, and that is the sin that infects us all. Some of our hymns compare leprosy to sin that makes us unclean and unwhole in the sight of God. Jesus came not just to temporarily heal us of our diseases; Jesus came to save us from our sins. This is the reason for Jesus' life and death. This is the gift Jesus gives us today.

When healed, we should not be surprised that only one out of ten returned to say "Thank you" to Jesus. Parents often have to remind children to say "thank you" when they receive a gift. We often forget to thank Jesus for all the things He does for us. The nation of Old Testament Israel reveals the sad principle of human behavior that the more God gives us, the less we return thanks to Him. Thanksgiving is an acknowledgement that everything we have comes from God. God has given us so much.

It might be helpful to have the children list the blessings both spiritual and material that they have received from God. Then have them list ways that they can show their thanksgiving to God.

## PASSAGES
**These passages can be assigned as memory work or simply discussed in class as to how they fit the lesson.**
**Psalm 103:1-5** - "Bless the LORD, O my soul; And all that is within me, bless His holy name! {2} Bless the LORD, O my soul, And forget not all His benefits: {3} Who forgives all your iniquities, Who heals all your diseases, {4} Who redeems your life from destruction, Who crowns you with lovingkindness and tender mercies, {5} Who satisfies your mouth with good things, so that your youth is renewed like the eagle's."
**Psalm 136:1** - "Oh, give thanks to the LORD, for He is good! For His mercy endures forever."
**Philippians 4:6** - "Be anxious for nothing, but in everything by prayer and supplication, with thanksgiving, let your requests be made known to God."

## HYMN CHOICES
Come to Calvary's Holy Mountain - THL #149 v.2
Now Thank We All Our God - TLH #36
Let All Things Now Living - Worship Supplement #792

## 33

**STORY**
Jesus Talks About Taxes and Offerings - Mark 12:13-17, 41-44

**TEACHER PRAYER**
Oh, All-Providing God in Heaven, you do daily provide all we need whether it be earthly possessions or Your blessed holy Word. The children you have entrusted to my care this morning need to know You as that loving always-caring God in Heaven. Help me to use Your holy Word to impress on their hearts this important truth. In Jesus' name. Amen.

**INTRODUCTION**
In today's story Jesus talks about taxes and our offerings.  I think you know what offerings are. Offerings are the money we put in the offering plate on Sunday at church.  Who is the offering money for?  If the offerings are for God, how does the church give the money to God?  (Explain how churches use the offerings to serve God and His kingdom.)Do you know what taxes are?  Taxes are the money we pay to our country's government.  You pay taxes when you buy something at the store. (Briefly present a small item such as a book.  Explain that it costs $1.00.  Show  the dollar you would have to pay the cashier and the extra pennies (sales tax) that you would have to pay.  Explain that the extra money goes to our government to pay for policemen, firemen, fire trucks, soldiers, building roads and schools, etc.  Explain how necessary these things are for our lives.  Explain good and bad attitudes people have about paying taxes.)

**PRESENTATION**
Use dollars, coins, pennies, and an offering basket to tell the story.  If you  don't have real dollar bills, then use Monopoly money.

**THE STORY**
Jesus had many enemies who hated Him.  They hated Him so much they wanted to kill Him. These enemies were looking for a reason to kill Jesus.  They tried to find a hard question for Jesus so that they could get Him in trouble.

First they said nice things to Jesus to try to trick Him.  They said, "Teacher, we know that you always tell the truth and teach God's Word rightly.  Jesus knew that they didn't really mean these nice things that they said.

Then they asked, "Should we pay taxes to our rulers or not?"  They were trying to get Jesus in trouble.  Most Jews hated their ruler and did not want to pay taxes to him.  If Jesus said, "Yes, you should pay taxes," then the Jewish people would not like Jesus.  If Jesus said, "No, don't pay taxes to the ruler," then the ruler would be angry at Jesus and might put Him in jail.

Jesus could look into His enemies' hearts.  He saw how much they hated Him and were trying to trick Him so they could kill Him.  Jesus knew this was a sin.  He tried to warn them to be sorry about their bad sin. He said, "Why are you trying to trick me?  Bring me a coin.  I want to see it."

They brought Jesus the coin.  Jesus asked them, "Whose picture is on this coin?"
The enemies said, "Our Ruler's."
Jesus answered, "Give to your ruler what belongs to the ruler, and give to God what is due to God."

The enemies were amazed at how wisely Jesus spoke.  They were not able to trick Him or get Him into trouble.

Later, Jesus was sitting in the temple watching people put their money in the offering boxes. Because He is God, Jesus could look into each person's heart and mind as they were giving their offerings.

Many rich people gave large amounts of money.  But a poor widow came who put two small coins in that were worth even less than a penny.

Jesus called His disciples to Him and said, "I tell you the truth, this poor widow has given more than all the other people. All the other people gave some of the money they had left over after they bought for themselves what they wanted. But she put in all her money, even though she needed it for herself to live on."

## LEVEL 1

### REVIEW
Why did the enemies want to kill Jesus? *(They hated Him.)*
What was in their hearts to make them feel that way? *(Sin)*
Did Jesus still love His enemies? *(Yes)*
How did Jesus show His love for His enemies? *(He warned them of their sin. He wanted them to see their sin and be sorry for it. Unfortunately, they weren't sorry.)*
What did Jesus say we should give to our rulers? *(taxes [money])*
What did Jesus say we should give to God? *(The First Commandment gives us our answer: "You shall have no other gods. What does this mean? We should <u>fear, love, and trust</u> in God above all things." Offerings and good works are a <u>fruit of faith</u> that show our fear, love, and trust for God.)*
Do you think the widow ever sinned? *(Yes)*
Who did she pray to when she was sorry for her sins? *(God)*
Who forgave her sins? *(God)*
How did this make her feel? *(happy, relieved)*
Where would she go when she died because her sins were forgiven? *(heaven)*
How did this make here feel? *(happy)*
How did she show her love and thankfulness to God for eternal life? *(She gave all she had.)*
Was Jesus pleased that the widow had faith in Him? *(Yes)*
Was Jesus pleased with the widow's offering? *(Yes)*

### OUTER AIM
**Jesus was pleased with the widow's offering because she gave it with love and thankfulness.**

### APPLICATION
Do we ever sin? *(Yes)*
How often do we sin? *(Many times each day)*
Can we go to heaven if we are full of sin? *(no)*
What should we tell God when we sin? *(I'm sorry, please forgive me.)*
How did Jesus pay for our sins? *(by dying on the cross)*
Who washes away our sins? *(Jesus)*
When our sins are washed away and we believe in God, can we go to heaven? *(Yes)*
How can we show God we love Him and are happy that we'll go to heaven? *(Many ways – prayers of thanksgiving, praise, obedience, sharing the Gospel, and also giving offerings)*
When we give offerings in church what are we showing God? *(love and thankfulness)*

### INNER AIM
**We show our love and thankfulness to God by giving Him offerings.**

### MEMORY WORK
We love Him because He first loved us. 1 John 4:19

Oh, give thanks to the Lord, for He is good! For His mercy endures forever. Psalm 107:1

We should fear, love, and trust in God above all things. (Luther's explanation to the first commandment)

Hymn: #442 v. 1-2

Lord of Glory, who hast bo't us
With Thy life-blood as the price,
Never grudging for the lost ones
That tremendous sacrifice;
And with that hast freely given
Blessings countless as the sand
To th' unthankful and the evil
With Thine own unsparing hand;

Grant us hearts, dear Lord, to yield Thee
Gladly, freely, of Thine own;
With the sunshine of Thy goodness
Melt our thankless hearts of stone
Till our cold and selfish natures,
Warmed by Thee, at length believe
That more happy and more blessed
'Tis to give than to receive.

## PRAYER

Dear Heavenly Father, You have given us so much. The whole world was created by You as a gift for us. Thank You for the many gifts you give us of food, clothes, family, and homes. Thank you also for Your best gift of all, Your Son, Jesus Christ. Through Jesus' death on the cross You have given us the gift of forgiveness and eternal life. We give You our offerings because we love You and want to thank you. Please accept them for Jesus' sake. Amen.

---

## LEVEL 2

## REVIEW

Why did the enemies want to kill Jesus? *(They hated Him.)*
What was in their hearts to make them feel this way? *(Sin)*
Did Jesus still love His enemies? *(Yes)*
How did Jesus show His love for them? *(He warned them of their sin.)*
What was Jesus trying to show them was in their hearts? *(Sin)*
Were they sorry for their sin? *(No)*
What did Jesus say we should give our rulers? *(taxes [money])*
What did Jesus say we should give to God? *(We should give God what is due Him. The First Commandment tells us what is due God: "We should have no other gods. What does this mean? We should fear, love, and trust in God above all things." Good works and offerings are a fruit of faith.)*

## OUTER AIM

**We should pay taxes to our rulers and give offerings to God.**

Did the widow give an offering to God? *(Yes)*
Was it very much money? *(No, worth less than a penny)*
Did the rich people give offerings to God? *(Yes)*
Were their offerings very much money? *(Yes)*
Who did Jesus say gave more, the rich people or the widow? *(the widow)*
How could the widow's offering be more if she gave so little money? *(She gave God all the money she had.)*
Who was showing more love for Jesus, the widow or the rich people? *(widow)*
Did the rich people have enough money to buy all the things they wanted and needed? *(Yes)*
Did the widow have enough money to buy all the things she needed? *(No)*
How much money did she have left for herself after she gave her offering? *(Nothing)*
Was she worried about how she would buy food to eat? *(No)*
Who did she trust would give her the food and the clothes she would need? *(God)*
Was the woman angry at God that she was poor or had lost her husband? *(No)*
She was showing respect for God in the way He was directing her life. Another word in the Bible for this respect is **fear**. When the Bible says we should fear God it means that we should respect Him, stand in awe of Him, and want to obey Him as our ruler.

Let all the earth fear the Lord; let all the inhabitants of the world stand in awe of Him. Psalm 33:8 (We should fear God.)

The widow, by giving her offering, was showing fear, love, and trust for God.

## INNER AIM
**We should fear, love, and trust in God above all things.**

## APPLICATION
Do you think the widow always feared, loved, and trusted God as she should? *(No)*
Do you think she may have been worried sometimes? *(Yes)*
Do you think she may have loved other things or people more than God sometimes? *(Yes)*
Do you think she may have showed a lack of respect for God by disobeying Him sometimes? *(Yes)*
What do we call it when we worry, love others more than God, and disobey God? *(Sin)*
What do you think the widow did when she sinned? *(Asked God to forgive her)*
Who forgave her sins? *(God, for Jesus' sake)*
Do we ever show a lack of respect for God by disobeying His commands? *(Yes)*
Do we ever worry? *(Yes)*
Do we sometimes love things or ourselves more than we love God? *(Yes)*
What do we call it when we do those things? *(Sin)*
What should we do when we sin? *(Tell God we're sorry and ask Him to forgive us)*
Will God forgive us? *(Yes)* Why? *(He forgives us because Jesus paid for our sins on the cross.)*
Who always respected God and kept all of His commandments? *(Jesus)*
Who always trusted the Heavenly Father for all He needed? *(Jesus)*
Who always loved God above all things? *(Jesus)*

**Jesus always feared, loved, and trusted God above all things <u>for us</u>.**

We call this Jesus' righteousness. All the <u>right</u> things Jesus did, He did for us, because He knew we couldn't keep all of God's commandments. Now when God looks at us, He doesn't see all our sin. Jesus washed those away. Instead God sees all the right things Jesus did for us.
Because God forgives our sins and makes us righteous, where will we go when we die? *(heaven)*
How does this make us feel? *(happy, thankful)*
How can we show God we are thankful and happy? *(Many ways – offerings, thanks and praise in our prayers, tell others the Gospel, obey God, help at church, help other people)*

## MEMORY WORK
Let all the earth fear the Lord; let all the inhabitants of the world stand in awe of Him. Psalm 33:8 (We should fear God.)

We love Him because He first loved us. 1 John 4:19 (We should love God.)

Our help is in the name of the Lord, who made heaven and earth. Psalm 124:8 (This is the God we trust in.)

1st Commandment
You shall have no other gods.
     *What does this mean?*
We should fear, love, and trust in God above all things.

Hymn: #442 v. 1-2

Lord of Glory, who hast bo't us
With Thy life-blood as the price,
Never grudging for the lost ones
That tremendous sacrifice;
And with that hast freely given
Blessings countless as the sand
To th' unthankful and the evil
With Thine own unsparing hand;

Grant us hearts, dear Lord, to yield Thee
Gladly, freely, of Thine own;
With the sunshine of Thy goodness
Melt our thankless hearts of stone
Till our cold and selfish natures,
Warmed by Thee, at length believe
That more happy and more blessed
'Tis to give than to receive.

**PRAYER**

Dear Heavenly Father, We are sorry when we don't respect (fear) You enough to obey Your commandments. We're sorry when we love other things or people more than You. We're sorry when we don't trust You. Please forgive us for Jesus' sake. Thank You for sending Jesus who perfectly feared, loved, and trusted You in our place. Help us to show our love and thankfulness to You in our offerings, prayers, and obedience to Your commands. In Jesus' name we pray. Amen.

## 34

### STORY
Jesus Talks About the Signs and the Day of His Second Coming - Luke 21, Matt. 25

### TEACHER PRAYER
Lord, we will all die and meet our Judge and Lord and Savior, Jesus Christ. When believers die, you take their souls into your bosom. O Christ, grant this to us and all believers. Amen.

### VOCABULARY
*Kingdom* - nation, country
*Famine* - not enough food to eat
*Pestilence* - sickness, disease, plague
*Adversaries* - enemies
*Perplexity* - confused, mixed up
*Apprehensive* - afraid
*This generation* - from Christ until now (including us)
*Dissipation* - scattered aimlessly

### OUTER AIM
Christ gives us the signs and terms of His second coming to judge the earth.

### INNER AIM
By parables, Christ shows that faith (the talents, sheep) will be the only thing that will let us and you enter heaven.

### BACKGROUND
Because Jesus had predicted the distraction of the beautiful temple of God's people, the disciples asked when would this take place and what would be the signs accompanying it. That was answered by the two parables, the talents, the sheep and the goats, and the various signs in heaven and earth that would precede His second coming.

### STUDENT PRAYER
  Lo, O Lord, help us to make proper use of the signs You gave us concerning Your second coming to judge the world. Help us be prepared for that day by keeping us constantly in Your Word so that we, too, may enter the gates of Heaven with all believers. Amen.

### PRESENTATION
Jesus gives us these stories so that we may be better prepared for Judgment Day. When we look at the signs given us in these various parts; namely, wars of nation against nation, earthquakes, famines, and pestilence like the flu, Aids, polio, cancer. All of these have taken place in the world at one time or another in history. As these signs have been fulfilled, may we the more take warning of the Judgment Day that is to come soon.

Everything in this world will pass away by fire. Only God's Words will endure through this world and into eternity. Christ predicts a great persecution of believers in those last days and many wars throughout the world as there are today. These serve as a warning to us to be prepared for Judgment Day always. That is why we must carry faith and the Word of God in our hearts always so that like the sheep and the two faithful servants we, too, may enter heaven with Christ on Judgment Day.

Because we knew and confessed Christ, God, the Father, will also know and confess us. May Christ be our badge of honor all our lives so we, too, enter eternal bliss and happiness.

## APPLICATION
We can be prepared for Judgment Day by hearing, reading, and studying God's Word every day.


## PASSAGES
**These passages can be assigned as memory work or simply discussed in class as to how they fit the lesson.**

II Tim 2:11-12 - This is a faithful saying: For if we died with Him, We shall also live with Him. If we endure, We shall also reign with Him. If we deny Him, He also will deny us.

Heb 12:2-3 - looking unto Jesus, the author and finisher of our faith, who for the joy that was set before Him endured the cross, despising the shame, and has sat down at the right hand of the throne of God. For consider Him who endured such hostility from sinners against Himself, lest you become weary and discouraged in your souls.

Mark 4:25 - For whoever has, to him more will be given; but whoever does not have, even what he has will be taken away from him.

I Thes. 4:16 - For the Lord Himself will descend from heaven with a shout, with the voice of an archangel, and with the trumpet of God. And the dead in Christ will rise first.

II Cor 5:10 - For we must all appear before the judgment seat of Christ, that each one may receive the things done in the body, according to what he has done, whether good or bad.


## HYMN CHOICES
And Will The Judgment Descend - TLH #610
The Day Is Surely Drawing Near - TLH #611
That Day Of Wrath, That Dreadful Day - TLH #612

## 35

## STORY

Jesus Institutes the Lord's Supper – Matthew 26:17-29; Mark 14:10-25, Luke 22:14-23, John 13:18-30

## TEACHER PRAYER

Dear Lord Jesus, help me to appreciate the great love You have for sinful mankind. On the very night You were handed over to die for sinners, You left us with one of the most valuable gifts we can imagine, Your body and blood in Holy Communion. Help me to convey Your great love for us sinners to my students. I pray that You would work through me to help prepare these young lambs for the day when they come before Your altar. Help them to prepare now, that they might learn to rightly examine themselves later, never communing in an unworthy manner. Bless my imperfect efforts with Your divine power. Amen.

## VOCABULARY

*Unleavened* – bread made without yeast

*Passover* – Jewish religious festival begun in Egypt on the day the Lord passed over the houses with blood on the doorposts and lintels.

*Covenant* – an agreement between two parties. Two types of covenants are found in the Bible: Suzerain-vassal (conditional) and Royal Grant (unconditional). There are two Bible examples of conditional covenants: 1.) Between God and Abraham in Genesis 17, where God promised to bless Abraham and his descendants on the condition of circumcision as a symbol of complete consecration to the Lord and his commands. 2.) Between God and the Children of Israel in Exodus 19-24, where the condition was devotion to the Lord on the part of the Jews. The other covenants were all unconditional. They include covenants between God and the following: Noah (Genesis 9), Abraham (Genesis 15), Phinehas (Numbers 25), David (2 Samuel 7), and all believers in the New Covenant (Jeremiah 31:31-34). Here (in a figure of speech) Jesus speaks of the container for the wine as it were the wine when He calls the cup the blood of this same "new covenant."

## OUTER AIM

Jesus instituted the Lord's Supper as a Means of Grace. The Means of Grace is the Gospel as it is found in Word and Sacraments.

## INNER AIM

Holy Communion gives and assures us of the forgiveness of sins, life, and salvation,

## BACKGROUND

*(Rupprecht Bible History References Vol.2, pp. 337-346)*

We read in Luke 22 that the disciples had been arguing about who was greatest among them. To demonstrate the kind of humility Christians should have, Jesus washed His disciples' feet and (in John 13:14) told the disciples to do likewise. Our name for this day, Maundy Thursday, comes from the Latin word for "command" – mandatum. Some believe it is named for Jesus' "command" to wash one another's feet. More likely is that the day was originally named for the "new commandment" Jesus gave on this night in John 13:34, "A new commandment I give to you, that you love one another..."

The Lord's Supper was instituted during the Passover celebration. The Passover had been observed by the faithful since the exodus from Egypt. God Himself gave directions in Exodus 12 on how the Passover was to be celebrated. That is how we know exactly what elements Jesus used when He instituted His Supper. We know that the bread He used was unleavened since no yeast was to be used (or even found in the house) for seven days. We know Jesus used wine, not only because that was what was used by the Jews to celebrate the Passover, but also because Jesus himself called it "the fruit of the vine" in Matthew 26:29.

v. 17-20

▸ The Feast of Unleavened Bread, which lasted seven days, began with the eating of the Passover meal. (Cf. Exodus 12)

▸ Jesus demonstrated His power and omniscience here (as He did before entering Jerusalem on Palm Sunday) by knowing in advance that the man who owned the upper room would make it available to them.

▸ It is possible that Jesus arranged this ahead of time with the man, but that only gives evidence that Jesus foreknew His own death.

▸ Prearranged or not, only Jesus could have known in advance about the man carrying the pitcher of water (Mark 14:13).

▸ Part of the preparation made by the disciples here was to purge the house of all yeast, in accordance with God's command in Exodus 12.

v. 21-25

▸ Jesus knew ahead of time not only that His time to die was at hand, but also which of His disciples would betray Him.

▸ In love He reached out to Judas with the law ("but woe to that man...")

▸ Note that Jesus did not offer the words of the gospel of forgiveness to an unrepentant sinner.

▸ John in his Gospel tells us that Judas went out immediately after receiving the sign from the Savior that he was the betrayer (John 13:30).

▸ This seems to indicate that Judas was not present at the time. Luke 22:21, on the other hand, seems to indicate that Judas was present, we admit that Luke's account might not be chronological, and John does not specifically mention at what point the Supper was instituted, whether before or after Judas left.

v. 26-28

▸ Jesus here used the word "is" when instituting His Supper: "This is my body...this is my blood..."

— Is means is. There were other words He could have and would have used if He had meant "represents," "symbolizes," "becomes," or "is changed into."

▸ Based on Jesus' own words, we believe that His true body and blood are present "in, with, and under the bread and the wine when we eat and drink."

▸ Jesus' true body and blood are present in a heavenly, miraculous way.

▸ They cannot be seen or tasted. This is called "real presence" and we accept it by faith in Jesus' clear words.

▸ Note that when we drink the cup, we drink the blood of the New Covenant.

▸ Jesus here tells us that we are to drink from the cup, which is His blood of the New Covenant.

▸ It was His blood that "was shed for (the) many for the remission of sins."

▸ The word "many" here is not meant to limit the number of people for which Jesus was to shed His blood. He clearly died to pay for all sins, as He taught in john 3:16, John 1:29, etc. An easy way to understand it is "the many."

▸ The eating and drinking of the very body and blood of our Lord gives and assures us of the forgiveness of sins earned for us by Christ's crucifixion.

▸ By faith the Christian believes and trusts that Holy Communion gives the forgiveness of sins.

v. 29-30

▸ Jesus referred to the cup as "the fruit of the vine."

▸ That this drink contained alcohol is beyond serious dispute, for without refrigeration grape juice will naturally ferment. (cf. 1 Cor. 11:20-21)

▸ This natural process is a blessing from God because fermentation kills the harmful organisms in the water.

- Jesus here prophesied that He would not repeat this celebration with the disciples until they share it in heaven.
- Indeed only hours later Jesus was arrested, tried, and executed.

## STUDENT PRAYER

Dear Jesus, thank You for the precious gift You gave to us on Maundy Thursday. On the very night You were betrayed to Your enemies You were thinking about us and what we would need to be strengthened while on earth. While I am young, each time the Lord's Supper is celebrated, help me to remember how You suffered and died for my sins. When I am older, help me to come to Holy Communion in a worthy manner – sorry for all my sins, trusting You for forgiveness, and certain that I am receiving Your true body and blood when I eat the bread and drink the wine. Amen.

## PRESENTATION

The Words of Institution are very precise and very important. If you tell the story in your own words, it would be a good idea to read at least the words of Institution from Matthew 26.

**ACTIVITY TWO**- Teacher: Have students color the picture, using the questions below to guide the activity.

1. Color the part of the picture that Jesus tells us to take and eat. (bread)

   What does Jesus also give us when we eat the bread? (His body)
2. Color the part of the picture of which Jesus tells us to drink. (cup)

   What is in the cup? (wine) What does Jesus give us with the wine? (His blood)
3. Jesus gave His body for us and shed His blood for us on the ____. Draw a cross in the empty box .

   The cross reminds us that our sins are forgiven.

## APPLICATIONS

1. Are we today obligated to wash each other's feet? What other loving actions could we do for each other today? Note that such things are only pleasing when they are done willingly, never by force or from a feeling of obligation.
2. Note that there was never a question if Jesus and the disciples would celebrate the Passover, only where (Matthew 26:17). So too there should never be a question about going to church each time we are able.
3. An unrepentant sinner like Judas needs to hear the threat of the law, not the pronouncement of forgiveness found in the gospel. Only the law can crush the proud, rebellious, sinful human heart. Unless the sinner first recognizes and repents of his sin, the news of a Savior can have no effect on him.
4. Jesus paid for all sins when he died on the cross. As children of God we don't have forgiveness for just some of our sins; we have forgiveness for all of our sins. Yet since we still have our sinful nature, Jesus gives us His Holy Supper as a Means of Grace which gives and assures us of the forgiveness of sins, life and salvation.

## PASSAGES

These passages can be assigned as memory work or simply discussed in class as to how they fit the lesson.

<u>Lower</u>

Luke 22:19 - This is My body which is given for you; do this in remembrance of Me.
John 15:5 - Without [Jesus] you can do nothing.
Philippians 4:13 - I can do all things through Christ who strengthens me.

<u>Middle</u> any of the above and...
Romans 4:5 - But to him who does not work but believes on Him who justifies the ungodly, his faith is accounted for righteousness.
Ephesians 1:7 - In [Christ] we have redemption through His blood, the forgiveness of sins, according to the riches of His grace.
Matthew 26:28 - For this is My blood of the new covenant, which is shed for many for the remission of sins.

<u>Upper</u> any of the above and...
1 Corinthians 10:16 - The cup of blessing which we bless, is it not the communion of the blood of Christ? The bread which we break, is it not the communion of the body of Christ?
Romans 6:22- But now having been set free from sin, and having become slaves of God, you have your fruit to holiness, and the end, everlasting life.
1 Peter 1:18-19 - Knowing that you were not redeemed with corruptible things, like silver or gold...but with the precious blood of Christ, as of a lamb without blemish and without spot.

## HYMN CHOICES

"The Death of Jesus Christ our Lord" (TLH #163:1-2)
"Redeemed, Restored, Forgiven" (TLH #32:1,4)
"Glory Be to Jesus" (TLH #158:1-4)

## 36

## STORY

Jesus in the Garden of Gethsemane, His Betrayal and Arrest - Matthew 26:14-16, 36-56, Mark 14:10-11, 32-50, Luke 22:39-53, John 18:1-11

## TEACHER PRAYER

Dear Father in heaven, I come to You now as Your Son came to You in the Garden on the night He was betrayed, humble and asking for Your help. I come on behalf of the children - Your little lambs - whom I am called to teach. Give me, I pray, wisdom and understanding that I might present to them Your words and Your will in all their truth and majesty. I pray that Your Holy Spirit might work through me to bring the power of Your Word to bear on their little hearts. Bless my instruction of these precious little ones. Let them see Your hand in their lives. This I ask in Jesus' name. Amen.

## VOCABULARY

*Legion* - Although a full Roman legion had 6,000 men, this word could also refer to simply a great multitude. (cf. Mark 5:9)

## OUTER AIM

Jesus prayed in the Garden of Gethsemane, was betrayed by Judas and arrested.

## INNER AIM

Jesus submitted to His Father's will to save mankind.

## BACKGROUND

*(Rupprecht Bible History References Vol. 2, pp. 346-360)*
Jesus had just celebrated the Passover with His disciples and had instituted the Lord's Supper. Surely the disciples must have been confused by Jesus' words: "Take eat, this is My body which is broken for you." "This is My blood of the new covenant, which is shed for many for the remission of sins." They were soon to find out just what Jesus meant by those words. Jesus and the eleven traveled from the upper room where they celebrated the Passover to a place they had used many times - the Garden of Gethsemane. Judas went out from the upper room and went straight to the chief priests and elders, who assigned to him a "great multitude" of men charged with arresting Jesus.

v. 14-16

▸ Judas' act of betrayal was calculated and premeditated rather than spontaneous.

▸ We cannot say for certain exactly what his motives might have been.

▸ Certainly money played a role, but Judas was a complex character, and there could well have been other factors that prompted his decision.

▸ The infamous thirty pieces of silver were worth about 120 denarii. A denarius was generally considered to be equal to one day's wage.

v. 36-39

▸ Gethsemane was probably more like a small park than a garden.

▸ Once again Jesus left the majority of the disciples behind (perhaps at the outer edge of the park) and took only Peter, James, and John to be near Him.

- Jesus did this not only to have someone close to Him in this time of great anguish, but also so that there might be witnesses for future generations.
- Few (if any) men can say that they have known this kind of sorrow.
- Jesus was not so full of grief that He wanted to end His own life to escape.
- Jesus was to the point where the anguish itself could kill Him.
- Perhaps this is why an angel was sent to strengthen him (cf. Luke 22:43).
- Luke also records that "His sweat became like great drops of blood, falling to the ground." Many believe that Luke is here simply telling us that Jesus was sweating profusely. There is, however, a medical condition known as *hematidrosis* where under conditions of great stress or anguish blood can actually mix with sweat.
- Jesus here demonstrated for all mankind the model prayer.
- As a true man, Jesus was suffering as no other man has or will. He openly expressed His will to His Father, that "this cup might pass from Me."
- Yet note well His unwavering submission to His Father's will: "Nevertheless, not as I will, but as You will."

v. 40-41
- How Jesus, as true man, longed for the companionship and support of His closest men.
- They failed Him, as all men failed Him. Jesus was utterly alone when He carried our sins to the cross. "God made Him who had no sin to be sin for us."
- Even His heavenly Father forsook Him on the cross.
- With His words "Watch and pray" Jesus here advocates that which has been all but lost to our modern society: self-discipline and self-denial.
- We can sympathize with the disciples who were very tired after a long day and a big meal.
- Jesus tries to impress upon them the seriousness of the occasion and the critical importance that they "watch and pray." The flesh is indeed weak.

v. 42-46
- The fact that Jesus repeated the same prayer three times is telling.
- God wants us to be persistent when we pray, so long as we add the words Jesus added: "Your will be done."
- It is probably incorrect to imagine that Jesus went to the spot where He prayed (about a stone's throw from the three), spoke only the few words recorded in our text, and came right back.
- He may have repeated these words many times. He may have added others, which would explain the slightly different wording in the three accounts.
- The fact is His prayers must have taken some time, since not only had His men fallen asleep, they apparently slept for some time.
- Jesus seemed surprised to find that the disciples were still sleeping when He came back the third time: "Are you still sleeping and resting?"

v. 47-50
- The chief priests and elders were not about to take any chances.
- That is why they not only hired Judas, but they also sent "a great multitude" to arrest a gentle man like Jesus.
- John alone recorded the amazing spectacle of how this rough, tough, well-armed band of ruffians retreated and fell to the ground when Jesus told them who He was.
- The message here is clear. No matter how tough or well armed, these men had no power over Jesus. Jesus willingly placed Himself under their power.

- Judas identified Jesus with a kiss - not an uncommon greeting in those days. His brazen hypocrisy, however, is not lost on Jesus, who yet in love calls him "friend."

v. 51-54
- All twelve of the Apostles were together now.
- Peter, still emboldened by the Lord Jesus, who stood at his side, swung with a clumsy fisherman's hand at one of the guards, Malchus, and cut off his right ear.
- Healing the ear by the power of His touch, Jesus assures His men that He could have any number of angels at His disposal.
- Twelve legions, in Roman terms, was equal to 72,000 soldiers. One single angel would have been more than a match for even this great crowd.
- Jesus willingly gave His life for us sinners.

v. 55-56
- Jesus shamed the men who came out to arrest Him.
- He reminded them that He had been with them daily in the temple, but they hadn't the courage to arrest Him there, in the daylight.
- They were operating instead under the cover of darkness, the favorite time of evil men.
- This was very likely not a quiet, gentle arrest, though Jesus would certainly have gone with them without a struggle.
- The disciples, we are told, did not simply wander off. They fled for their lives.
- One of them (most believe it was Mark) was grabbed by the mob. In terror and shame he left his cloak and fled naked into the night. Jesus was alone, in the midst of the hostile crowd.

## STUDENT PRAYER

Dear Jesus, I can't even imagine how much You suffered for me in the Garden of Gethsemane and on the cross of Calvary. I'm sorry that my many sins made it necessary for You to have to suffer as You did, but with all my heart I thank You for doing it. I could never have done what You did, and I surely did not deserve to have You suffer like that in my place. Thank You, dear Jesus, for suffering the punishment of hell for my sins. Amen.

## PRESENTATION

If your students enjoy acting out the Bible stories, this lesson certainly lends itself to that. Otherwise it is best to tell this lesson in your own words since there are many interesting facts in the different accounts that should be included.

**ACTIVITY ONE** - Use the cover picture and the questions and directions below to help students review the lesson.

1. Draw a line under the people Jesus took with Him into the garden. What were their names? What did Jesus ask them to do while He prayed?
2. Draw an X on the picture of Jesus praying to His Father. What did He ask His Father to do for Him? How did He end His prayer? To whom do we pray for help? How should we end our prayer?
3. Draw a circle around the part of the picture that shows what Jesus found His disciples doing when He went back to them. How did Jesus feel?
4. Draw a box around the part of the picture that shows what made all the noise at the gate of the garden. Why did the crowd have swords and spears?

5.   Make a red dot under the person who showed the enemies where to find Jesus.  What was his name?

6.   Jesus did not use His great power to escape.  He did not let His disciples fight to rescue Him.  Why was Jesus willing to be captured?

**ACTIVITY TWO** - The figures below may be cut out and used to dramatize the story.  Figures may be glued to craft sticks to make puppets, or moved around on a flat surface, or they may be glued in place on a large sheet of paper, to recreate the story setting.  If there is time in class, they could be used for review instead of the question/activity at the top of the page.  If not, give each student an envelope so that the pieces may be taken home and used to retell the story with the child's family.

## APPLICATIONS

1.   Just as Jesus reached out to Judas, so also He calls out to us through His Word when we are in danger of falling into sin. If we deprive ourselves of a regular study of His Word, we cut ourselves off from His words of warning and encouragement. Many times we have to receive this strengthening before the temptation comes. The disciples trusted in their own strength and thought they could handle the temptation. They were wrong.

2.   Picture for the children the extreme suffering of Jesus, together with why He had to suffer as He did. Note too that the suffering was mental, emotional, and physical. Illustrate by asking how they would feel if all their friends abandoned them when they were in trouble and needed help.

3.   No matter how much we might want something in this life, we ought always to follow Jesus' example and pray, "Your will be done." Jesus knows what is best for our spiritual well-being. Ask your students to think of examples of things they might pray for and why God might say, "No." (ie. you might get injured if you had your own car or horse; you might skip church on Sundays if you had your own cabin, etc.)

4.   We can never stress often enough or strongly enough the tremendous love Jesus had for us to endure what He did. Note also the power that was His. How tempting it would have been for us to strike back at anyone who tried to treat us as he treated Jesus.

## PASSAGES

These passages can be assigned as memory work or simply discussed in class as to how they fit the lesson.

Lower
Mark 14:38 - Watch and pray, lest you enter into temptation.
1 Tim. 1:15 - Christ Jesus came into the world to save sinners, of whom I am chief.
Romans 4:24-25 - Jesus our Lord... was delivered up because of our offenses.

Middle any of the above and...
Matthew 26:41 - Watch and pray, lest you enter into temptation. The spirit indeed is willing, but the flesh is weak.
Luke 24:26 - Ought not the Christ to have suffered these things and to enter into His glory?

Upper any of the above and...
1 John 3:1 - Behold what manner of love the Father has bestowed on us, that we should be called children of God!
Hebrews 2:18 - For in that He Himself has suffered, being tempted, He is able to aid those who are tempted.

## HYMN CHOICES

"Go to Dark Gethsemane" (TLH #159:1,4)
"Christ, the Life of All the Living" (TLH #151:1-2,7)
"Glory Be to Jesus" (TLH 1#58:1-4)
"Abide with Us, the Day is Waning" (TLH #194:1,3)

## STORY

Jesus Before the High Priest and Peter's Denial— Matthew 26:57-75; 27:3-10; Mark 14:53-72; Luke 22:54-71; John 18:12-27

## TEACHER PRAYER

Dear Lord Jesus, as I read once again how You suffered great humiliation to pay for my sins, my heart is filled with gratitude. As I read once again how Your disciples all abandoned and denied You, I am filled with awe that still You remained faithful. As I contemplate all that You suffered for my sins, it is my desire now to thank You with my life. It is therefore my prayer that I might continue to experience Your hand in my life, as I struggle to teach Your little lambs the truth concerning Your suffering and death. Work powerfully in their hearts through Your Word, and make me an able witness. Amen.

## VOCABULARY

*Sanhedrin* — The Jewish Supreme Court, made up of 70 men of pure Jewish descent plus the High Priest. The Sanhedrin tried cases that did not fall under Roman jurisdiction, such as heresy and idolatry. They had their own police force and could both make arrests and pronounce the death sentence, but they had no authority to carry out such a sentence.

*Adjure* — to place someone under oath. This was the Jewish equivalent to swearing in.

*Blasphemy* — speaking evil of God, or claiming for oneself anything that belongs to God, especially His power, praise, or glory. For the Jews this was a crime punishable by death.

## OUTER AIM

Jesus was tried and abused by the Jews and denied by Peter.

## INNER AIM

Though forsaken and abused by all mankind, Jesus chose to lay down His life for us all.

## BACKGROUND

*(Rupprecht Bible History References Vol.)*

It was Thursday night (early Friday to the Jews) about 3 a.m. when Jesus was arrested. It was a mixed crowd of both Romans and Jews that took captive the Son of God. Jesus was taken first to Annas, the former high priest, who was the father-in-law of the high priest that year, Caiaphas. Annas was the real power behind the office. Ironically, the Jews broke several of their own laws in their attempt to convict Jesus of criminal activity. Preliminary examination of the accused was forbidden by Jewish law — which is exactly what took place when they took Jesus to Annas. Nor were the Jews permitted to convene the Sanhedrin before the morning sacrifice (which they did anyway) or on the day of, or prior to, any major festival. The Jews were therefore breaking several of their own laws in their irrational attempt to convict and condemn the sinless Son of God.

v. 57-58
- ▸ Matthew, Mark, and Luke do not mention the illegal preliminary examination of Jesus before Annas. Why the arresting party would take Jesus to Annas first is uncertain. It could be an indication that Annas still represented the real power of the office of high priest.
- ▸ (Note that the officer who slapped Jesus in John 18:22 even referred to Annas as if he were still the high priest.)

133

- ▸ Or it could have been that they took Jesus there simply because Annas' residence was closest to Gethsemane, where Jesus was arrested.
- ▸ Jesus was then taken to Caiaphas, where the scribes and elders had gathered. - Peter did not immediately abandon Jesus. In fear, however, he distanced himself from his Lord.

## v. 59-63
- ▸ This was the epitome of an unfair trial.
- ▸ Those entrusted with justice in Israel were in no way concerned with the truth.
- ▸ They did not weigh the evidence to establish a just verdict.
- ▸ They first established a false verdict and then brought false evidence to support it.
- ▸ It is no wonder therefore that their false witnesses could not agree.
- ▸ Note that Jesus never said anything about destroying the temple in Jerusalem. The temple He was going to rebuild after three days was His own body.
- ▸ How frustrating to the high priest that Jesus would not answer these false charges.
- ▸ The evidence was not there to convict Jesus.
- ▸ The high priest no doubt hoped that Jesus might say something in their presence that they could then use to convict Him. Caiaphas therefore placed Jesus under oath in an attempt to elicit a statement.

## v. 64-66
- ▸ Jesus accepted the fact that Caiaphas has placed Him under oath and spoke the truth, proclaiming Himself to be the Christ, the Son of God.
- ▸ The high priest tore his clothes to dramatize his "horror" at what he called "blasphemy" on the part of Jesus.
- ▸ Note that this too was an illegal act on the part of the high priest, who was strictly forbidden from doing so (cf. Leviticus 21:10).

## v. 67-68
- ▸ Spitting in someone's face was considered the worst insult possible by the Jews.
- ▸ Once the death sentence was pronounced, Jesus became fair game for any and all abuse and ridicule, though this treatment also preceded His sentence.
- ▸ What hatred they displayed toward the sinless Son of God, their own Savior!

## v. 69-75
- ▸ John, who was known to the high priest, arranged for Peter to be admitted into the courtyard of the high priest. (John 18:15-16)
- ▸ Nothing is known of John's words and actions while Peter was denying his Lord.
- ▸ Note the progression of Peter's denial. He began with a simple denial. The second time he denied with an oath. Finally he added cursing and swearing to make himself believable.
- ▸ Peter's Galilean accent gave him away, no doubt as conspicuous in Jerusalem as a southern accent in the northern United States or a northern accent in the South.
- ▸ While Mark records that Jesus said, "Before the rooster crows twice you will deny me three times," the other three gospels record only one crowing of the rooster.
- ▸ Jesus no doubt said both things in the course of His conversation with Peter. Mark, who was probably guided by Peter in the writing of his Gospel, records finer detail.
- ▸ Matthew, Luke, and John record only "the crowing of the rooster" as Jesus' reference to sunrise.
- ▸ Thus Jesus very likely first said to Peter, "Before the rooster crows (i.e., before the sun rises) you will deny me three times."
- ▸ We could imagine Peter's objection. Mark then records Jesus' further statement, "Before the rooster crows twice you will deny me three times." Both statements are true. Matthew, Luke, and John refer to sunrise, Mark to the actual sound of a rooster crowing.
- ▸ Luke records for us that the Lord turned and looked at Peter after the third denial.
- ▸ What a dagger to the heart of proud Peter!
- ▸ He went out and wept bitterly, knowing, unlike Judas, that he could do nothing to pay for his sin.

## STUDENT PRAYER

Dear Jesus, thank You for suffering so much to pay for my sins. Give me a strong, humble faith that I might never deny You as my Lord and Savior. Help me to remember how important it is for me to boldly tell others that I believe that You are the only Savior of the world. When I do fall into sin, help me to repent of my sin as Peter did. Amen.

## PRESENTATION

Since there are important parts of this lesson scattered throughout the four gospels, the teacher should use the harmony that has been prepared or tell the story in his/her own words — taking note of the various points found in the four different accounts.

## APPLICATIONS

1.  Jesus, in answering the "I adjure thee" of the high priest, took an oath. We can learn from this that taking an oath is not a sin. It is swearing falsely or frivolously that is a sin. We may in good conscience take an oath when necessary for the glory of our God or the good of our neighbor. In our everyday conversation however, our yes should be yes, and our no, no. (See Matthew 5:37 below.)

2.  Telling the truth was so important to God that He dedicated a commandment to it. God hates a false witness in part because it was false witnesses who condemned His own Son.

3.  The Jewish leaders were willing to sin to accomplish their goals. Jesus said in Matthew 7:20, "By their fruits you will know them." Those who will sin to get what they want are not working to please their Lord, who desires obedience from His children. List some ways we might be tempted to sin to get what we want.

4.  We are the ones who should have been put on trial, not Jesus. We have sin, he had none. We deserve to be punished, Jesus did not. Yet Jesus was guilty! Not according to the justice of man, but according to God's justice. God made Jesus to be sin for us. Because of this, Jesus was made the worst sinner the world has ever seen. How the Father must have loved us to condemn His own Son in this way!

## PASSAGES

These passages can be assigned as memory work or simply discussed in class as to how they fit the lesson.

Lower
Exodus 20:16 - You shall not bear false witness against your neighbor.
Proverbs 16:18 - Pride goes before destruction, and a haughty spirit before a fall.
Isaiah 53:6 - The LORD has laid on Him the iniquity of us all.

Middle any of the above and...
Matthew 5:37 - But let your 'Yes' be 'Yes,' and your 'No,' 'No.' For whatever is more than these is from the evil one. 2 Corinthians 5:21 - For (God) made Him who knew no sin to be sin for us, that we might become the righteousness of God in Him.
Proverbs 19:5 - A false witness will not go unpunished, and he who speaks lies will not escape.

<u>Upper</u> any of the above and...

Isaiah 53:7 - He was oppressed and He was afflicted, yet He opened not His mouth; He was led as a lamb to the slaughter, and as a sheep before its shearers is silent, so He opened not His mouth.

Romans 3:23-24 - For all have sinned and fall short of the glory of God, being justified freely by His grace through the redemption that is in Christ Jesus.

Matthew 26:64 - Jesus said to him, "......I say to you, hereafter you will see the Son of Man sitting at the right hand of the Power, and coming on the clouds of heaven."

## HYMN CHOICES

"O Dearest Jesus, What Law Hast Thou Broken?" (TLH #143:1-3)

"Christ, the Life of All the Living" (TLH #151:1,2 & 5)

"Go to Dark Gethsemane" (TLH #159:1-2)

## STORY
Jesus Before Pilate - Matthew 27:1-2, 11-31; Mark 15:1-20; Luke 23:1-25; John 18:28-19:16

## TEACHER PRAYER
Dear Heavenly Father, when I hear again just how much Your Son suffered for me, I am ashamed of how little love I return to You and to my neighbor. Though I can never offer anything to You as payment for what You have done to save me, I desire now to show my love to You and to my neighbor by teaching Your little lambs the truths of this Bible lesson. Guide me, I pray, by Your Holy Spirit that the words of my mouth and the meditations of my heart might be acceptable in Your sight, and that these precious souls might be led aright through me. I ask this in Jesus' saving name. Amen.

## VOCABULARY
*Governor* - the Roman administrator in a conquered country, also called a praetor. The Roman government, in an attempt to pacify the people in a conquered land, most often allowed the original government structure to stand, but only as a relatively powerless figurehead. Thus Israel was allowed its own kings, councils and judges. The real power, however, rested with the Roman government, represented by the consuls and regional governors or praetors. The governor's function was most judicial.

*Sedition* - inciting others to resist or overthrow established authority. This was one of the crimes of which Barabbas was accused.

*Praetorium* - the official residence of the Roman Governor or Praetor.

## OUTER AIM
Jesus was tried by the Roman governor and, though found to be innocent, was condemned.

## INNER AIM
Jesus willingly suffered under Pontius Pilate on His way to the cross.

## BACKGROUND
*(Rupprecht Bible History References Vol. 2, pp.376-384)*

Jesus had been condemned to death by the Jewish Sanhedrin (Supreme Court) and was sent to the Roman governor, Pontius Pilate, to carry out the sentence. The Jewish courts could sentence someone to death, but under Roman law they could not carry out such a sentence. Thus the Jews had to do business with the hated Roman government. Their hatred of Jesus was so great they would stoop to any level to see Him executed.

v. 1-2, 11-14
- Jesus appeared before Pilate from 6-9 a.m. on Friday morning.
- Jesus respectfully answered Pilate's questions when it was necessary, but he refused to defend himself against the charges of the Jews.
- This demonstrates again that Jesus went to his death willingly to save mankind.
- Pilate was obviously not used to such calm silence on the part of an accused man.
- He marveled that Jesus did not defend himself. How differently the believer and the unbeliever view physical death.

v. 15-18
- In what was no doubt another attempt at keeping a conquered people pacified, the Roman governor in Jerusalem released a prisoner at the request of the people during the Feast of Unleavened Bread.
- Seeking to release Jesus, whom he believed to be innocent, Pilate probably chose the worst criminal in his prison as the only alternative to Jesus. The people picked him anyway.

v. 19-23

▸ Pilate's wife sent word to him that she had been warned in a dream about Jesus. Note the opposing forces at work here. Pilate's wife and his own conscience were opposed by the people and his own desire to appease them. God gave Pilate every opportunity to do the right thing. He chose expediency.

▸ Pilate probably asked his questions to the people so many times in the hope that they might change their minds, or at least to attempt some sort of compromise. So also Pilate offered to whip Jesus and then release Him. What strange justice Pilate sought to impose on the man he had declared to be righteous!

▸ The gospel of Luke records another feeble attempt by Pilate to avoid making the right decision. When he heard that Jesus might fall under Herod's jurisdiction (since He was a Galilean), he sent Jesus to Herod, the governor of Galilee who was also in Jerusalem at that time. This was the same Herod who had ordered John the Baptist beheaded.

▸ Herod was pleased to see Jesus, he wanted to see some miracle done by Jesus, but he was also pleased because he saw this as a statement by Pilate affirming Herod's rulership over all things pertaining to Galilee. Remember that Jesus, though born in Judea, had moved with His parents to Nazareth in Galilee shortly after Jesus was born.

▸ Herod returned Jesus to Pilate when Jesus refused to perform for him, but not before he had treated Jesus shamefully. From this point on Pilate and Herod, who had been enemies, became friends. No matter how bitterly unbelievers disagree, they unite in their opposition to Jesus.

v. 24-25

▸ Pilate knew that condemning an innocent man is wrong, yet he refused to render the correct verdict. Though he did what he knew to be wrong, like all unbelievers he did not want to feel guilt over his actions, or to suffer the consequences.

▸ Yet how foolish is Pilate's notion that by washing his hands before the people he would somehow absolve himself of this great evil.

▸ What ominous words the Jews utter here when they shouted: "His blood be on us and on our children!" Jesus knew the horrible consequences of such words, so also in great love He later prayed, "Father forgive them, for they do not know what they do."

▸ John records how the Jews were even ready to claim the hated Caesar as their king rather than Jesus: "The chief priests answered, 'We have no king but Caesar!'"(John 19:15) How desperate were these men and how great their hatred of Jesus to so prostrate themselves before the pagan Romans.

▸ v. 26-31

▸ The true nature of Pilate and his men is revealed in these verses. These were barbaric men who enjoyed inflicting pain upon others.

▸ Though Pilate knew that Jesus was innocent, he did not simply condemn Him; he also gave his permission to his men to torture and mock Jesus before the actual crucifixion. Roman scourging was a supremely inhumane form of punishment. They did not use simple cords of leather in their whip. They imbedded sharp pieces of bone and metal into the cords to lay open the flesh of the one who was whipped. Backs were frequently laid open to the bone. Even strong men often died from this cruelty.

▸ The robe and the crown of thorns served as a mockery of Jesus' claim that He was a king. The thorns of the crown were likely pushed into Jesus' flesh when they put it on His head. They were certainly driven into His flesh when the soldiers struck him with the reed. This is how they treated the Son of God and Savior of the world.

## STUDENT PRAYER

Dear Jesus, I'm sorry that my sins caused You so much pain. Thank You for willingly suffering all that You did to pay for those sins, especially Your crucifixion on the cross. Please help me now to tell everyone I know what You have done for all of us. Amen.

## PRESENTATION

Once again it is recommended that the teacher use the combined account prepared for you in presenting this lesson. No single gospel account includes every important point.

## PASSION WEEK BOX (p. 3)

Use these pictures to review what happens to Jesus during Passion Week. Have students color these pictures. Cut out along dark outer lines and fold on dotted lines to make a box. Glue tabs behind pictures. These may be hung up with fish line.

## APPLICATIONS

1. Why did Pilate condemn Jesus to death? (Answer: He wanted to please the crowd) Think of some ways we might be tempted to deny Jesus and go along with the crowd.
2. Jesus was falsely accused even though He was perfect. We are sinners and deserve punishment. We are to learn from Jesus to accept persecution and lies from the unbelieving world patiently, without trying to retaliate or take vengeance.
3. Impress on your students the need to do the right thing in God's eyes, without looking first to the possible consequences of doing that right thing. Pilate got himself into trouble because he knew the right thing but failed to carry it out because he feared the consequences.

## PASSAGES

These passages can be assigned as memory work or simply discussed in class as to how they fit the lesson.

Lower
Acts 5:29 - We ought to obey God rather than men.
1 John 4:19 - We love Him because He first loved us.
1 John 4:11 - Beloved, if God so loved us, we also ought to love one another.

Middle any of the above and...
Matthew 6:24 - No one can serve two masters; for either he will hate the one and love the other, or else he will be loyal to the one and despise the other. You cannot serve God and mammon.
Acts 8:33 - In His humiliation His justice was taken away, and who will declare His generation? For His life is taken from the earth.
1 Peter 2:21 - For to this you were called, because Christ also suffered for us, leaving us an example, that you should follow His steps.

Upper any of the above and...
Isaiah 53:5 - But He was wounded for our transgressions, He was bruised for our iniquities; the chastisement for our peace was upon Him, and by His stripes we are healed.
1 Peter 2:23 - (Jesus), when He was reviled, did not revile in return; when He suffered, He did not threaten, but committed Himself to Him who judges righteously.
Hebrews 5:8-9 - Though (Jesus) was a Son, yet He learned obedience by the things which He suffered. And having been perfected, He became the author of eternal salvation to all who obey Him.

## HYMN CHOICES

"Oh, for a Thousand Tongues to Sing" (TLH #360:1,4 & 6)

"Chief of Sinners Though I Be" (TLH #342:1-2, 5)
"Jesus, Refuge of the Weary" (TLH #145:1,3)

## 39

## STORY
The Crucifixion of Jesus- Matthew 27:32-44; Mark 15:21-32; Luke 23:26-43; John 19:17-27

## TEACHER PRAYER
Dear Lord Jesus, may the love that You demonstrated for me on the cross fill my heart with love and appreciation. Truly You have rescued my soul from hell through Your innocent sufferings and death. I desire now to show my love to You by teaching the blessed truths of Your crucifixion to my students. As Your Holy Spirit has already worked faith in my heart, so also I pray that He might now work through me to strengthen the faith of these little ones. Give success to my humble effort for Your name's sake. Amen.

## VOCABULARY
*Cyrene* – an important city in Libya, North Africa.
*Gall* – a poison which when used in small portions and diluted with wine or vinegar became a mind-numbing narcotic. Jewish women often gave this drug to the condemned.
*Cast lots* – an ancient form of gambling.

## OUTER AIM
The Crucifixion of Jesus, the Son of God.

## INNER AIM
Jesus allowed Himself to be crucified to pay for the sins of the world.

## BACKGROUND
*(Rupprecht Bible History References Vol. 2, pp. 395 - 403)*
It was about 9:00 a.m. when Jesus and the two criminals were nailed to their crosses. Crucifixion was most often reserved for the very worst criminals, and then only for slaves and non-Roman citizens. The hatred of the Jews is demonstrated in that they not only wanted Jesus executed, they delighted in His suffering and asked for crucifixion.
V. 32 (On the way to Calvary, Simon of Cyrene, the women who mourned)
- ▸ It was customary for the condemned criminal to carry his own cross to the place of crucifixion.
- ▸ Jesus, however, was exhausted. Not only was He sleep deprived and in anguish of soul, He had also been whipped by the Romans – a particularly brutal form of punishment.
- ▸ When Jesus collapsed under the load of the cross, the Romans conscripted Simon of Cyrene to carry the cross.
- ▸ Simon, a Jew from northern Africa, was just entering Jerusalem, probably on his way to celebrate the Feast of Unleavened Bread.
- ▸ Mark further explains that he is the father of Alexander and Rufus. Most believe that this is the same Rufus mentioned later by Paul in Romans 16:13 – one who had obviously been converted to Christianity.
- ▸ Jesus was followed by a great multitude, including women who mourned for Him.
- ▸ We can not be sure of the makeup of this group of women but we are told that the women took pity on Jesus being a condemned man.
- ▸ Thinking not of Himself but of these women, Jesus turned to them and warned them of the disaster about to befall Jerusalem.
- ▸ This prophesy was fulfilled forty years later (70 AD) when the Romans under Titus laid siege to Jerusalem and destroyed the temple.
- ▸ Indeed the eyewitness accounts from the historian Josephus tell us that the suffering in Jerusalem was

unparalleled.

- ▸ Cannibalism was rampant, proving Jesus' words that the women would wish they had never given birth.

V. 33-36 (The nailing to the cross, the wine and gall, the dividing of his garments)

- ▸ They crucified Jesus on the hill outside of Jerusalem called Golgotha, meaning "The Place of the Skull." The place today is also known in the Christian Church as Calvary, taken from the Latin Calvaria, meaning "the Skull."

- ▸ Heavy iron nails were used to fasten the condemned to the cross. These nails were most often driven through the wrists and heels. In Jesus' case we know that the nails did not break a bone (cf. John 19:33-36 and Psalm 34:20).

- ▸ This helps also to complete the picture of Jesus as our Passover Lamb. No bone of the Passover lambs in the Old Testament could be broken. (Ex. 12:46 & Num. 9:12)

- ▸ Nails could have been driven between the radius and ulna in the wrist or between the metacarpal palm bones of the hand without breaking a bone. Likewise a nail could be driven between the metatarsal foot bones or between the Achilles tendon and the tibia without breaking a bone.

- ▸ Several types of crosses were used by the Romans in crucifixion.

- ▸ Since Pilate attached a sign to the cross above Jesus' head, we can be fairly confident that the common Latin cross design was probably used.

- ▸ Jesus refused to drink the wine or vinegar mixed with gall since it was a mind-numbing narcotic. He wanted to drink the cup of suffering to the last drop, in full possession of all His faculties.

- ▸ It was the privilege of the Roman soldiers to divide the meager possessions of the one crucified. Gambling was a favorite pastime among them. This too was in fulfillment of a prophesy in Psalm 22:18.

V. 37 (The sign on the cross above Jesus)

- ▸ Pilate wrote the sign in three languages to ensure that everyone passing by could read what it said.

- ▸ This was meant as an insult to the Jews, whom Pilate blamed for the death of this innocent man.

- ▸ The Jews wanted the sign changed to "He said, 'I am the King of the Jews.'" In a rare show of resolve, Pilate refused to change what he had written.

V. 38-44 (Jesus' first words, "Father forgive them," the mocking and blasphemy)

- ▸ Only Luke records Jesus' first words from the cross, "Father, forgive them, for they do not know what they do."

- ▸ In the midst of such great agony Jesus' thoughts and prayers are for His tormenters.

- ▸ What perfect love! Jesus recognized what the soldiers and the Jews did not – the enormity of the sin of crucifying the very Son of God. In great love Jesus wanted even this great sin to be charged to His own account.

- ▸ The soldiers, the Jews watching, the people passing by, even the two criminals crucified with Him began to mock and blaspheme Jesus as He hung on the cross.

- ▸ The cruelty directed against the perfect, meek, loving Savior of all mankind is beyond our comprehension.

- ▸ Truly the evil hatred of man and devil was being meted out upon the sinless Son of God.

Luke 23:39-43 (Jesus' words to the repentant criminal)

- ▸ The words and actions of Jesus have the desired effect upon one of those crucified with him.

- ▸ In faith the man defends Jesus from the blasphemy of the other malefactor and asks Jesus to remember him.

- ▸ In telling the man that he would be with him "today in paradise" Jesus signifies the transition at death from time to eternity. Jesus said "today" because time stopped for the man at death. This was to be his last day, for he was about to enter eternity. It is difficult for our human minds to comprehend timelessness, and how there is no passage of time for those who through death are carried into eternity.

John 19:25-27 (Jesus' words to His mother Mary and John)

▸ Several believers were also present in the crowd near the cross, among them were Jesus' mother and the Apostle John.
▸ Even at this point in His suffering Jesus' thoughts center on the needs of others.
▸ In tender love He considers the sorrow of his dear mother.
▸ Mary loved Jesus as no other mother could love her child, for she loved Him both as her own son and as her Savior.
▸ Jesus offers to His mother the Apostle John as her son.
▸ To John (the disciple Jesus loved) Jesus offered Mary as his mother. Jesus knew that John would not be martyred but would live to be an old man.
▸ He was the perfect choice to care for Mary as she grew old.

## STUDENT PRAYER

Dear Jesus, when I hear again all of the misery You had to suffer because of what I have done wrong, it makes me feel very sorry and ashamed. Please forgive me for causing You such agony by my sins. Though You suffered greatly for me, now I also know that You rose again from the dead and now live glorified in heaven! Help me always to repent of my sins, and to look only to You for forgiveness and eternal life. How I look forward to seeing You as You are now in heaven! Please hold me in Your hand until that day. Amen.

## PRESENTATION

Present the story in all its various points using the harmony prepared for that purpose.

## APPLICATIONS

1. Whom would we probably be thinking about if we had to suffer like Jesus? (Ourselves.) Whom did Jesus think about? (Everyone else.)
2. The example of Jesus on the cross teaches us that even when we are punished unjustly we are still never to seek revenge. Think of all that was done to Jesus. What caused His suffering? (My sins.) Has anyone ever done anything to us as bad as what we caused Jesus to suffer? What then should we do to people who hurt us, no matter what they do? (Forgive them, as Jesus did.)
3. There is nothing to indicate that the repentant thief was baptized, yet Jesus said that he would go to heaven. What does this tell us about baptism?

## PASSAGES

These passages can be assigned as memory work or simply discussed in class as to how they fit the lesson.

Lower
Mark 16:16 - He who believes and is baptized will be saved; but he who does not believe will be condemned.
John 1:29- Behold! The Lamb of God who takes away the sin of the world!
Ephesians 1:7 - We have redemption through His blood, the forgiveness of sins.

Middle any of the above and...
1 John 2:2 - And He Himself is the propitiation for our sins, and not for ours only but also for the whole world.
Matthew 20:28 - The Son of Man did not come to be served, but to serve, and to give His life a ransom for many.

Upper any of the above and...

2 Corinthians 5:19 - God was in Christ reconciling the world to Himself, not imputing their trespasses to them, and has committed to us the word of reconciliation.

1 Peter 1:18-19 - ...Knowing that you were not redeemed with corruptible things, like silver or gold, ...but with the precious blood of Christ, as of a lamb without blemish and without spot.

## HYMN CHOICES

"When I Survey the Wondrous Cross" (TLH #175)
"On My Heart Imprint Thine Image" (TLH #179)
"Lord Jesus, We Give Thanks to Thee" (TLH #173)

## 40

## STORY
The Death and Burial of Jesus - (Matthew 13, Mark 14, Luke 23, John 19)

## TEACHER PRAYER
Lord Jesus, help me to bring into focus for these children the wonderful, self-sacrificing attitude You had even as You died on the cross, and please send Your Spirit to capture their hearts with Your love for them. Amen.

## OUTER AIM
Jesus suffered, died, and was buried.

## INNER AIM
God's plan for our redemption required that One Substitute must die for the sins of the world, and we are happy that Jesus died for us.

## BACKGROUND
*(Rupprecht Bible History References Vol.2, pp. 412-422)*
Just a quick review of a couple of minutes at Calvary as we hear Jesus say goodbye to his mother. His foster-father Joseph was no longer alive; Jesus' younger brothers and sisters (Mt.13:55) were not yet converted to His fellowship (Jn.7:5), so Jesus provided Mary with the support of a Christian son (John); His younger siblings became members of the Christian Church sometime later(Acts 1:14). John was happy to become her adopted son.

**Application:** This is a practical example of spiritual (church) fellowship applied in real life by Jesus Himself! St. Paul did not invent the doctrine of church fellowship, for Jesus already here was practicing it in a most personal way. We are closer to Jesus than His blood relatives were, as He Himself claims in Mt. 12:46-50. What an honor for us!!

**At the scene of Jesus on the cross,** from about noon until 3:00 pm, Jewish Standard time:
Luke 23:44-45 tells us that there was darkness at midday over all the earth, for the sun was darkened (obscured) as in a total solar eclipse, yet this was not the moon obscuring the sun, because Passover was always at full moon, when the moon and sun are on opposite sides of our planet. This miracle was recorded even by heathen writers, for it darkened the whole hemi-sphere of the planet facing the sun for three hours. Comment: Perhaps this miraculous darkness was a byproduct of the struggle of Jesus against the "Prince of darkness," who was doing his infernal worst to penetrate Jesus' self-sacrificing attitude of love for us. The light of heaven was denied Jesus, as it would be denied to us if He had not endured this brush with hell.

Mt.27:46
▸　"And about the ninth hour (with no sun shining, it would have been difficult to be very precise about "clock" time), Jesus cried out with a loud voice..."
▸　Even after three hours of losing blood and his cardio-vascular system going into shock, He summoned enough energy to call out with a LOUD voice "My God, My God, why have You forsaken Me?" In Hebrew/Aramaic *El* is the form of direct address for *God*, and the *i* suffix means *my,* as Jesus spoke the words of Ps. 22:1 when He felt the pain of being abandoned by His own Father in heaven.
▸　We will never plumb the depth of what Jesus felt, but we may ponder: "Why..."-- ( What have I done to deserve this treatment?) have You -- (You, the eternal Creator and Architect of the plan of salvation, the merciful God who does not desire the death of even the wicked) forsaken--(abandoned, cut off from all rescue or desire to salvage) Me?"-- (the one Person

who has done nothing to deserve being cast overboard like this, the only totally flawless, blameless human who has ever lived.)

Matt 27:47
▸ "Some of those who stood there, when they heard that, said: 'This man is calling for Elijah.'" These Scripturally illiterate bystanders did not recognize Ps.22:1 and perhaps mistook *Eli* as a shortened form of *Elijah*.

John 19:28
▸ "After this, Jesus knowing that all things were now accomplished, that the Scripture might be fulfilled, said: 'I thirst.'" Again Psalm 22 came to Jesus' mind as it befit His agony of thirst (due to the parching effect of raging fever and heavy panting in pain).
▸ We most note that "knowing that all things were now accomplished" carries a depth of meaning: by the Spirit John reports that Jesus had arrived at the conviction that His sufferings had accomplished their purpose, for He had gone through the torments of hell, and nothing was left undone that He had been commissioned to do as the Lamb of God for sinners slain. The life He had lived in perfect loving obedience and self-sacrifice could now come to a successful close.

John 19:30 and Luke 23:46 tell us that when He had received the sour wine, He cried with a loud voice, "It is finished!" and "Father, into Thy hands I commend My spirit" (cf. Ps.31:5); He then breathed His last and gave up His spirit. These are the sixth and seventh "words" from the cross, and both of them came during His last conscious moments.

"It is finished" means more than "I am a goner," for it is a loud echo of "all things are now accomplished.." In spiritual content, everything that had ever gone wrong and needed righting in the court of divine justice had been taken care of and properly completed; the obstacle of sin, sins, and sinfulness was successfully removed to the last iota in that moment of His death. The head of Satan had been crushed, and Paradise opened for all mortals. The loudness of His vigorous announcement should ring from every Christian pulpit and echo in every sinner's heart, as Paul expresses: "But thanks be to God, Who gives us the victory through our Lord Jesus Christ!" (I Cor.15:57).

When His spirit (soul, "ghost") left His earthly body, the God-man really died. He entrusted His eternal future into the loving care of His Father, and OUR Father. Hallelujah!

Mt. 27:51
▸ "And behold, (the Spirit expressly points these out as deserving our attention, due to their import) "the veil of the temple was torn in two from top to bottom."
▸ This three-inch thick, 60' tall by 30' wide room divider between the Sanctuary and the Most Private Sanctuary normally protected the privacy of God's Ark of the Covenant from any intrusion, symbolizing God's unapproachable presence. The only exception was that once a year on the Day of Atonement *(Yom Kippur)* the High Priest was authorized to come in with sacrificial blood to sprinkle on the "Mercy Seat" (place of mercy) for atonement of sins.
▸ Since Jesus "by His own blood entered in once [and that was enough!] into the Holy Place, having obtained eternal redemption for us" (Heb. 9:12), the obstructive curtain had no further function; the Old had been superseded by the New!
▸ --"and the earth quaked and the rocks were split" in testimony that a corner of history had been turned; a new Era had been opened by God's almighty hand.
▸ "...and the graves were opened and many bodies of the saints who had fallen asleep were raised, and coming out of the graves after His resurrection, they went into the holy city and appeared to

many."

▸ First of all, we remember that these were not underground graves, but grottos in hillsides; in these little caverns our brothers and sisters came alive, and on Easter morning they got out to return to their old neighborhoods and their families to prove that the Resurrection was no theory!

▸ Thus God added a few more instruments of orchestral accompaniment to the grand symphony of victory over death and the grave--in resurrecting some Christian folks who knew from personal experience that Jesus was indeed Savior and LORD.

Mt. 27:54

▸ The earthquake and its impact on the cemetery scared these tough soldiers, for they made the correct connection between Jesus and God, recognizing that His death had disturbed the universe. Luke comments that the centurion "glorified God" by his recognition that Jesus was a righteous man.

▸ Perhaps we shall see this man in heaven, a firstfruit of Jesus' promise: "If I be lifted up from the earth [upon the cross], I will draw all persons unto Me" (Jn.12:32).

Luke 23:48

▸ "And the whole crowd who came together to that sight, seeing what had been done, beat their breasts and returned."

▸ Perhaps they felt as did the Publican of Luke 18, sorry for their cruelty and repentant of their guilt in participating in Jesus' crucifixion.

v.49:

▸ "But all His acquaintances, and the women (among whom were Mary Magdalene, Mary mother of James and Joses, and the mother of Zebedees' sons--Mt.27:56) who followed Him from Galilee, stood at a distance, watching these things."

**The *coup de grace*: John 19: 31-37**

Saturday, the Sabbath, was only a couple of hours away, since it started at sundown. Mosaic Law required that a corpse not be left exposed overnight (Deut. 21:22-23), so the Jewish officials wanted to move quickly. First, they would brutalize the three men crucified so as to snuff out any flicker of aliveness from their bodies. Breaking their thigh bones with a sledge-hammer would do it, and so this was done with the two criminals.

"But when they came to Jesus and saw that He was already dead, they did not break His legs." They could see that Jesus had stopped breathing, and other clinical clues [not to be discussed with children] told them that He was past further torture.

"But one of the soldiers pierced His side with a spear, and immediately blood and water came out." This was a fail-safe and less strenuous way to be sure He was dead; one sharp jab up under the ribcage would puncture liver or heart or aorta; the blood did not spurt as from a beating heart, but as from a pool in one of the ventricles. It is more difficult to figure whether this and the water (clear fluid?) was a miracle or not; the prophecies that were fulfilled as to His bones not being broken (Ex.12:46 as the Antitype of the Passover Lamb) and His side being pierced (Zech. 12:10) are called to our attention, but we have no prophetic notation about the blood or water. Jesus still retains the five deep wound-marks on His glorified body and will retain them through Judgment Day as testimony to both believer and unbeliever (Rev.1:7) of His self sacrifice for sinners.

Matt. 27:56-61 Jesus' corpse awaited claiming by family or friends. The three hours between His death and sundown was a busy time. Joseph went to Pilate with his request to be allowed to claim the body;

Pilate sent for the centurion in charge to see if Jesus had already died; he reported the fact that Jesus was dead; Pilate authorized Joseph's claim to the body, and Joseph (with help from others--though none of the eleven, probably) proceeded with such meager funeral preparations as he could for a hasty entombment so that he and the others could get home yet before sundown.

We are told that Nicodemus (John 19:39-40) was another attendant in this last-hour rush to place Jesus' body to rest. This is the same Nicodemus who had gotten acquainted with Jesus early on (John 3) and was also a member of the Council, who nevertheless had defended Jesus at a Council meeting some six months earlier (Jn.7:50-53) who now came to His side with a large amount (70 to 100 pounds) of pickling spices to pack around the corpse to delay decay; this was the normal Jewish practice for embalming a corpse. Close by was the "garden" with Joseph's cemetery plot, so they could manage to do all this and still get home by sunset if they hurried; whatever else needed doing to complete the burial would have to wait for later, because the Law forbade physical activities on Saturday, the Sabbath.

[ Of course, by time they got back to the grave site very early on Sunday morning, it was absolutely too late for a funeral, because Jesus was up before anybody else, wide awake in His glorified body which had been miraculously kept from cellular decay (Ps.16:10)!! ]

Joseph of Arimathea deserves some attention because he was also a member of the Supreme Council (Sanhedrin), was a righteous--rather than a hypocritical--Pharisee, had voted against the Council's condemnation of Jesus (Mk.14:64), and had become convinced that the Messiah he had long expected had now arrived in the person of Jesus. In devoted love he quickly wrapped Jesus' body in a clean linen shroud, with helpers carried it to the tomb recently carved out of the rocky hillside for his own use, hurriedly laid the body there, intending to return on Sunday morning to continue the burial (Luke 23:55-56); he (and helpers ?) closed the opening with a large slab of rock that could be rolled into its groove to keep varmints out of the gravesite, and they went home, feeling pretty sad about everything.

## STUDENT PRAYER
I am ready and willing to search the scriptures today for the truth about my Savior, and to reflect on who I am in His sight. I want to know Jesus first, myself second, and then everyone else as people You have loved so unselfishly. Amen.

## PRESENTATION
Present the lesson by telling the account as a harmony of the four gospels.

## APPLICATIONS
1.  Regarding Christian funeral, burial, interment: as our Savior brought life and immortality to light, , our death and burial are actually but a process by which we will receive our share in His life and immortality. Our bodies will sleep in the graves until Christ awakens them on Resurrection Morning; until then our souls will be in His keeping pending reuniting with our glorified bodies at the Judgment. Because we don't understand eternity, we don't know how to describe the condition of souls between death and Judgment Day.
2.  Further, Jesus' life, death, and resurrection are the three great pillars of Biblical truth and thus of Christian theology. His life, in obedience to the will of God filled up the defects of our sins; His death was a final requirement as payment for the debt of sins; His resurrection provides public notice that the whole program of salvation was successful. The apostle Paul in particular was sponsored by Jesus to spell it out (justification, redemption, atonement, reconciliation) from

a variety of angles and aspects, as we read in the epistles to the Roman and Galatian congregations.

## PASSAGES

These passages can be assigned as memory work or simply discussed in class as to how they fit the lesson.

<u>Lower</u>
Phil. 2:8 - He humbled Himself and became obedient to the point of death, even the death of the cross.
Heb. 2:9 - ...that Jesus...by the grace of God...might taste death for everyone.

<u>Middle</u> any of the above and...
Jn.10:17 - Therefore my Father loves Me, because I lay down my life that I may take it again.
II Tim. 1:10 - Our Savior Jesus Christ has abolished death and brought life and immortality to light.
Jn.12:32 - And I, if I am lifted up from the earth, will draw all peoples to myself.

<u>Upper</u> any of the above and...
Rom.6:23 - For the wages of sin is death, but the gift of God is eternal life in Christ Jesus our Lord. Heb. 9:12 - With His own blood He entered the Most Holy Place once for all, having obtained eternal redemption.
I Cor.15:56-57 - The sting of death is sin, and the strength of sin is the law.  But thanks be to God, who gives us the victory through our Lord Jesus Christ.

## HYMN CHOICES
Come to Calvary's Holy Mountain, Sinners Ruined by the Fall (TLH #149)
Alas! And Did My Savior Bleed and Did My Savior Die (TLH #154)
Lord Jesus, We Give Thanks to Thee (TLH #173)
On My Heart Imprint Thine Image (TLH #179)
Lamb of God, We Fall Before Thee (TLH #358)

## STORY

The First Appearance of Our Living Lord after His Death  -  Matthew 28:1-15, Mark 16:1-11, Luke 24:1-12, John 20:1-18

## TEACHER PRAYER

Dear Father in Heaven, bless my study of Your Word with the gift of Your Holy Spirit. Please guide and direct me to present the saving truths of this story in a direct and faithful manner to my students. I thank You for the assurance that Your word will never return to You void, but always accomplish Your good will. In Jesus' name. Amen.

## VOCABULARY

MATTHEW:

*Sabbath* - With reference to the seventh day when God rested (ceased) from His creating work. The people of God were to observe the Sabbath Day (Saturday) as a day of rest, ceasing from their labors. The Third Commandment calls for the observance of that day. The Old Testament Sabbath was a shadow of things to come, but the body (making the shadow) is Christ's: Colossians 2:17. He is our Sabbath, for He brings us rest for our souls Matthew 11:28.29.

*Countenance* - Appearance, the "look" on a person's face.

*Brethren* - The brother-in-faith, spiritual family brothers.

*Elders* - Generally, an older person. Here, used with reference to the Jewish Old Testament officers known as the "Elders." For example," rulers" of the synagogue and the "elders" of the people  were one and the same.

*Appease* - To pacify, to quiet, to satisfy.

*Make you secure* - Keep you out of trouble, see to it that you will not be court-marshaled.

MARK

*Anoint* - To apply oil upon someone in a ceremonial manner, to dedicate someone to a special calling. Here, perfumed (spiced) oils were applied to the dead body to cover the odors of death and decay.

*Demons* - Used with reference to the fallen angels (Matt. 25:41; Rev. 12:7—9), ministers of the devil. Satan is called the prince of the demons (devils).

LUKE

*Perplexed* -  Puzzled, full of doubts, confused.

*Idle tales* - Nonsense, gossip

## OUTER AIM

To teach us to believe that Jesus, who died on Friday, appeared alive on Sunday as He had promised.

## INNER AIM

To recognize God's hand in our lives: Jesus, who died to save us, arose from death as our living Savior.

## BACKGROUND

*(Rupprecht Bible History References Vol. 2, pp. 422-434)*

We have heard how God sent His only Son, Jesus, to pay for our sins by His suffering and death. On the cross Jesus said, "It is finished!" The payment for our sin was completed by His death. But Jesus not only died for sin, but He was victorious over death. Today we learn about this victory as He showed Himself alive to some disciples on Easter morning.

The ransom for our souls was paid by Jesus through His suffering and death. As He promised, on the third day He arose from death. He was victorious over sin and death. Jesus lives, the victory's won! And because He lives, we also have life; life now, and life forever with Him in His heavenly Home.

- The Sabbath (no-work day) was over.
- At the "first light" of Sunday morning the women, who followed and ministered to Jesus with their material things, went to the tomb with "sweet spices" to embalm Jesus' body for burial.
- Mary of Magdala (Mary Magdalene) may have gone to the tomb before sunrise, for she found the tomb empty and hastened with her cry of sorrow to Peter and John, assuming that the body of Jesus had been stolen.
- During her absence from the tomb, the other women arrived and even entered into it.
- There they saw the two angels (Matthew and Mark refer to only one angel, the one who was the spokesman).
- The angel's message was: "He is not here, for He is risen.. .go quickly and tell His disciples that He is risen from the dead.. .He is going before you into Galilee; there you will see Him!"
- Meanwhile Peter and John were hurrying to the tomb, followed by Mary.
- John arrived first and paused for a time outside the tomb, but when Peter arrived he went directly into it.
- John joined him to observe that the body of Jesus had not been stolen, for the tomb did not appear to have been burglarized.
- They silently pondered the discovery as they returned again to the city.
- Mary arrived at the tomb after Peter and John had left.
- She lingered there, weeping over what she believed to be her losses: first, the living Jesus; now, even His dead body.
- Once more, two angels appeared and addressed Mary: "Woman, why are you weeping?"
- Mary replied: "Because they have taken away my Lord, and I do not know where they have laid Him."
- She turned away as if to find the body of Jesus in another place and, suddenly, Jesus stood before her in His living presence.
- Tearful and sorely grieved, Mary did not recognize Jesus.
- She thought it was the gardener, so she begged information concerning the whereabouts of Jesus' body so she could take Him away.
- She again turned toward the tomb and now Jesus spoke to her: "Mary!"
- She immediately recognized His voice and with great relief uttered the comforting word: "My Lord!" (Rabboni, Aramaic; Rabbi, Hebrew.)
- We recall that Jesus had taught: "My sheep hear My voice...and they know me."
- Mary was the first to whom the risen and living Jesus revealed Himself.
- After that He met the other women who were returning to Jerusalem pondering the wondrous message of the angels.
- Jesus instructed them:: "Rejoice! Do not be afraid. Go and tell my brethren to go to Galilee, and there they will see Me."
- We are told that while Mary's report caused Peter and John to run to the tomb, the other disciples considered the report from the other women to be astonishing, but utter nonsense.
- They did not even go to the tomb out of curiosity.
- The disciples isolated themselves in their room to agonize in their grief over the loss of their Master, Jesus.
- They forgot that He had told them that He would rise again on the third day and go before them into Galilee.

## STUDENT PRAYER

Lower Level: Dear Jesus, You died for me that I may live. You live to lead me Home.
Teach me to follow You. Amen.

Upper Level: Lord, give me ears to hear Your word and a heart that believes Your word.
You died to save me, You live to lead me. Teach me to follow You. Amen.

## PRESENTATION

Tell the story with the same emotion and excitement as if you were there. Tell the story in your words, but be faithful to the account that God recorded through the four evangelists.

## APPLICATIONS

1.  The ransom for our souls was paid by Jesus through His suffering and death. As He promised, on the third day He arose from death. He was victorious over sin and death. Jesus lives, the victory's won! And because He lives, we also have life; life now, and life forever with Him in His heavenly Home.
2.  That is why we confess in the Apostles Creed: "I believe in the resurrection of the BODY". Our souls do not die and are not buried. When God takes us to Himself, He leaves our corrupted bodies on earth to return to dust. But on the last day our glorified bodies will be raised unto life with Him. This is our joy, our comfort, and our hope.

## PASSAGES

These passages can be assigned as memory work or simply discussed in class as to how they fit the lesson.

Lower
John 14:19 - Jesus said: "Because I live, you will live also!"
Hymn 200, Stanza 1: I know that my Redeemer lives; What comfort that sweet sentence gives! He lives, He lives, who once was dead; He lives, my everliving Head.

Middle any of the above and...
John 11:26 - Whoever lives and believes in Me shall never die.
Hymn 211, stanza 4: The power of death He broke in twain When He to life arose again. Hallelujah! To Him all praise be given!

Upper any of the above and...
John 11:25.26 - I am the resurrection and the life. He who believes in Me, though he may die, he shall live. And whoever lives and believes in Me shall never die.
Hymn 206, stanza 2: Jesus, my Redeemer lives; I too unto life shall waken. Endless joy my Savior gives; Shall my courage then be shaken? Shall I fear, or could the Head Rise and leave His members dead?

## 42

## STORY
Emmaus Disciples - Mark 16:12, 13; Luke 24:13-35

## TEACHER PRAYER
Lord, Abide with us as You stayed and taught the Emmaus disciples. Help us to use Your Word to teach those You have given unto us to teach in our Sunday School class. Let us never forget Your sacrifice for our sins, nor Your return on the third day as our victorious, living Redeemer. Bless our preparations and the teaching of Your Easter history that we may give a message to share with those who do not yet know You as their living Savior. Amen.

## VOCABULARY
*Restrained* - The Emmaus disciples were prevented from recognizing Jesus. Jesus wished to open their spiritual eyes by teaching from His Word.
*Constrained* - The disciples invited, begged, urged Jesus to stay.

## OUTER AIM
Jesus gladdened the hearts of two disciples by telling them about their risen Savior.

## INNER AIM
God's Word makes us certain that Jesus is our risen Savior.

## BACKGROUND
*(Rupprecht Bible History References Vol. 2, pp. 435-441)*
We have heard how Jesus appeared to Mary and the other women early on Easter morning. Today we hear that Jesus appeared to two other disciples going it Emmaus.. They were sad as they talked of the events that had happened in Jerusalem. Jesus will gladden their hearts by His message from God's Word and by His showing Himself alive to them.

▸ The two disciples were Cleopas and an unnamed disciple, who were not members of the twelve.
▸ It was now early afternoon on that first Easter Sunday.
▸ The town of Emmaus was six or seven miles from Jerusalem.
▸ We can see and hear the despair of the two disciples. They are confused because their faith is floundering. The words of the women and the news of Peter and John's visit to the empty tomb seemed to these two men like nonsense. (V. 11)
▸ Jesus, as only He can do, opened the Scriptures to these men. Beginning from the books of Moses and continuing through the prophets Jesus taught them about the Savior.
▸ At the meal the Lord acted as host, not guest, and when their eyes of faith were opened the Lord also opened their physical eyes to see their Savior.
▸ With ecstatic joy they ran back to Jerusalem to tell the other disciples the great news. There they heard the good news that Jesus had also appeared to Peter sometime that day.
▸ The Lord is risen!

## STUDENT PRAYER
Lower: Dear Father in Heaven,
Abide with us as You stayed with the Emmaus disciples. Help us listen to, learn and live Your Word. Help me also to tell others about the Savior who died and rose again to pay for the sins of the world. Please keep our faith strong. In Jesus' name we ask. Amen.

Upper: Lord Jesus, I thank You that You died for my sins and rose again with the victory over death. In You I have life! Thank You for giving me parents, pastors and teachers to teach me Your Word. Make me a faithful witness of this Good News to all people. Amen.

## PRESENTATION

Tell the story with the same emotion and excitement as if you were there. Tell the story in your words, but be faithful to the account that God wrote through Luke and referred to in Mark.

## APPLICATIONS

1.  How hopeless, helpless, joyless we would be if Jesus had not risen from the dead! (1 Corinthians 15:17) However, we can be assured by God's Word that our faith is not in vain. Christ is alive! All we need to do is turn to the Word of God for proof. God's Word makes us certain that Jesus is our risen Savior. (John 5:39; Romans 10:17)

2.  When our parents, teachers, and pastors teach us the Word of God it is like Jesus speaking to us Himself, just like He did to the disciples in our lesson. That is why we should hear His Word in church, in school, and at home. We need to know that Jesus is our Savior. He suffered, died, and rose again to pay for all of our sins and to conquer death and hell.

3.  The Old Testament is filled with Prophecies concerning the Messiah. They are all fulfilled in Jesus. May we learn them for our strengthening and comfort.

4.  This lesson shows us the ecstatic joy of the disciples. We too can have this same joy as we learn of our Savior.

## PASSAGES

These passages can be assigned as memory work or simply discussed in class as to how they fit the lesson.

Lower
Romans 10:17 - "So then faith comes by hearing, and hearing by the word of God."
John 5:39 - "You search the Scriptures, for in them you think you have eternal life; and these are they which testify of Me." (You may want to take only the first part for a memory verse.)
TLH Hymn #53, stanzas 1 & 4

Middle any of the above and...
Matthew 16:16 - "You are the Christ, the Son of the living God."
TLH Hymn# 552, stanzas 1, 3, 8

Upper any of the above and...
1 Corinthians 12:3 - "No one can say that Jesus is Lord except by the Holy Spirit."
TLH Hymn# 552, stanzas 1, 3, 6, 8

## 43

## STORY
The Appearance to Disciples in Galilee- John 21:1-17

## TEACHER PRAYER
Dear Savior, You appeared to Your disciples and Peter in Galilee to comfort them and to strengthen their faith. You also called Peter, who denied You three times, to become a shepherd of souls. You have also called me to help in teaching the children in our Sunday School. Send Your Holy Spirit that I may be a faithful teacher of Your children in my preparations, in my teaching, and in my daily life. Amen.

## VOCABULARY
*Sea of Tiberias* - Another name for the Sea of Galilee. At Jesus' time Tiberias was the name of one of the nine smaller communities around the Sea of Galilee. One historian, Josephus, states that it was built by Herod Antipas and was named by him in honor of the emperor Tiberias. Many of the inhabitants of Tiberias were Greeks and Romans, so foreign customs prevailed there. "Sea of Tiberias" was used by John only (21:1).

*200 cubits* - A cubit is an ancient measure of length, about 18-20 inches; originally the length of the arm from the end of the middle finger to the elbow. 200 cubits is about 100 yards.

*Gird yourself* - The term, "gird up" and "gird up your loins" called for one to use a belt or sash to gather up the length or fulness of a garment to be ready for any service or activity that might be required.

*Simon, son of Jonas* - By these words Jesus addressed Peter. "Peter" was the name of honor (Rock) that Jesus gave to Simon. Jesus used his original name in order to remind Peter that he had, by denying Jesus three times, reverted to his natural state and disposition.

*The disciple whom Jesus loved* - John never refers to himself by name in his writings. He usually referred to himself as "that other disciple" or "the disciple that Jesus loved." By that term John did not suggest that he was Jesus' favorite disciple, or that Jesus loved him more than others. John believed on Jesus as the Savior of all people, even John! It is a humble confession of his faith when he includes himself in Jesus' love.

## OUTER AIM
The resurrected Savior appeared to His disciples at Galilee as He promised. There, He reminds them of His loving care and forgiveness in directing His called shepherds to "Feed My lambs and feed My sheep."

## INNER AIM
To recognize God's Hand in our lives: the forgiving love and the life-giving care of Jesus for His disciples and all people.

## BACKGROUND
*(Rupprecht Bible History References Vol. 2, pp. 447-452)*
Jesus appears to His disciples in Galilee as He had promised. There He comforted Peter and called him to be a shepherd of His sheep. Before He had been crucified Jesus had promised His disciples that He would

rise again the third day and go before them into Galilee. On Easter Sunday Jesus showed himself alive to the women and the disciples. He continued to appear to them in order to reinforce their faith. In our lesson today, we join the disciples as they go fishing while they wait for Jesus to appear in Galilee. When Jesus appeared to His disciples in Galilee, He reminded them of His great love and power. He assured Peter of forgiveness for his denials, and called him to be a shepherd (pastor) of His lambs and sheep.

▸ When Jesus was tried before the High Priest, Peter in the courtyard denied even knowing the Lord. Peter was sorry for this sin and wept bitter tears of repentance.

▸ Our Bible account for today shows Jesus' great love for Peter by letting him know his sin was forgiven and that he was being called to serve Jesus as a shepherd of His sheep.

▸ Jesus had told the disciples that after His death He would go before them into Galilee.

▸ After Jesus appeared to them in Jerusalem, they waited for His appearance in Galilee.

▸ Peter decided to use the time by continuing to work at his old profession of fishing, and the disciples went with him. They could not locate fish to net.

▸ As they were rowing to shore, suddenly Jesus appeared on shore, but they did not recognize Him.

▸ He called out, "Children, have you any food? They replied: "No!" He directed them to cast their net out of the right side of the boat. They did this and, as the net became very heavy with the weight of fish, they knew that the One on shore was Jesus.

▸ Knowing this, Peter plunged into the sea and hurried to shore.

▸ The disciples brought the boat to shore with a net full of 153 fish, yet the net never split open.

▸ Jesus invited them to a breakfast that was already prepared for them.

▸ After they had eaten, Jesus spoke privately to Peter, calling him Simon (not Peter, the "Rock"). Jesus said, "Simon, do you love me more than these?" Peter is asked to rank his love in a scale of comparison to others.

▸ He replied, "Yes, Lord, You know I love You."

▸ Jesus said to him, "Feed My lambs."

▸ Jesus asked him again, "Do you love me?" No comparison is asked for here; no ranking of its value. It is just a question for what love he had in the most essential, simple way.

▸ When he replied: "Yes, Lord, You know that I love You", Jesus said, "Tend My sheep."

▸ When Jesus asked him a third time, "Do you love (even like) Me?" The verb changes - as Jesus asked for the presence of even an affection between companions. That's what really stung!

▸ Peter replied, "Lord, You know all things; You know that I love You."

▸ Jesus said, "Feed My sheep." Jesus gives Him the assurance that even that last "like" sort of love is still of use for the service of feeding His flock the precious Word of Truth.


## STUDENT PRAYER

Lower: Jesus, we thank you for forgiving us our sins, and making us lambs in Your flock. Lead us safely Home. Amen.

Upper: Lord Jesus, we too have often sinned by denying You. Thank you for forgiving us and for being our Good Shepherd. Lead us safely Home to You. Amen.

## PRESENTATION

Tell the story with the same emotion and excitement as if you were there. Tell the story in your words, but be faithful to the account that God wrote through the evangelist John.

## APPLICATIONS

As God brings us to faith in our Savior, we become the lambs and the sheep of His flock. He leads us with the assurance of the forgiveness of our sins and a love for our souls. He therefore continues to call shepherds (pastors and teachers) to help care for His flock, that they may follow Him all the way Home.

## PASSAGES

These passages can be assigned as memory work or simply discussed in class as to how they fit the lesson.

<u>Lower</u>
Psalm 23:la and 6b - The Lord is my shepherd... I will dwell in the house of the Lord forever.

Hymn 428, stanza 4: I am trusting Thee to guide me; Thou alone shalt lead; Ev'ry day and hour supplying All my need.

<u>Middle</u> any of the above and...
Psalm 23:1-3 - The Lord is my shepherd; I shall not want. He makes me to lie down in green pastures; He leads me beside the still waters. He restores my soul; He leads me in the paths of righteousness For His name's sake.

Hymn 428, stanzas 1-3: I am trusting Thee, Lord Jesus, Trusting only Thee; Trusting
Thee for full salvation, Great and free.
I am trusting Thee for pardon; At Thy feet I bow, For Thy grace
and tender mercy Trusting now.
I am trusting Thee for cleansing In the crimson flood; Trusting Thee to make me holy By Thy blood.

<u>Upper</u> any of the above and...
Psalm 23 - The Lord is my shepherd; I shall not want. He makes me to lie down in green pastures; He leads me beside the still waters. He restores my soul; He leads me in the paths of righteousness for His name's sake. Yea, though I walk through the valley of the shadow of death, I will fear no evil; For You are with me; Your rod and Your staff, they comfort me. You prepare a table before me in the presence of my enemies; You anoint my head with oil; My cup runs over. Surely goodness and mercy shall follow me all the days of my life; and I will dwell in the house of the Lord forever.

Hymn 428, stanzas 4-6: I am trusting Thee to guide me; Thou alone shalt lead, Ev'ry day and hour supplying All my need.
I am trusting Thee for power; Thine can never fail. Words which Thou Thyself shalt give me Must prevail.
I am trusting Thee, Lord Jesus; Never let me fall. I am trusting Thee forever And for all.

## STORY

The Ascension of Jesus - Matthew 28:16-20; Mark 16:19.20; Luke 24:44-53; Acts 1:1-12

## TEACHER PRAYER

Dear Savior, You have called your believing children to be witnesses of the Gospel. You have assured them that as they witness Your words, the Holy Spirit will cause them to be effective and never return to You void. Lord, give us this faith that we may be faithful witnesses to the students in our Sunday School. Let us witness with boldness and joy, for You ascended into glory, and will come again to receive us unto Yourself that, where You are, we will also be eternally. Amen.

## VOCABULARY

*Endued* - Provided with, gifted with, endowed with.

*Confirming* - Establish the truth of that which was doubtful or uncertain, verify, support, strengthen, prove valid.

*Opened their understanding* - Human understanding (reason) is corrupted by sin and does not receive the truths from God, but rejects them. For example, God creating all things in six days. The Holy Spirit, working in the Word from God, causes our ears to hear, our eyes to see, our hearts and minds to understand by faith the things of God. The Spirit "opened their understanding."

*Comprehend* - To grasp mentally, to understand, to catch on. When effected by the Word of God, we recognize this happens by faith, the work of the Holy Spirit.

*Promise of My Father* - With reference to the promise to send the Holy Spirit who will cause unbelieving hearts to believe the truth from God. Isaiah 44: "I will pour My Spirit on your descendants.. .one will say, 'I am the Lord's; another will write with his hand, 'The Lord's." Ezekiel 36: "...I will give you a new heart and put a new spirit within you... I will put my Spirit within you and cause you to walk in my statutes. . ." Acts 2: (Quoting the Prophet Joel) "I will pour out my Spirit on all flesh... I will pour out my Spirit in those days..."

*Tarry* - To linger, wait for, to stay longer than originally intended.

*Infallible* - incapable of error, never wrong, thus dependable, reliable, sure.

## OUTER AIM

To record for our learning the Homecoming of Jesus in Glory after He had completed His saving work. To remind us that He commissioned all believers to be His faithful witnesses who, by the gift of the Holy Spirit, would share His saving Word with all people.

## INNER AIM

That we who have been brought to Jesus may boldly and with great joy share the Good News with all people. God loved the world; Christ died and rose again for the world; by the witness of His Word, the world is to be called unto faith and be saved.

## BACKGROUND

*(Rupprecht Bible History References Vol.2, pp.453-460)*

For background to the Ascension account: Matthew 28:16-20; Mark 16:15-18; I Corinthians 15:6-7. In these lessons we hear Jesus commission (call) His disciples to make disciples of all nations by baptizing them and teaching them all things that He had commanded them. Jesus said: "He who believes and is baptized will be saved; but he who does not believe will be condemned". In the letter to the Corinthians Paul reviews the number of witnesses to Jesus' resurrection: Peter, the twelve disciples, 500 Christians at one time, James, and then all the apostles.

The Ascension account: Mark 16:19.20; Luke 24:44-53; Acts 1:1-12. Jesus concluded His post-Easter work on earth (40 days) by leading His disciples to the Mount of Olives. There He underscored their call as His witnesses of the Good News to all nations. He assured them of His blessing, the gift of the Holy Spirit to make their witnessing effective, and then ascended into the glory of heaven.

Jesus continued to reinforce the faith of His disciples with many appearances and with teachings of Holy Scripture concerning His work as the Messiah, the Savior. As He prepared to return to His heavenly home, He commissions His disciples to be His witnesses to all people. Their works would be supported by the gift of the Holy Spirit. Then He ascended to His Father.

Jesus prepared His disciples to be His witnesses, pastors, teachers, and missionaries. He promised them divine help with the presence of the Holy Spirit. Since God loved the world, and Jesus died and arose for the world, the world must also have the work of the Spirit of God in order to believe such Good News. By making all believers His witnesses, His word and Spirit does go forth into all the world, to call sinners to believe and be saved.

▸ Jesus had completed His Savior work by His death and resurrection.
▸ The sins of the world had been paid for in full and the Father transferred the perfect righteousness of His Son to every cleansed sinner.
▸ Those who were born in sin and lived their life in sin were now declared by God to be "not guilty".
▸ As righteous children adopted by the heavenly Father, we brothers and sisters of Christ, are to be His witnesses on earth until it is the time of our Homecoming.
▸ Mark records Jesus' ascension and tells us that the disciples (believers) "went out and preached everywhere, the Lord working with them and confirming the word..."
▸ Luke records that just before the ascension of Jesus, He reminded His disciples of the things that had been written about Him in the Law of Moses and the Prophets and the Psalms.
▸ He further instructed them, "Thus it is written, and thus it was necessary for the Christ to suffer and to rise from the dead the third day, and that remission of sins should be preached in His name to all nations..."
▸ Jesus concluded with the words, "You are witnesses of these things. Behold, I send the Promise of My Father upon you..."
▸ Luke then tells how Jesus led His disciples toward Bethany.
▸ There He blessed them, was parted from them and carried up into heaven.
▸ The disciples returned to Jerusalem with great joy, and were continually in the temple praising and blessing God as they awaited the outpouring of the Holy Spirit.
▸ In the Book of Acts, Luke refers to the promise of the Holy Spirit: "You shall be baptized with the Holy Spirit not many days from now... You shall receive power when the Holy Spirit has come upon you; and you shall be witnesses of Me."
▸ Luke tells us a bit more about the ascension of Jesus: "While they looked steadfastly toward heaven as He went up, two men stood by them in white apparel, who also said, 'Men of Galilee, why do you stand gazing up into heaven? This same Jesus, who was taken up from you into heaven, will so come in like manner as you saw Him go into heaven.'"

### STUDENT PRAYER
Lower: Dear Jesus, You went back to Your home in heaven. You told Your children on earth to tell about You. Help us to be faithful in telling others that You are their Savior. Amen

Upper: Dear Jesus, You ascended to your home in glory. You called the believers on earth to be Your witnesses. You promised to bless their witness with Your Holy Spirit. Make us faithful witnesses and bless us in like manner. Amen

## PRESENTATION
Tell the story with the same emotion and excitement as if you were there. Tell the story in your words, but be faithful to the account that God wrote through His evangelists Mark and Luke.

## APPLICATIONS
You and I have been called to Jesus by the Holy Spirit. As believers in Jesus we are His disciples. All His disciples have been called to be His witnesses: in our family, neighborhood, school, place of work, recreation. And how about YOU becoming a pastor, teacher, or missionary witness? Why hesitate to become such a witness  -  He promises to bless those who are doing His work, giving them the ability, strength, guidance, and correction as needed. His Holy Spirit, abiding in the word we witness, assures success for those souls who need their share in Jesus success!

## ANSWERS TO EXERCISES
Recalling Details
1. Where did Jesus meet with His disciples? Near Bethany on Mt. Olivet
2. What authority did Jesus claim to be his? All authority in heaven and on earth
3. How did the disciples understand the Scriptures about Jesus? And (Jesus) opened their understanding (of the Scriptures)
4. Why did Jesus have to suffer and die? That repentance and remission of sins should be preached
5. Where and why were the disciples supposed to wait? In Jerusalem, for the gift of the Holy Spirit
6. What instructions did Jesus have for His disciples? Be witnesses, make disciples of all nations, baptize, teach, preach the Gospel
7. How did Jesus visibly leave this earth? He rose into the clouds
8. Who appeared after Jesus' ascension? Two angels
9. What message did they have for the disciples? Jesus will return.
10. Why is this message also a comfort for us? Jesus will take us to Himself in heaven some day
11. What does Jesus want us to do while here on earth? Preach the Gospel to all creatures
12. How do we know that Jesus is still here, though we can't see Him? And lo, I (Jesus) am with you always, even to the end of the age

**Review - Match the statement with the passage reference that best fits.**

1. __C___ Jesus had to suffer and die.
2. __A___ Jesus reclaimed His rightful authority.
3. __B___ Jesus is sitting at the right hand of God the Father.
4. __E__ The disciples were given clear instructions by Jesus.
5. __D__ The disciples appreciated the blessings they had received.
6. __F___ The disciples could be comforted that Jesus had left them only visibly.

**A. Matt.28:18**         **B. Mark 16:19**         **C. John 24:46**

**D. John 24:52-53**      **E. Matt. 28:19**         **F. Matt. 28:20**

## PASSAGES

**These passages can be assigned as memory work or simply discussed in class as to how they fit the lesson.**

<u>Lower</u>

Acts 2:32 - This Jesus God has raised up, of which we are all witnesses.

Hymn 215, Stanza 1:    Draw us to Thee, For then shall we

Walk in Thy steps forever
And hasten on Where Thou art gone
To be with Thee, dear Savior.

<u>Middle</u> **any of the above and...**

Acts 1:9 - Now when He had spoken these things, while they watched, He was taken up, and a cloud received Him out of their sight.

Hymn 215, Stanzas 2-3:    Draw us to Thee, Lord, lovingly;
Let us depart with gladness
That we may be Forever free
From sorrow, grief, and sadness.

Draw us to Thee, Oh, grant that we
May walk the road to heaven!
Direct our way Lest we should stray
And from Thy paths be driven.

<u>Upper</u> **any of the above and...**

Acts 1:11 - This same Jesus, who was taken up from you into heaven, will so come in like manner as you saw Him go into heaven.

Hymn 215, Stanzas 4-5:    Draw us to Thee That also we
Thy heavenly bliss inherit
And ever dwell Where sin and hell
No more can vex our spirit.

Draw us to Thee Unceasingly,
Into Thy kingdom take us;
Let us fore'er Thy glory share,
Thy saints and joint heirs make us.

## 45

## STORY
Pentecost - Acts 2:1-42

## TEACHER PRAYER
Dear Father in heaven, I know that by my very best efforts I cannot make my students believe Your saving truths. But I have great confidence in teaching them Your word, for thereby the Holy Spirit will do His work of converting human reason to child-like faith in whatever God tells us. Without the work of the Spirit, all our efforts are in vain. Thank You for the gift of Your Holy Ghost! Amen.

## VOCABULARY
*Pentecost* - The term itself means "fifty". Originally, it was the name for a Jewish harvest festival which took place fifty days after the Passover. For us this tenth day after Jesus ascended into heaven is the day on which Jesus sent the Holy Spirit upon the disciples so that they could effectively spread the Gospel. This same "festival of the Holy Spirit" is also known among us as Whitsunday (accent on "it"). This term had reference to "White Sunday," the day of Pentecost when the candidates for Holy Baptism were dressed in white gowns.

*Devout* - Pious, religious, showing reverence.

*Proselytes* - A person who has been converted from one religion to another.

*New Wine* - The word used may refer to new, or sweet wine. From its use here we know that it was recognized to be intoxicating. Third hour of the day: According to our measure of time, 9:00 AM.

*Attested* - Bear witness, declare to be true or genuine. Acts 2:23: "Him, being delivered by the determined purpose and foreknowledge of God, you have taken by lawless hands, have crucified, and put to death;". Also correctly translated: "This man was handed over to you by God's set purpose and foreknowledge; and you, with the help of wicked men, put Him to death by nailing Him to the cross."

*Patriarch* - The father and ruler of a family or tribe, as one of the founders of the ancient Hebrew families. In the Bible Abraham, Isaac, Jacob, and Jacob's twelve sons were patriarchs.

*Exalted* - Praise, glorify, elevate with honor.

*Promise of the Holy Spirit* - With reference to the promise to send the Holy Spirit who will cause unbelieving hearts to believe the truth from God. Isaiah 44: "I will pour My Spirit on your descendants.. .one will say, 'I am the Lord's'; another will write with his hand, 'The Lord's.'" Ezekiel 36: "...I will give you a new heart and put a new spirit within you... I will put my Spirit within you and cause you to walk in my statutes. . ." Acts 2: (Quoting the Prophet Joel) "I will pour out my Spirit on all flesh... I will pour out my Spirit in those days...".

*Exhort* - Urge earnestly by advice or warning, strongly admonish.

*Perverse* - Deviating from what is right or good. Something wrong, improper, corrupt, wicked.

*Steadfast* - Firm, fixed, settled, not changing, constant.

*Breaking of bread* - Instead of being sliced, pieces of bread were "broken." Note the use of this expression in the account of the Lord's Supper.

## OUTER AIM
Jesus told His disciples to wait in Jerusalem until He sent the Hold Spirit to them.

Upper - The Holy Spirit was poured out on His believers to enable them to witness about Jesus Christ.

## INNER AIM
God, the Holy Spirit, comes to create and strengthen faith through the peaching and teaching of His word.

Upper - The Holy Spirit has called us through baptism and God's Word to be witnesses for Jesus Christ.

## BACKGROUND

*(Rupprecht Bible History References Vol. 2, pp.461-472)*

When we heard about the Ascension of Jesus, we heard Jesus promise to send the Holy Spirit upon His disciples. Ten days later, as they were gathered together with other followers of Jesus, it happened! The Holy Spirit came upon them with some miraculous signs: the sound of loud wind, tongues of fire on the heads of the apostles, and everyone heard them witness God's truth to them in their very own languages.

Recall the Holy Spirit's three miracles on the day of Pentecost: He caused the disciples to witness the word of God in many languages; He gave them courage and faith to witness His word; He caused many people (3000 that day) to believe and to be baptized.

v. 1-13

▸ The promise to send the Holy Spirit upon the disciples was to enable them to make disciples from all nations.

▸ This outpouring of the Holy Spirit was accompanied with external signs: the sound of a loud wind, tongues of fire set on the heads of the apostles, and they were able to witness in other tongues (known human languages).

▸ The Spirit of God had been active in Old Testament times, indicated by words such as: "the Spirit of the Lord was upon him."

▸ But now the word would not be confined to God's Old Testament people in Israel.

▸ It was to spread through all the world. Therefore, the emphasis is not on the gift of speaking in tongues, but on the preaching of the Gospel in words that people could hear in their own languages.

▸ As a result of this Pentecost miracle of language abilities, mockers accused the disciples of being full of sweet wine!

v. 14-36

▸ Peter delivered a sermon wherein he tied what was happening into what the prophet Joel had written about the pouring out of the Spirit (Joel 3:1ff).

▸ The work of the Holy Spirit, working in and through the witnessing, preaching, and teaching of the word from God, would continue until the second coming of Jesus in glory.

▸ Peter did not dwell upon the signs (tongues) of the Spirit, but underscored the saving work of Jesus who had been crucified.

▸ Peter convicted them of their sin of crucifying the Messiah, the Lord of Glory. But this was all part of God's foreordained plan.

▸ Through Jesus' suffering and death sinners would be redeemed from sin, ransomed from death, and saved.

▸ Peter also pointed to the resurrection.

▸ In Psalm sixteen God told His people the Lord would not leave "His Holy One" in the grave (hell), nor would His body see corruption.

▸ The resurrection of Jesus was the witness of God that Jesus of Nazareth was His Son, the promised Messiah.

▸ Peter's sermon contained both law (with reference to sin and death) and Gospel (God's love in Christ for all sinners — to redeem, reconcile, and give Life to them).

v. 37-42

▸ After the sermon a question was asked: "What must we do?" Answer: "Repent and be baptized for the remission of sins.. for the promise is to you and to your children."

▸ The Holy Spirit worked mightily in the word that was preached, and three thousand souls were added to the Lord, for they gladly heard His word and were baptized.

- The believers (the congregation) in Jerusalem were all brought to faith by the Holy Spirit and He joined them in a unity of faith (fellowship).
- They are described by the words: "They continued steadfastly in the apostles' doctrine and fellowship, and in breaking of bread and prayers."
- People were amazed by the love of the early Christians who generously shared their daily bread with one another.

## STUDENT PRAYER

Lower: Jesus, You called me to be Your witness. My words cannot make someone believe. Send Your Holy Spirit to make me a good witness, by sharing Your word with others. By Your word, the Spirit makes believers out of unbelievers. Amen.

Upper: Dear Father in heaven, thank you for sending Your Holy Spirit to turn our sinful hearts into believing hearts, cleansed and ready to serve as witnesses. May the Spirit bless my witness of Your word, by working faith in unbelieving hearts. This is Your good will, Your will be done! In Jesus name. Amen.

## PRESENTATION

Tell the story with the same emotion and excitement as if you were there. Tell the story in your words, but be faithful to the account that God wrote through His apostle, Luke.

## APPLICATIONS

1. In the explanation to the third article of the Apostles Creed we confess: "I believe that I cannot by my own reasoning or effort believe in Jesus Christ, my Lord, or come to Him. But the Holy Spirit has called me by the Gospel..."
2. How thankful we are that our unbelieving hearts did not turn from the Gift of God which is eternal life through our Lord Jesus Christ. With the Holy Spirit present in God's word, He calls, gathers, enlightens, and sanctifies us and the whole Christian Church on earth... and He keeps us in that saving faith through the word until Jesus comes again in glory to take us Home.

## PASSAGES

These passages can be assigned as memory work or simply discussed in class as to how they fit the lesson.

Lower
I Cor. 12:3 - No one can say that Jesus is Lord except by the Holy Spirit.
TLH # 229, Stanza 1: Holy Spirit, hear us On this sacred day; Come to us with blessing, Come with us to stay.

Middle any of the above and...
Romans 8:16 - The Spirit Himself bears witness with our spirit that we are children of God.
TLH #229, Stanza 2: Come as once Thou camest To the faithful few Patiently awaiting Jesus' promise true.

Upper any of the above and...
Titus 3:5 - According to His mercy He saved us, by the washing of regeneration and renewing of the Holy Spirit.
TLH #229, Stanzas 3-4: Up to heav'n ascending, Our dear Lord has gone; Yet His little children Leaves He not alone. To His blessed promise Now in faith we cling. Comforter, most holy, Spread o'er us Thy wing.

## 46

## STORY
Ananias and Sapphira - Acts 4:31-5:11

## TEACHER PRAYER
Almighty God, heavenly Father, by the work of Your Holy Spirit I have been brought to Jesus. I enjoy the unity of faith in the fellowship within the visible assembly of the church. Teach me to resist the traps set by Satan, the peer pressures of the world, and my own weak flesh with Your word. Day by day, keep me in a child-like faith that trusts the power of Your word for absolute security all the way Home. In Jesus' name. Amen.

## VOCABULARY
*Levite* - One of the descendants of Levi (descendant of Leah, Jacob's wife), also the distinctive title of that portion of the tribe which was set apart for the service of the sanctuary subordinate to the priests. A Levite's period of service was from age 25—50, after which he became an overseer. The function of the tribe was to preserve the Law of Jehovah in all its integrity and purity.

## OUTER AIM
Ananias and Sapphira lied to Peter and to the Holy Spirit.

\* We use terms such as the "visible assembly of believers", "visible congregation", "visible church on earth", etc, to distinguish them from the "Holy Christian Church" which is made up of all believers in heaven and on earth; they are known only to God who knows the hearts of all. (I know if I believe, but beyond that I only know of others who profess to believe. I take their word concerning their faith, but I cannot read another's heart. It may therefore happen that there are hypocrites in the visible Christian church on earth.)

## INNER AIM
God, the Holy Spirit, gives us the power to be truthful in our dealings with one another.

## BACKGROUND
*(Rupprecht Bible History References Vol. 2, pp. 480-486)*
Every believing child of God confesses that despite the good he desires to do, he sins. The wages of sin is death. The Lord does not wish to have the sinner die, but to repent of his sin, believing that in Jesus he has forgiveness.

In our lesson, we are told about a husband and wife who posed as Christians, but lied to the Holy Spirit. They did not repent of their sin, believing in Jesus for the forgiveness of their sins. They, therefore, suffered instant death. This was a warning to the early church and to us of the fatal folly of a worship of God and a following of Jesus that is only a pretense.
▸ The Holy Spirit produced a unity of spirit and a boldness of witnessing among the early Christians.
▸ Their faith and unity were such that they shared all things in common.
▸ The people brought what they had, and this was distributed as each had need.
▸ This communal sharing was an expression of the oneness of faith of the believers.
▸ This "system" of care for one another in the church worked for a while, but did not last for long.
▸ Part of the reason for its short life is found in this record.
▸ Note that this was not an enforced "communism," but a love - prompted voluntary sharing with others in need.
▸ Joses (Barnabas) had set a good example of such Christian charity in the congregation.

- We are told that also Ananias and Sapphira sold their property and brought the money to the Apostles.
- They claimed that they were bringing the entire amount of money.
- Their sin was not that they kept back part of the money for Peter pointed out that the property and money always were theirs.
- But in pretending to bring the entire amount, they were lying, not just to the congregation, but to the Holy Spirit.
- Satan had turned their hearts to lie to the Holy Spirit.
- The consequences show that death is the wages of sin.

## STUDENT PRAYER

Lower: Holy Spirit, You have called me unto faith in Jesus. Keep me in that faith, by my use of God's word. In Jesus' name. Amen.

Upper: Holy Spirit, You have called me unto faith in Jesus and to be His witness. The devil, the world, and my flesh are against my listening to Your voice and following You. Keep me in the faith that trusts in Jesus and His word. Remind me of what my God has said, whenever I am tempted to sin. I ask this in the name of Jesus, my Savior. Amen.

## PRESENTATION

Tell the story with the same emotion and excitement as if you were there. Tell the story in your words, but be faithful to the account that God wrote in Acts 4:31—5:11.

## APPLICATIONS

1. Let us daily examine our hearts, that we do not fall into sins of unbelief or self-deception or hypocrisy. Lip service to God is a mockery of Him; He will not allow that. Being a Christian, means that the Holy Spirit has given us a heart that repents of sins and trusts in Jesus for forgiveness. Such a heart will ask the Holy Spirit to cause us to follow our Good Shepherd, faithfully listening to His voice.
2. To warn the believers that there can be hypocrites in the visible church* on earth. In like manner, to warn against the fatal danger of lying to the Holy Spirit.
3. To remind us that the church on earth is made up of those who profess to believe. We are yet in our weak flesh, in a world of unbelieving peers, and subject to Satan who constantly seeks to devour us. All these we are to resist by clinging to our Savior in child-like faith, and to grow in our relationship with Jesus by using God's word, which is "our trusty shield and weapon."

## PASSAGES

These passages can be assigned as memory work or simply discussed in class as to how they fit the lesson.

Lower
Proverbs 19:5b - He who speaks lies will not escape.
TLH #323, stanza 1: With broken heart and contrite sigh, A trembling sinner, Lord, I cry. Thy pardoning grace is rich and free, O God, be merciful to me!

Middle any of the above and...
Ephesians 4:25a - Putting away lying, let each one of you speak truth with his neighbor.
TLH #323, stanza 2: I smote upon my troubled breast, With deep and conscious guilt opprest; Christ and His

cross my only plea, 0 God be merciful to me!

Upper any of the above and...
Matthew 15:8 - These people draw near to Me with their mouth, and honor Me with their lips, but their heart is far from Me.
TLH #323, stanzas 4 and 5: Nor alms nor deeds that I have done Can for a single sin atone. To Calvary alone I flee, 0 God be merciful to me!
And when, redeemed from sin and hell, with all the ransomed throng I dwell, My thankful song shall ever be, God has been merciful to me!

## 47

## STORY

Stephen, God's Child Martyred - Acts 6:8-7:60

### TEACHER PRAYER

Lord Jesus, I thank You for how You kept Stephen from feeling abandoned when he needed You most. I thank You for this example of the strength of heart You can give to one of Your own. If it pleases You to give me similar stresses, I trust You to give me what You gave Stephen to carry him through to glory. Bless my heart and mouth as I serve You today in my classroom. I need You every hour. Amen.

### OUTER AIM

Stephen was condemned and executed for preaching Jesus-Savior, but Jesus came to his rescue.

### INNER AIM

God gave Stephen enough love for even his enemies so that after he explained how God had given them a Savior (long sermon!) he was taken home to be with Jesus.

>     **or:**

The way our Lord Jesus cared for His people in Jerusalem seems self-defeating in that He let Stephen get killed early in life, but this was God's way of blessing Stephen–who was taken to heaven– and God's way of reaching out to other souls, because Christians who fled for their lives "went everywhere preaching the word." (8:4)

### VOCABULARY & BACKGROUND

Further study sources: Rupprecht, *Bible History References*, Vol. 2, 491-497; a good Bible dictionary such as the *Westminster Dictionary of the Bible*, or a Bible Handbook.

v. 8

▸ When the home congregation in Jerusalem grew in membership quickly, the pastors had to ask for help in some of their work--so the congregation agreed to help by electing seven assistants.

▸ One of them was Stephen, who was blessed with extraordinary faith, power, wisdom, and spirituality.

v. 9

▸ *Synagogue of the Freedmen* - one of the congregations in Jerusalem whose membership was made up of Jews from foreign countries: Their congregation's name tells us that they wanted to be identified as people not of the lower class, but as first-class citizens in the Roman world.

▸ These hostile people enjoyed the challenge of attacking Stephen's person, message, and success.

v. 9, 10

▸ Soon Stephen's sermons and miracle-working got the attention of others who were convinced that Jesus was a false prophet, and that Stephen was also.

▸ This mob of independent tough guys did not know God's Word as well as Stephen did, and since they were losing their debates, they decided to play dirty by hiring false witnesses to accuse Stephen of a number of scary sins:

v. 11, 12

▸ That he had bad-mouthed (blasphemed) Moses, God, and the "holy place" (Temple). On these charges they brought Stephen to trial before their ecclesiastical court.

▸ *elders and scribes* - the Jewish professional class of clergy and teachers of Scripture.

▸ *the council* - the supreme court of the Jewish church (the Sanhedrin, not a civil court), and testified that they had heard him say:    a) Jesus of Nazareth shall destroy this Temple, and                    b) Jesus shall change their church's customs and rituals.

v. 13

- ▸ *blasphemy* - the awful sin of bad-mouthing God's person or word or work.
- ▸ We note that in regard to point a), they had misunderstood--or chose to misrepresent--what Jesus had said about His own approaching death and resurrection in John 2:19-22. In regard to point b), they did not understand that Jesus had come to fulfill the Mosaic Law in the place of all Law-breakers. That made the ceremonial regulations--as prefiguring types of Himself-- no longer functional, either.

v.15
- ▸ The Holy Spirit here points up the contrast between Stephen and these evil-minded Jesus-haters, who now "saw his face as the face of an angel."
- ▸ We know little about the face of an angel, but we do know that angels have appeared in phosphorescent, radiant clothing (Luke 24:4), and that when Moses had received the Law from God, his face was shiny (Ex.34:35).
- ▸ This seems to be a God-given way for Stephen to get their full attention.
- ▸ Stephen certainly had the work of an angel (a messenger from God on high) cut out for him.

Ch.7:
- ▸ Stephen was on the witness stand long enough (fifty verses!) to make a good case that the charges against him were falsified.

vv. 2-8
- ▸ He makes the point that he serves (rather than blasphemes) the LORD God, who chose Abraham to carry forward His gracious plans for a special people...

vv. 9-18
- ▸ He makes the point that he reveres the God who preserved His people through His special servant Joseph.

vv. 20-40
- ▸ He makes the point that it is the Jewish nation that should be on trial, for when God appointed Moses as their "ruler and deliverer," he was rejected; and then the greater "ruler and deliverer" who had been with them in the wilderness was discarded in favor of heathen idols.

vv.44-50
- ▸ He makes the point that God was not as interested in the temple as they made Him out to be.
- ▸ At this point Stephen's sermon/testimony takes an abrupt turn.

v.51
- ▸ Why does Stephen here break out into a scathing denunciation of the council for resisting the Holy Ghost?
- ▸ We deduce that during his sermon they had been shaking their heads or showing their bad attitude in other ways...until Stephen could no longer ignore their response.
- ▸ Their attitude toward God and His messenger Stephen was so bad that....

v.51-55
- ▸ Now they had to be told that they are resisting God's own Holy Spirit, who yearns for their salvation.
- ▸ They were copying the bad example of their parents and forebears who had murdered God's preachers, and now they had even become guilty of doing the same to God's "Just One," the sinless Messiah Himself!
- ▸ Note: It was not Stephen who was guilty of a bad attitude toward God, Moses, and the Temple, but the Jewish leadership that was guilty--guilty of even more sin than all the other sins during all the centuries of Jewish history.

v.51
- ▸ *Stiff necked* is the opposite of bowing the head in humility; and *uncircumcised in heart and ears* means they were unconverted, undedicated to God.
- ▸ Note: To oppose God's messages brought by God's spokesmen IS to oppose the Holy Ghost, who uses the means of grace to get into sinful hearts and turn them around upside-down.

v.54
- ▸ This is not the response we would like to see, for it was seething anger that exploded in Stephen's face.

v.55

▸ How wonderful that God drew Stephen's attention away from this hellish scene of mad-dog snarling and snapping, and gave him a glimpse into the heavenly Jerusalem--actually letting him look into the sanctuary of God's throne-room--with Jesus standing at attention at the place of honor and privilege, ready and waiting for Stephen's arrival home.

v. 56

▸ Stephen couldn't help but blurt out in excited amazement and joyous surprise, ("LOOK!") and evidently expected the others also to see the wonderful vision that he saw.

v. 57

▸ They, of course, not having Jesus in their hearts, could not see Him in heaven either.

▸ Explore these thoughts with the class: Why did they holler and put their fingers into their ears and assault Stephen? Why were Stephen's message and conduct so frightening to them?

v. 58

▸ Even though they had no legal right to execute anyone, the Jews were so mad at Stephen that they took the law into their own hands.

▸ In the Old Testament times, God allowed this style of execution for blasphemers (Lev. 24:14-16).

▸ But in doing this to Stephen, they had become carbon copies of their evil forefathers (cf. v. 51-52).

▸ Note: Stephen is the central character here, of course, the hero of faith who may be included in the Hebrews 11:33-40 listing of such champions whom God supported.

▸ Which verse could be a reference to Stephen?

▸ Stephen died from brain concussions when his skull was smashed by the rocks they threw.

▸ Thus, vv.55-56 and 59-60 deserve our closest attention, for here we have an example of how a Christ-like heart reacts to the most horrendous mistreatment.

▸ True religion is to forgive from the heart--to want God to bless such evil men--to call upon our God to carry us through every obstacle when we are truly serving Him--to beseech the LORD to include such sins in/with/under His redemptive mercy and to keep on with His program of seeking lost souls, even in Jewry.

▸ Finally, true religion is to commit ourselves, body and soul and all things into His keeping--so that we can fall asleep in Jesus, Who has stood by us through everything else and will receive us before the throne of our Father, to introduce us there to the rest of the family of God.

## STUDENT PRAYER

If you have perceptive and thoughtful students, they can be asked to compose prayers of their own for use by the class. If it is up to the teacher to provide one, it should be simple and short.

## PRESENTATION

With Stephen's sermon included, this gets to be one of the longest New Testament stories in the series; so you should summarize. But for the Upper Level give the gist of his defense-strategy to show Stephen's concern that his listeners would review God's blessings on Israel, blessings which were often not appreciated. Many of our own sermons are meant to work the same way.

## APPLICATIONS

1. In our society, are Christians protected by law from being attacked as Stephen was? Yet, since Satan and his crew do their dirty work anyhow, what might happen to a Christian in any of the following situations,... and how would YOU handle a bad response?

   -A Christian business-person makes the Savior known among the other office personnel.

   - Co-workers enjoy discussing a subject that God answers in the Bible.

   -A Christian delivery van driver shares Bible testimony with customers on his route.

   -A Christian student shows disapproval of the dirty talk and jokes of other students.

   -A Christian student has a quiet moment of prayer at the lunch-table.

   -A Christian is asked his opinion on socially-acceptable sins such as abortion, alcoholism, gambling, drug abuse, living together without marriage, etc.

2. How do you as a young Christian feel about your parents (or your pastor or teacher) when they want to talk with you about something you did that needs correcting?

3. If you get into trouble because of your own sinfulness, might you feel "persecuted"? What causes a person to become angry--such as the council members were--when you are scolded or disciplined? Explain:

## PASSAGES

These passages can be assigned as memory work or simply discussed in class as to how they fit the lesson.

### Lower

Acts 4:12 - Nor is there salvation in any other, for there is no other name under heaven given among men by which we must be saved.

I Tim. 6:12a - Fight the good fight of faith, lay hold on eternal life....

### Middle any of the above and...

Luke 12:8 - Also I say to you, whoever confesses Me before men, him the Son of Man also will confess before the angels of God.

Matt. 5:44 - But I say to you, love your enemies, bless those who curse you, do good to those who hate you, and pray for those who spitefully use you and persecute you.

I Thess. 4:14 - For if we believe that Jesus died and rose again, even so God will bring with Him those who sleep in Jesus.

### Upper any of the above and...

Romans 1:16 - For I am not ashamed of the gospel of Christ, for it is the power of God to salvation for everyone who believes, for the Jew first and also for the Greek.

Luke 2:29-32 - Lord, now You are letting Your servant depart in peace, according to Your word; for my eyes have seen Your salvation which You have prepared before the face of all peoples, a light to bring revelation to the Gentiles, and the glory of Your people Israel.

II Tim. 4:18 - And the Lord will deliver me from every evil work and preserve me for His heavenly kingdom. To Him be glory forever and ever. Amen!

## HYMN CHOICES

"Am I a Soldier of the Cross" (TLH #445:1,4)

"Fight the Good Fight with All Thy Might" (TLH #447:1,2,4)

"Stand up!--Stand Up for Jesus" (TLH #451:1,4)

## 48

## STORY
Philip and the Man from Ethiopia - Acts 8:26-39

## TEACHER PRAYER
Lord Jesus, today is another opportunity for me to share what You want these children to absorb into their hearts. One of them may not yet know You as Savior, so I want to help as Philip did. Others may be ready to go to a neighbor or acquaintance and present Your Word in a better way because of Philip's example. I follow where You direct and ask You to bless every step of my way. Thank You. Amen.

## OUTER AIM
God saved a non-Jewish foreigner by means of a Christian missionary.

## INNER AIM
God sends us to preach the gospel to all people.

## BACKGROUND
*(Rupprecht Bible History References Vol.2, pp. 498-505)*
v. 26
▸ Stephen (a Greek name) was the second in the listing of those chosen to supervise the Jerusalem Christian food pantry and see to it that the Greek widows were not overlooked.
▸ An angel came from heaven with a special assignment for Philip--one that would take him out of town onto the Jerusalem-Gaza federal highway going to the southeastern corner of Judea.
▸ The passing comment that "this is desert" sets the stage as a place where one person will offer aid to a stranger in need.
▸ Yet it was not Philip, the man on foot, who needed a helping hand; it was the rich man in the chariot who needed help to find the road that leads from one's own spiritual desert into God's well-watered Paradise.

v. 27
▸ *Eunuch*, a man usually of the slave class, castrated in order to guarantee that women he served/guarded would be safe from rape, as well as to protect him from false accusations of rape.
▸ He had risen to a high position in government civil service, for as Secretary of the Treasury, he was a Cabinet member of the government of *Ethiopia*, a gentile nation in Africa (probably Meroe, in S.Nubia, not modern Ethiopia) that had a succession of women as rulers during the first century AD.
▸ This first angel directive said nothing about mission work or preaching to anyone.
▸ But Philip obeyed, of course. (If we wonder why the angel could not carry out the mission himself to the Ethiopian man without Philip's help, apparently God wants to use us humans to reach other humans.
▸ Angels do God's messenger service, but humans are used for intensive instruction or the long-term soul-care that we Christians render to one another.)
▸ This man was not only a foreigner to Jews, he was also of the Negroid race; thus no Jew would have selected him as mission material unless by direct order from God.
▸ Yet an unusual case such as this was soon to become usual for mission outreach, as Christians discovered that people of the Jewish race were less receptive than folks of different race and nationality.
▸ The eunuch was not ignorant of the God of Abraham.
▸ He evidently was a convert to the Jewish worship of Jehovah and had made a special trip of many hundreds of miles to get to Jerusalem to worship (for the Passover or Pentecost festival) as every devout Jew (or proselyte) wanted to do.

- He had bought a hand-printed copy of the book of the prophet Isaiah, the premier Old Testament book of the Gospel of the Savior.
- As his chauffeur handled the horsepower, he occupied himself in reading this gospel.
- He valued God's Word even though he did not understand everything he read, and at this decisive moment he needed help in understanding a crucial truth which God was about to give him by the hand of Philip

v. 29

- Up to now Philip did not know his assignment on the highway that day, so the angel told him his next move was to get going and catch up to that chariot on the road ahead .

v.30

- So Philip broke out into a jogging trot and soon caught up with the idling chariot and its occupants.
- Evidently the black man was reading the text of Isaiah out loud--and Philip deduced that the man was puzzled about the wording or the meaning of the words.
- (This would be a good time to ask the students if they have ever been puzzled about something in the Bible--perhaps a passage they have heard in church, or been told to memorize, etc., or even Isaiah 53...*and* what they have done to solve the puzzlement.)
- Philip "cut to the chase" with no delay for chit-chat about the heat or the man's fine vehicle. "Do you understand...?" is a fine non-challenging approach because any response is OK.
- We teachers do well to regularly ask this question in our classes of religion, literature, math, science...and then run with the ball. Invite dialogue rather than pursue a monologue. It is not enough to teach the Bible as one would train a parrot. It is not enough to assert, declare, and drill Bible truths. We must discover whether we have brought the student to understand what God wants him to understand.)

v. 31

- What a wonderful, ingenuous, sincere reply! And what a motto for every classroom!

v. 32-34

- The instruction class began at Isaiah 52:7-8, prophesying Jesus' last hours on Maundy Thursday and Good Friday.
- (Ask the class if anyone knows the answer to the man's question. Who is the person referred to as the *sheep*, the *lamb* who had received no fair trial, no justice, and whose life was taken from him...and when was all this to take place?)
- The eunuch and Philip were ready for the key question: Is Jesus the embodied fulfillment of the human tragedy here predicted by Isaiah?

v. 35

- Philip's heart was already open, and now his voice opened the mysteries of God's redeeming love in Jesus the Messiah.
- Starting at the puzzling text, he followed Scripture's signposts to lead the eunuch to deduce that Jesus the Nazarene was none other than the long-awaited Messiah.
- (The class may be asked to come up with additional Scriptures that Philip probably used to draw this man to Jesus as his Savior. If we note that no mention is made here of sins, judgment, repentance, or any other Law-word, it becomes clear that at such a time in his life, what the eunuch needed was not a stronger thirst, but a good long drink of the Water of Life.)

v. 36- 38

- During the process of this Bible class, the eunuch's heart became convinced that Jehovah had given Jesus to be the Messiah-Savior, and thus Jesus was his personal Savior. He had also become ready to commit himself, body and soul, into Jesus' hands by Holy Baptism.
- The question, "What hinders me from being baptized?" may indicate a concern that perhaps his Gentile or Negro heritage could be an obstacle to his being accepted into the Christian fellowship. It would not, of course.
- Note: Though v. 37 is not found in the most reliable ancient texts, it is consistent with common practice that such a confession would be asked of and given by the convert about to be baptized. As to the mode of

baptism (either immersion or hand application of the water) the wording of the text tells us only that what was done by the one person was <u>likewise</u> done by the other ("both Philip and the eunuch went down,...they came up out of the water"). Those who hold to the theory that this was an immersion style baptism should admit that this would require <u>the pastor to be immersed along with</u> the convert, which is rather unlikely.

▸ This entire encounter lasted only a few hours, but it brought this soul to the Savior, who claimed the eunuch for all eternity.

v. 39

▸ As Philip was spirited away to do other privileged work, the eunuch steered his vehicle homeward, absolutely thrilled over what he had received from God and ready to share with folks back home.

▸ Although he did not have the support of a Christian congregation when he arrived home, we expect that--due to his government position and his joy-filled heart--he would be able to gain an audience for the Scriptures.

▸ We also expect that many souls in that heathen foreign land were led to the Savior by his service to Jesus, and we will someday meet these folks who are now awaiting our arrival at the throne of grace.

## STUDENT PRAYER

Teacher: Lord, don't give up on anyone who gets a hold of a Bible; give him/her the urge to read the parts that tell of Your love in Jesus, and send someone like me to help him understand what Jesus is all about. Amen.

Student: Lord, don't give up on me when I don't understand something in Your Word. Get my brain working on it, and get my heart open to accept what You want to tell me. Especially bless my pastor and teacher to get my attention and to hold it when they tell me Your Word. Thanks and Amen.

## PRESENTATION

The story should be told in the words of the teacher using appropriate background information from the Background section. The Middle and Upper levels could read the story from the student folder.

## APPLICATIONS

1. We all have to start somewhere in our Bible studies. Where do YOU want to start?

2. When a person searching for relief from a sin-burdened conscience, salvation from a bad life, and freedom from evil influences, finally discovers that God has already taken care of all this for him in Jesus, he can hardly *slouch* his way through life after such a discovery.

3. We want to be ready to present Jesus at any time to anyone. Thus we want to prepare in advance for such "chance" encounters by studying the Bible as God's personal Word on everything of value for souls headed into eternity.

4. We may meet someone new to us at school, at a sports event, during a vacation, at the place we work, at the dentist's office, or on the Internet. Let's keep an eye and an ear open for an opportunity to share a Bible thought or to ask the other person's opinion on a moral subject. This can lead to searching the Bible for God's viewpoint.

5. The way God works to save souls is to send a Christian to individuals who do not yet understand God's Word, especially the parts about our Savior. God does not want us to hold back from these opportunities to serve people of a different race from a foreign country, for He can open hearts when people understand what He has done for their salvation.

6. There can be no greater goal in life than to aid a soul in finding the Savior and there is no greater pleasure than being God's spokesperson in using His Word to enlighten and nurture another soul in God's will and ways. And the Christian person <u>can do it</u>. Remember? *Ask, and it will be given to you; seek, and you will find; knock, and it will be opened to you." (Mt.7:7)*

7. Besides, if challenged without advance warning, we have this assurance: *"But when they arrest you, and deliver you up, do not worry beforehand, or premeditate what you will speak. But whatever is given you in that hour, speak that; for it is not you who speak, but the Holy Spirit." (Mark 13:11)* All glory to God, Amen!

8. For an adult who has already been brought to faith, Baptism serves as a wonderful means of grace through which God offers and gives spiritual and eternal blessings.
   a. On Pentecost, the apostle Peter said to his adult listeners, "Repent, and let every one of you be baptized in the name of Jesus Christ for the remission of sins; and you shall receive the gift of the Holy Spirit." (Acts 2:38)
   b. Ananias said to Paul who had already come to faith, "Arise and be baptized, and wash away your sins, calling on the name of the Lord." (Acts 22:16)
   c. Finally, Jesus gave this wonderful promise, "He who believes and is baptized will be saved." (Mark 16:16a)

## PASSAGES

These passages can be assigned as memory work or simply discussed in class as to how they fit the lesson.

Lower
Acts 8:37 - I believe that Jesus Christ (Messiah) is the Son of God
Acts 4:20 - For we cannot but speak the things which we have seen and heard.

Middle any of the above and...
Acts 4:12 - Nor is there salvation in any other, for there is no other name under heaven given among men by which we must be saved.
Acts 2:38-39 - Repent, and let every one of you be baptized in the name of Jesus Christ for the remission of sins; and you shall receive the gift of the Holy Spirit. For the promise is to you and to your children, and to all who are afar off, as many as the Lord our God will call.

Upper any of the above and...
Acts 10:42-43 - And He commanded us to preach to the people, and to testify that it is He who was ordained by God to be Judge of the living and the dead. To Him all the prophets witness that, through His name, whoever believes in Him will receive remission of sins.
Eph.2:11-13 - Therefore remember, that...at that time you were without Christ, being aliens from the commonwealth of Israel and strangers from the covenants of promise, having no hope and without God in the world. But now in Christ Jesus you who once were far off have been made near by the blood of Christ.
James 5:19-20 - Brethren, if anyone among you wanders from the truth, and someone turns him back, let him know that he who turns a sinner from the error of his way will save a soul from death and cover a multitude of sins.

## HYMN CHOICES
"Today Thy Mercy Calls Us" (TLH #279)
"God's Word is Our Great Heritage" (TLH #283)
"We have a Sure Prophetic Word" (TLH #290)
"Spread, Oh, Spread, Thou Mighty Word" (TLH #507)

## 49

**STORY**
Peter Heals the Lame Man - Acts 3-4

## TEACHER PRAYER

Lord, grant me the spirit and power of Peter to boldly proclaim your name and your salvation to all men and especially to my students this day. May the beauty, love, gift, and power of Your salvation fill the hearts of my students for You. In Jesus' name we pray.

## VOCABULARY

*Beautiful Gate* - main gate on the east side of the temple. Each side had a main gate besides other smaller gates. All gates were usually guarded to prevent trouble. A gift from one Nicanor who built this gate.

*Hour of prayer* - ninth hour (3 p.m.) One of the times when sacrifices were offered at the temple. Often called evening sacrifice. Since they no longer sacrificed, because Christ's death was their sacrifice, they entered for prayer.

## OUTER AIM

God gave Peter the gift of healing and the boldness to preach and to spread the message of the Word of God.

## INNER AIM

Since we have been healed from the disease of sin, we should desire to spread the message of salvation.

## STUDENT PRAYER

Lord, help us for we are sinners, lame of faith and poor in grace! Strengthen our faith so we look only to Your grace and salvation for the hope of eternal life. Make us bold as Peter was to speak of Your name to all people we meet. Only in You is there salvation and hope for eternity. In Jesus' name we pray. Amen.

## PRESENTATION

Through the power of the Holy Spirit and in the name and power of Jesus Christ, Peter and John heal a 40-year-old man. This attracted much attention in the temple, as everyone knew he was lame, and now they were amazed to see him walking and jumping around giving God, Peter, and John praise and thanks for his healing.

Peter used the opportunity to preach Law and Gospel, Christ and Him crucified for their sins. He also reminded them that they were responsible for Jesus's crucifixion. Unless they repented, God would be severely angry with them and punish them with hell in eternity. So Peter urged them strongly: "Repent and be converted that your sins may be blotted out." About 5,000 men, women and children came to faith at that time. God does work in mysterious, wondrous ways-way beyond our understanding, comprehension, talents and abilities.

But such popularity made others very jealous as were the Jewish authorities and Jewish upper echelon. They feared for their own worldly respect, honor and authority. People would flock to the disciples and not to them. They were angry and afraid, so in the evening they had the disciples arrested.

The next day they released the disciples, however, for fear of the people who looked to the disciples for spiritual guidance and blessing. Yet before the disciples were released the authorities tried to instill in them the Sanhedrian version of the "fear of God," but to no avail.  It only gave opportunity for the disciples to preach and accuse them of crucifying Christ, which offended God and brought condemnation from God upon them.  Yet Peter preached the Gospel to them for their benefit also telling them in Acts 4:12: "Nor is there salvation in any other (Christ) for there is no other name (again, Christ) under heaven given among men by which we must be saved."  What a bold, beautiful statement.  Too bad it had little or no spiritually uplifting effect on its hearers.  Instead, the disciples were commanded to no longer speak or teach in the name of Christ.

This the disciples did not heed, but they comforted one another with Words from Psalm 2 and prayed together.  The building they were in shook.  The disciples and all believers continued preaching, teaching, and doing miracles by God's help.  God caused many to "give money" to and for the "church" and apostolic work.  Let God be praised for His mysterious, wondrous ways.  Amen!

## ACTIVITY (Level 2)
(Some answers should include: telling others that they are sinful, Jesus's love, Jesus's forgiveness.  Other answers might be, Jesus rose from the dead, God created all things, we are going to heaven.  There can be an unlimited number of answers.)

## APPLICATION
How ready are we to endure shame, persecution and jealousy for displaying our faith without using rancor, bitterness or revenge?  We should learn to suffer many things and still endure while confessing the truth of Christ and His Word.  To be able to do that, we must study God's Word as Christ and the apostles did.  Note what keen memory the disciples had.  They quoted Scripture exactly without any text before them.  We should know all of God's Word.  May the Holy Spirit so bless us as He did the disciples in witnessing.

The Holy Spirit was also active in every act and word spoken by the apostles and believers in this story.  We too, often underestimate and forget His involvement in our faith and its works.

## PASSAGES
**These passages can be assigned as memory work or simply discussed in class as to how they fit the lesson.**

Ps. 50:15 - Call upon Me in the day of trouble; I will deliver you, and you shall glorify Me.

Matt 10:32-33 - Therefore whoever confesses Me before men, him I will also confess before My Father who is in heaven.  But whoever denies Me before men, him I will also deny before My Father who is in heaven.

Acts 4:12 - Nor is there salvation in any other, for there is no other name under heaven given among men by which we must be saved.

Romans 10:17 - So then faith comes by hearing, and hearing by the word of God.

James 1:15 - Then, when desire has conceived, it gives birth to sin; and sin, when it is full-grown, brings forth death.

Acts 4:19-20 - But Peter and John answered and said to them, "Whether it is right in the sight of God to listen to you more than to God, you judge.

## HYMN CHOICES

Praise To The Lord, The Almighty - TLH #39
Lord, Keep Us Steadfast In Thy Word - TLH #261
A Mighty Fortress Is Our God -  TLH #262
O Little Flock, Fear Not The Foe - TLH #263
God's Word Is Our Great Heritage - TLH #283
Chief Of Sinners Though I Be - TLH #342
Oh, For A Thousand Tongues To Sing - TLH #360
What God Ordains Is Always Good - TLH #521

## 50

**STORY**
Peter Delivered from Prison - Acts 12

**TEACHER PRAYER**
Triune God of heaven, look upon us and gird us with Your Spirit so we may endure under the trials and tribulations You allow to come our way. Give us the strength to help others and to bear their burdens with them. In this way we, too, may be strengthened in the faith of Your forgiveness and Your great sacrifice for us on the cross. Help us never to despise or despair regardless of how severe and painful our trials may be. In the name of the Father, Son and Holy Spirit. Amen.

**VOCABULARY**
*Harass* - persecute

*Days of unleavened bread* - precedes the fourth day of the Passover celebration

*Squad* - more than one soldier. In this case perhaps two by the door and one at each gate.

**OUTER AIM**
God does not tempt or try believers (including us) beyond what they or we are able to bear.

**INNER AIM**
God delivers His chosen ones from all evil by giving them power to overcome that evil.

**BACKGROUND** This takes place well after Christ's persecution, death, resurrection, and ascension which gained salvation for all sinners of all times, including you and me. It takes place before the three so-called journeys of Paul but after Paul's conversion, probably around the year 41 A.D.

Persecution of Christians was on the rise including the death and beheading of James. (Beheading was considered to be most disgraceful.) Little has been made of this death of James, who was the brother of Jesus' favorite disciple, John. Maybe that is why Jesus held John closely so that his faith would not fail him at the death of his brother. James is the first martyr of the 12 disciples. This is not the James that was the cousin or "brother" of the Lord. That James joined other martyrs of Bethlehem as well as Stephen as the early martyrs of Christianity.

**STUDENT PRAYER**
Lord, You have taught us that we should be willing to lose our lives for Your sake. Grant us the faith and spiritual strength never to waiver in our faith in You regardless of the severity of the trials and troubles You allow to come our way. Grant us a double portion of the Spirit that You sent to James and Peter that we, too, may spend eternity with You because of Your sacrifice for our sins. Grant us complete remission of all our sins. We trust You for our salvation. Amen.

**PRESENTATION**
The martydom of James by Herod Agrippa I (grandson of Herod the Great, who tried Jesus for Pilate) did not satisfy the unbelieving Jews. They and Herod sought more and got it. Imprison Peter. It was in pre-Passover days so Herod would send Peter to trial and put him to death after the Passover and so they would not defile the Passover celebration.
But God had other plans. A squad of four constantly guarded Peter. Two were chained to him and

one each was placed at the door and the prison gate. They changed shifts, but always four were with Peter while he was in prison.

Through an angel, God delivers Peter. The angel awakens Peter, not disturbing the sleeping squad of guards. Peter's chains fall off. There were no keys. The door opens and the prisoners leave the prison. All guards are still sleeping. Peter could not believe all this was happening, but he surely did like the "dream" he was having. The angel brings Peter to a familiar part of Jerusalem and then leaves him.

We also note that the other disciples and other Christians were fervently praying for Peter's deliverance. As James says (5:16), "The effective fervent prayer of a righteous man avails much." God did answer their prayer. He did deliver Peter from prison.

When the angels leave, Peter's "dream" ends; he finds he is truly delivered. He then is amazed and thankful and tries to get further away from the prison.

Peter goes to the home of John, Mark's mother Mary, where a certain servant girl, Rhoda, also was. She heard a knock on the door and recognized his voice when she asked who it was. But she did not let him in, so others found it hard to believe her. Yet when the knocking continued and the others finally answered, they were astounded to find Peter there.

They, too, were thankful and were anxious to keep Peter, but Peter under wisdom of God, left for another place to preach the Good News of forgiveness of sins to all and the promise of heaven to those who believe. He left Judea for Samaria and other regions so that it would make it harder for the enemies and opposers of Christianity to find him.

We are told Peter's persecutor, Herod, died a death by worms, inflicted by God, because Herod did not give glory to the God of heaven for his fame, but let others claim him (Herod) to be a god. He also had all the guards put to death for the escape of Peter.

## APPLICATION

God does not always let the wickedness and cruelty of men run rampant. In His way and at His time, He does all things for the spread of the Gospel.

When people like Herod try to oppose and hinder the spread of that Gospel news, God steps in with His way and at His time to continue the growth of his kingdom.

Even though trials and temptations may desperately seek to overwhelm us, like Peter and those other Christians we must persevere in prayer that God would help us so that we do not lose eternal life and the forgiveness of all our sins through Christ.

Like our early CLC fathers, we must hold faithfully to God's Word and promises so that we do not sacrifice heaven for some paltry offering the world may have to give, since all offerings of the world, even their best and greatest, are paltry compared to heaven and eternal life. Keep steadfast in the Word of God. You'll never go wrong, and it will never steer you wrong. It is truly our great heritage! Keep it and use it always in Christ's name!

## PASSAGES

**These passages can be assigned as memory work or simply discussed in class as to how they fit the lesson.**

Ps 50:15 - Call upon Me in the day of trouble; I will deliver you, and you shall glorify Me.

Matt 7:7 - Ask, and it will be given to you; seek, and you will find; knock, and it will be opened to you.

Matt 10:32-33 - Therefore, whoever confesses Me before men, him I will also confess before My Father who is in heaven. But whoever denies Me before men, him I will also deny before My Father who is in heaven.

Matt 18:20 - For where two or three are gathered together in My name, I am there in the midst of them.

Matt 24:35 - Heaven and earth will pass away, but My words will by no means pass away.

Mark 8:34-38 - And when He had called the people to Him with his disciples also, He said to them, "Whoever desires to come after Me, let him deny himself, and take up his cross, and follow Me. For whoever desires to save his life will lose it, but whoever loses his life for My sake and the gospel's, will save it. For what will it profit a man if he gains the whole world, and loses his own soul? Or what will a man give in exchange for his soul? For whoever is ashamed of me and My words in this adulterous and sinful generation, of him the Son of Man also will be ashamed when He comes in the glory of His Father with the holy angels."

## HYMN CHOICES

Lord, Keep Us Steadfast In Thy Word - TLH #261
A Mighty Fortress Is Our God - TLH #262
Little Flock, Fear Not the Foe - TLH #263
Thine Honor Save, O Christ, Our Lord - TLH #265
What Is The World To Me - TLH #430
What God Ordains Is Always Good - TLH #521
Be Still, My Soul - TLH #651
Now The Day Is Over - TLH #654
Onward Christian Soldiers - TLH #658

## 51

## STORY
Cornelius and Peter - Acts 10

## TEACHER PRAYER
Lord Jesus, since Your love is too deep, broad, high, and wide to be detoured by such trivialities as a person's age, sex, race, or position in life, help me to show your wider, broader, higher and deeper love for all peoples.  Use me as You used Peter wherever and however I may serve You by serving others. Amen.

## OUTER AIM
A veteran Roman army officer is brought to know Jesus as his Savior.

## INNER AIM
God's love for souls is wide enough and deep enough to seek out an officer in the military and bring him to salvation in Jesus. (see Eph. 3:18-19)

## BACKGROUND AND VOCABULARY
*(Rupprecht Bible History References Vol.2, pp. 520-530)*
It has always been God's desire to save all souls all over the world through all history.  But if the Jerusalem Christians did not get moving into other cities and then to other countries, such souls would not learn of their salvation.  So God had to give Peter and other disciples the thrill of discovering that gentile souls could also be saved through Jesus.  Then each convert could become a witness to Jesus in his own life situations, and so on and on...until today when even you and I are among the gentiles blessed with the Savior.
v.1
▶    *Caesarea* - The Roman capital of Palestine, named after Caesar Augustus, located on the Mediterranean seacoast about fifty miles NW of Jerusalem.
▶    a *centurion* is a Roman  army commander of about 100 troopers.
▶    the *Italian Regiment* -  these men were native Italians, not conscripted from a province.
v.2
▶    Although Cornelius was sincere, pious, and dedicated to the LORD Jehovah, he was still lacking what Peter could bring him--the revelation that the Savior had already arrived in the person of Jesus of Nazareth.
▶    Both Cornelius and Peter, the main characters in this story , needed to learn the scope of God's love for one and all.
v. 3-6
▶    Cornelius' prayers were reminders to God of His promises that included Gentiles in the width-depth-height of  His love for sinners.
▶    The angel made mention of these prayers to reassure Cornelius that he had been on the right track in his spiritual quest.
▶    God's next step was to enlist a Christian to come to his rescue.
v. 7-8
These details are rehearsed also in vv. 30-33.
▶    Since Joppa (modern Jaffa) lay about thirty miles south of Caesarea, and they had set out soon after 3:00 pm, they did not arrive at Joppa until early afternoon the next day.
v. 9-16
▶    Here the scene shifts to God's working to correct Peter's (natural and Jewish) misconception that God's mercies did not include Gentiles.
▶    That's why He put the disciples into training to enlarge their perception of His love.

- They were going to learn how far from Jerusalem God would go to save a soul--how deep down into the dregs of society He would reach to salvage a soul--how wide afield into the pagan wilderness His love would range.
- To get Peter's cooperation in reaching out to gentiles, God needed to make Peter's heart convinced about the scope of His redeeming love.
- That was the purpose of the vision of the critters in the sheet being lowered <u>from heaven</u> (God's throne) and the <u>heavenly</u> voice directing him to share in whatever <u>God</u> declared OK.

v.14
- Even in the trance,Peter's response came from an inbred "kosher" conscience.
- The term *common* indicates that it did not qualify for sacrificing, and *unclean* that it was unfit for human consumption at any level, being outlawed in Leviticus 11.
- The whole "kosher" arrangement was a constant reminder that God had His fingers on Jewish everyday life (their stomachs, vessels, water supply, clothing, farming and hunting activities, business dealings, social customs, etc.), and that He was in control of how He wanted people to worship Him.
- Yet Peter did not readily surrender to the heavenly insistence (in triplicate!) that God can revoke His own Levitical restrictions as He sees fit.
- Peter had to learn that when God declares He "has cleansed" something (to erase its unsuitability), no human has the right to still disapprove.
- After all, it is God who makes the rules for humans, not vice versa.

v. 17-18
- Since Peter had no stomach for nonkosher foods, he was confused as to whether he dared go against God's ancient regulations delivered through Moses.
- In the midst of his mental disarray, the delegation arrived from Cornelius.

v. 20ff.
- Peter's concern over the puzzling vision was "put on hold" while the Spirit directed Peter to attend to the visitor--with assurances that they had been sent by God to locate Peter, and that Peter could go along, free of conscience pangs about being in the company of gentiles.

v. 21
- Though Peter gave them a less-than-warm welcome when he saw the Roman soldier, he invited them to declare the purpose of their call.

v. 22
- They presented their cause to Peter, humbly petitioning him to speak whatever he wished.

v.    23
- It was by now too late in the day to set out on a ten-hour walk; moreover, by now God's directives and Peter's love for souls had put aside his narrow Jewishness about inviting "unclean" persons to share his friend's roof, his table, and his linens.
- The next day, in the right God-pleasing frame of mind, Peter set forth for Caesarea, accompanied by Christian friends.
- They were soon to get a new revelation of how God looked at gentiles, and that would redirect them in their mission to preach the Savior to all folks.

v. 24-33  *Peter meets Cornelius*
v. 24
- In the fourth day of this new chapter in Cornelius' life, he eagerly awaited the return of his servants with Simon Peter; he was prepared to greet them with a house full of relatives and close friends who shared his devotion to Jehovah, the Covenant God.

**v. 25**

Cornelius' prostrate welcome was corrected by a kindly but firm hand, as Peter permitted no popish adoration.

**v. 27-28**

▸ Peter, who had to overcome generations of Jewishness, had learned the lesson of the trance/vision, and he opened his heart as he explained this to the group.

**v. 29**

▸ Since God had not as yet spelled out what Peter should do when he met with these gentiles, Peter was obliged to ask what <u>they</u> had in mind.

**v. 30-33**

▸ So Cornelius rehearsed it (cf. vv.3-7) and invited Peter to deliver whatever it was that God had on His mind for Peter to tell them.

**vv. 34-43**

▸ *Peter's sermon to Cornelius'* household clearly reveals that he had come to learn God's love was broad and long enough to cross over the ethnic barrier between Jew and Gentile.

▸ Peter traced the length of God's love, which reached from Judea through Galilee (v. 37) to all points beyond; that "<u>whoever</u> (with no ethnic limitations) believes in Him will receive remission of sins."

▸ The Christian message always includes these historical events, with emphasis on the truth that Jesus of Nazareth (an unlikely person from an unlikely place) was indeed the "anointed" agent of God the Father (v. 38), who survived death in his resurrection (v. 40) and will function as Judge over humanity, to grant remission of sins to <u>whoever</u> believes in Him.

**v. 44-48**

▸ *The Holy Spirit comes* to the gentiles also in this "Epiphany of the Gentiles".

▸ This should dispel any doubt lingering in the minds of anyone past, present, or future that God's love was broad/deep/long enough to bring gentiles into His family, for here Jesus' promise to bestow His Spirit upon His people (Acts 1:5) was again honored as the "Holy Spirit fell upon all those who heard the Word."

▸ In other words, they were converted then and there from their Old Testament faith in the coming Messiah, as the Spirit brought them the assurance that Jesus was <u>already</u> Savior, and not for Jews only, but for them also.

**v. 45-46**

▸ This was a new and marvelous discovery for the Jewish-background Christians, who up to now had not fully realized that their Jewish "Jesus" was also the gentile "Savior."

**v. 46**

▸ Their "tongue-speaking" should not be interpreted as an unearthly lingo, for at such an emotional moment as this they simply broke forth into their mother tongues (Italian and other Mediterranean dialects of the Indo-European family of languages), all of which were "foreign" to the Hebrews, of course.

▸ This whole subject of "tongue-speaking" (as it happened also on the first Christian Pentecost--Acts 2:4-11) has been largely misunderstood and misrepresented by Pentecostals as heavenly languages unknown to this earth.

▸ Scripture gives us to understand that "speaking in tongues" means they spoke in languages or dialects foreign to the Palestinian Jew.

▸ The miracle of the "tongue-speaking" at the first Pentecost lies in this that in that instance God <u>also</u> broke the language barrier (a barrier to the Gospel ever since Babel) by enabling Hebrews to speak in foreign languages. But they were **human, earthly languages**, after all.

▸ And that's what happened here. As in their mother tongues these people of Cornelius' household glorified

God for reaching out beyond Jewry to salvage even them.

▸ (Years later in the Corinth congregation its polyglot members needed to be corrected from their misuse of "tongue-speaking," for they disturbed the worship service with personal messages blurted out in their mother tongue in the enthusiasm of the moment. See I Cor. 14)

v. 47

▸ Now then, since <u>God</u> had given them <u>His</u> five-star approval rating, who dared deny them acceptance into the earthly fellowship?

▸ So they were received into full membership in the company of saints via baptism, during which they also affirmed their faith in Jesus. Hallelujah!!

## STUDENT PRAYER

Dear Lord Jesus, thank You for saving Cornelius and his friends and relatives. Thank You for a love that sees past all the things that sometimes keep us from caring whether someone knows about You, their Savior, or not. Lord, we know that no one is saved without faith in You. Help us to love more so that we do care about the salvation of others and do share the truth about You. Amen.

## PRESENTATION

Teacher should present story by directly telling the story rather than reading it.

## APPLICATIONS

1. Our approach to the neighbor or stranger (even "God-fearing, church-going, decent people") avoids chastising them for what they may be lacking in their lives. Since we do not know if a person lacks the One Thing Needful, we find a way to present Jesus in a spirit of warmth, confident that our sharing the Scriptures and the Savior with them is a privilege entrusted to us by our God. Then we let the dialogue develop from there one step at a time.

2. We also do well to ferret out of our hearts any residual prejudice against others (Jews, Mexicans, Hmongs, Negroes, Poles, etc.). A bad attitude about Jews, Catholics, and "Polacks" (ala Archie Bunker, the clown-prince of Bigotry) could short-circuit an opening for the Spirit's working, making us unsuitable for His use. "He who says he abides in Him ought himself also to walk just as He walked." (I Jn.2:6) "We should love one another." (I Jn.3:11) Note: We learn from Scripture (John 5:23; 6:53-58; 8:24; 11:25; 14:6, etc.) that God does not value false religions, those not founded on Jesus as the Way, the Truth, and the Life--and no amount of devotion and piety can compensate for the loss of the Savior.

3. We can see that our social or cultural inhibitions hamper God's ministry of the gospel. The privileged responsibility (calling) of the Christian in this world is to respond to any request "as in the presence of God to speak all the things commanded us by God" as the occasion warrants (10:33). One-on-one is how we usually begin; sometimes a small group gathered in a private home asks for pastoral service: This is how many of our CLC congregations first assembled.

4. This military person in a foreign land did not give up his worship of Jehovah, but influenced his whole household to join him in God's kingdom. Cornelius serves as a "good conduct" example for anyone in the military.

5. God is indeed "impartial" (v.34), not prejudiced against any individual, race, or nationality. We in the CLC share that view, not resting on our family's bloodline, or our grandpa's status as a founding father in the CLC or some other status symbol of Lutheran patriotism. We realize that God looks on our heart for the right attitude ("whoever fears Him") and in our lives for the right effects ("and works righteousness") when He has a special assignment lined up for us. Whereas angels make announcements and give directions, God entrusts missionary and pastoral care as the Spirit's work through the <u>agency</u> of <u>fellow mortals</u>. Isn't that an amazing privilege for us?

## PASSAGES
These passages can be assigned as memory work or simply discussed in class as to how they fit the lesson.

<u>Lower</u>
I Thess. 5:17 - Pray without ceasing.
I Tim. 2:3-4 - God our Savior...desires all men to be saved and to come to the knowledge of the truth.

<u>Middle</u> any of the above and...
Isaiah 43:1 - Thus says the LORD, who created you..."Fear not, for I have redeemed you; I have called you by your name; You are Mine."
Eph. 2:13 - But now in Christ Jesus you who once were far off have been made near by the blood of Christ.
1 John 1:7 - The blood of Jesus Christ His Son cleanses us from all sin.

<u>Upper</u> any of the above and...
I Thess. 2:13 - When you received the word of God which you heard from us, you welcomed it not as the word of men, but as it is in truth, the word of God.
II Peter 3:9 - The Lord ... is longsuffering toward us, not willing that any should perish but that all should come to repentance.

## HYMN CHOICES
"Salvation Unto Us has Come"  TLH # 377
"By Grace I'm Saved, Grace Free and Boundless"  TLH # 373
"Come, Holy Spirit, Come"  TLH # 225
"Savior Sprinkle Many Nations" TLH #510

## 52

## STORY
Conversion of Saul to be God's Special Servant - Acts 9:1-19

## TEACHER PRAYER
Lord Jesus, I thank You for the love You gave to Saul, and that Your love supported him through all his trials as Your spokesman. I ask for a measure of that support for me in my teaching and living today. Open my mouth that I may present You to these children in all Your saving grace and loving care. As always, in Your Savior name. Amen.

## OUTER AIM
When God saved Saul's soul, He also prepared him to be the great Christian apostle and missionary Paul.

## INNER AIM
God's love is for all people, the Jew and Gentile.

## BACKGROUND
*(Rupprecht Bible History References Vol. 2, pp. 505-518)*

We have seen how God worked on a Christian Jew, Peter, to recognize the needs of the gentiles. The LORD had an even bigger job getting a non-Christian Jew, Saul, to see his own needs and God's love for him in Christ Jesus. Converting Saul was a special miracle of grace, and the apostle Paul said many times that if God saved him, God could save anyone. So saving Saul was one small step in God's larger program of saving souls--Jew and gentile--all over the world for centuries to come.

v.1,2
- Saul was a super-Jew, a premier champion of Pharisaism, which is the conscientious attempt to be "right with God" by the route of obedience to the commandments.
- This life-style attempts to prove to God that "I am a really good person" and God ought to reward me; it is, of course, in direct conflict with the Christ-centered approach: "God loves me, not because I'm a good person, but because He is such a wonderful Person to forgive me for what I am and what I do against Him."
- Saul had to learn this for himself before he could help others to learn it.
- Since Saul was actually convinced that Jesus was a false prophet, he volunteered for the privilege of persecuting His followers as far away as Damascus, 140 miles NE of Jerusalem.
- He was hoping to arrest and extradite such heretics back to Jerusalem, where they stood little chance of surviving the fate of Stephen--which, by the way, had been a pleasure for Saul to watch (ch.7:58-8:3).
- *"The Way"* is a term used to identify the Christian religion, which was not the way of the unbeliever, nor the way of the Jewish religion, but the Way of Jesus.

v.3-9
- Jesus stopped Saul and set him straight.
- Here Luke is reporting what Paul himself later told the Jerusalem mob (Acts 22) and again King Agrippa (Acts 26).
- We usually assert that Saul was converted on the highway by this confrontation with Jesus, but the text does not pinpoint the moment or hour or day when Saul's heart was won over to Jesus as his

Savior and LORD.

- ▸ It probably happened gradually during the three days of his anguish (blindness, nervous tension, isolation) after which Saul was given the Christian greeting "brother Saul," and received his sight and was baptized.

v. 3

- ▸ Jesus chose the time and place to arrest this "storm-trooper" in a reality check that would convince Saul that the Christians were correct, while he had been in the wrong.
- ▸ The intense, blinding light (ch.26:13) evidently hit so hard that he suffered a jarring fall from his horse.

v. 4

- ▸ There on the ground, disoriented and blinded, he knew that he was at the mercy of whoever was speaking.
- ▸ The voice from heaven called out his name in Hebrew with the soul-piercing question: "WHY ARE YOU PERSECUTING ME?"
- ▸ Indeed, WHY ME? What do you think you have to gain by this? What prompts such ungodly behavior against ME?

v. 5

- ▸ Because of the terrifying voice of the unidentified heavenly person, Saul knew that someone in heaven (Moses? Gabriel? Abraham?) was really angry with him.
- ▸ But to whom should he apologize? "Who are you, lord?"
- ▸ The answer: "I am Jesus of Nazareth, whom you are persecuting!" left Saul "trembling and astonished," because this meant that the Jesus he had rejected was not a false prophet at all, but was really reigning at the right hand of the Father in heaven!
- ▸ The awful truth now scalded Saul's heart that he had been duped by Satan to attack God Himself, and the horrifying dread possessed him that an angry God would exact a terrible payment from him for this sin.
- ▸ The statement "it is hard for you to kick against the goads" (just as an ox hurts himself if he kicks against a sharpened cattle-prod) reminded Saul that he had often heard the truth about Jesus from Christians, but had reacted angrily against the Spirit's prodding him to submit to the truth.

v. 6

- ▸ What penalty would be demanded from him?
- ▸ He had to find out.
- ▸ "Lord *(Master,* rather than *LORD Jehovah), what do you want me to do?*"--to make restitution for my vicious opposition to you and your people?
- ▸ We must say that this is not yet the response of a converted heart, for Saul still expected to appease God by his own personal payment.
- ▸ Jesus' answer "Arise and go into the city, and you will be told what you must do" still left him in the dark to wonder what an upset God was planning as a suitable "pay-back."

v. 7-8

- ▸ Everybody else in the group had also been knocked flat (ch.26:14), so Saul had to take charge to get them into Damascus, even as he remained blinded and helpless.
- ▸ They found lodging at Judas' house on Straight Street.

v. 9

▸ What the Spirit did for Saul during those three days and nights is not revealed to us.

▸ Yet it was prime time for God to work on Saul's heart.

▸ Saul would review the Scriptures he had in his memory banks, especially the prophecies of the Messiah and what he had heard about Jesus from His followers.

▸ He could not relax enough to eat--and perhaps slept but little--because he was totally absorbed in sifting through his guilt of disbelief, in recycling the meaning of the prophecies, and in rehearsing the Spirit's prodding.

v. 10

▸ God enlisted a mature Christian in His venture to reclaim Saul.

▸ Ananias' response "Here I am, Lord" came from a heart ready and willing to serve his Savior.

v.11-12

▸ Directions follow--the street and house address where he could find Saul, praying for the help God had available for him coming in the person of Ananias armed with God's love.

v.13-14

▸ It was natural that Ananias, under threat of persecution, would have reservations about approaching Saul, already notorious for his assaults on God's people.

v. 15-16

▸ Of course, Ananias did not know what God had already done to disarm Saul, so God briefly outlined His progress with Saul: (a) I have selected Saul as a chosen vessel of Mine; (b)I am authorizing him to represent Me wherever I send him, to Jew and gentile, the lowly and the regal; (c) and he will get rehabilitated under My chastisement.

v.17

▸ That evidently was enough to gain Ananias' support as a co-worker, so off he went, found Saul and gladly welcomed him into God's family as his brother in Jesus the Messiah.

▸ He continued with assurances that this meeting had been programmed in heaven by Jesus for the purpose of healing Saul's sight (both spiritual and physical) and giving him the Holy Spirit to fill the void left by his Pharisaism and then to empower Saul for God's service.

v.18

▸ The miracle followed, of course,--visible to Saul and to others.

▸ Baptism next--not to initiate faith, but to give Saul the assurance that his soul had been cleansed and to initiate him into the Christian fellowship with the saints of God.

v.19

▸ Breakfast next--with good Christian friends--and in a shared love that overcame emotional scars as they got to know one another better.

▸ Saul was on his way to becoming one of God's extra-special vessels (containers) that would pour out God's redeeming love to others. All glory to God in the highest!


## STUDENT PRAYER

Lord Jesus, I thank You for the love You showed me by making me one of Your dear children. Keep my soul free from Satan's grip until I will join You in our heavenly home. I ask this in Jesus' name. Amen.

## PRESENTATION

Tell the story in your own words with the same emotion and excitement as if you were there.

## ACTIVITY

- Color the picture on page 1. Carefully cut along the three dark lines. Fold along the one dashed line near the top of the flap you just made.
- At this point you may want the children to glue a second sheet of paper to the back of page one. This would make attaching the picture of Jesus somewhat easier.
- Color the picture of Jesus below. Cut it out. Glue this picture onto page one behind the flap that lifts up. Either glue it so that it is on the back of the flap that lifts up, or the picture could be glued to the backer sheet that you added. Whichever way you think looks best.
- Cut out the word box below. Glue it to the bottom of page one.
- Use you finished page one to tell the story of how Saul became a Christian.

## APPLICATIONS

1.     The subject of conversion is a natural with this Bible account, and Saul's dramatic case is recorded for a number of reasons. Primarily, it demonstrates that God is so filled with grace and love that He can salvage and rehabilitate the most perverse sinners, including blasphemers. Paul later referred to himself as an example of the way God's love reaches out to the "worst sinners."

2.     In addition, we may deduce some truths about conversion:   A) It is God's will and God's power that salvage a lost soul, turn it around, and then use the convert to help others. B) If a person begins to feel that he has made a contribution to his own conversion, he should review Paul's personal experience supported by the Spirit's testimony in Romans (esp. the close of ch.3, and ch.5:6-11) and the theme of God's grace promoted in every Pauline Epistle (see Eph.2:8-9). C) Current popular theology  that "you should accept Christ" or "make your decision for Christ" puts a dangerous *self-centered slant* on conversion; although this approach purports to be a gospel invitation,  it may also rob God of His glory.

3.     Few conversions are as dramatic as Saul's--simply because his case was so extreme that it required extreme measures to salvage him. So we refrain from using Saul's example as the paradigm of genuine conversions.

4.     Yet it has common denominators for adult conversions:  (a) the realization that one has been opposed to God's will and work in Jesus;   (b) soul-searching in the light of Scripture (which for Saul took three days), yielding repentance for having been God's enemy; and  (c)an application of assurance that God loves and forgives.

5.     God has a plan for each Christian's life;  a purpose for our existence on earth;  a calling, be it missionary, teacher, pastor, businessperson, homemaker, etc.;  His hand touches us at all stages of life-- teenager, parent, or grandparent--for God is always giving us openings to touch others as Ananias did to Saul, and as Saul did for others.

6.     Saul became the great Christian apostle and missionary Paul;  God also inspired him to write over a dozen of our New Testament books, filled with doctrine, instruction, explanations, etc., for upbuilding us even today. You can get better acquainted with this extraordinary person in a Bible dictionary or Rupprecht Bible History References, II, 506-507. We today are still receiving the blessed fall-out from what God did to him and for him.

7.     Jesus can overcome hatred and unbelief in any sinner's heart. God works this out in every conversion (also for infants), because a soul can be freed from Satan's grip only by a stronger hand--the hand of God's love. God pulled Saul dramatically free of Satan's grip, as this  record of Acts 9 shows us.

## PASSAGES

These passages can be assigned as memory work or simply discussed in class as to how they fit the lesson.

<u>Lower</u>
I Cor 6:11 - But you were washed, but you were sanctified, but you were justified in the name of the Lord Jesus and by the Spirit of our God.
I Cor. 15:10 - By the grace of God I am what I am, and His grace toward me was not in vain.

<u>Middle</u> any of the above and...
Gal. 1:15-16 - "...it pleased God, who separated me from my mother's womb and called me through His grace..."
Rom.10:4 - For Christ is the end of the law for righteousness to everyone that believes.
Eph. 1:3-5 - Blessed be the God and Father of our Lord Jesus Christ...as He chose us in Him before the foundation of the world...having predestined us to adoption as sons by Jesus Christ to Himself, according to the good pleasure of His will.

<u>Upper</u> any of the above and...
I Tim.1:15-16 - This is a faithful saying and worthy of all acceptance, that Christ Jesus came into the world to save sinners, of whom I am chief. However, for this reason I obtained mercy, that in <u>me first</u> Jesus Christ might show all longsuffering, as a pattern to those who are going to believe on Him for everlasting life.
Acts 26:18 - "...to open their eyes and to turn them from darkness to light, and from the power of Satan to God, that they may receive forgiveness of sins and an inheritance among those who are sanctified by faith in Me."
Phil. 3:7-8 - But what things were gain to me, these I have counted loss for Christ. But indeed I also count all things loss for the excellence of the knowledge of Christ Jesus my Lord, for whom I have suffered the loss of all things and count them as rubbish that I may gain Christ.

## HYMN CHOICES

"Chief of Sinners Though I be" (TLH #342)
"Grace! 'Tis a Charming Sound" (TLH #374)
"My God, Accept My Heart this Day" (TLH #336)

## STORY
Paul and the Jailer at Philippi - Acts 16:9-40

## TEACHER PRAYER
Lord Jesus, who came to Paul in a vision--to steer him to people whom he could help bring home to You--let my vision of You be strong and helpful to me so that I can carry You to others; and let me help bring them home to You also.  Thanks.  Amen.

## OUTER AIM
God used Paul to bring Jesus to a prison warden and then to his family.

## INNER AIM
God sends believers into the world with the Gospel message in order to rescue those lost in sin.

## BACKGROUND
*(Rupprecht Bible History References Vol.2, pp. 557-566)*
By now we have skipped over Paul's first missionary trip (chs. 13-14), the first convention of the Christian Church (ch.15), and part of the second missionary trip (15:36-16:30), which was a revisiting of congregations founded on the first trip.  The Spirit kept steering them down to Troas (Troy), where He sent Paul the vision of the Macedonian person pleading for Paul to sail over to Greece to preach the gospel of salvation to him and his countrymen.

v.9
- With this vision God guided Paul to Europe across the Adriatic to bring the Savior to gentiles there, and He did it with the plea: "Come over and help us!"
- We would no more turn our back on perishing souls than ignore a drowning person's frantic cries: "HELP! HELP!"
- *Macedonia* was a country north of ancient Greece, homeland of Alexander the Great, a northern portion  of the modern country of Greece. (cf. maps)

v. 10
- Paul never hesitated to obey Jesus, so with Luke, Silas, and Timothy, they got a coastal sailor going to Europe because someone there needed help.

v.12
- Philippi was the "county seat" of the eastern division of Macedonia, at that time a Roman colony;  so Paul's Roman citizenship would be an advantage in such a place.
- Foreign governments often restrict or revoke passports and visas; many heathen countries especially with Muslim heritage do not welcome Christians, whether as tourists or missionaries.

v.13
- The normal place to make contact would be the local Jewish synagogue; since there was none, they found a prayer group having Sabbath service at Riverside Park.
- As a rabbi in his own right, Paul got their attention and guided them into a conversation about the Messiah.
- We have no Synodical rule book for "How to start a mission." When we speak of our Savior with neighbors, at school, at work, at sports events--or invite people to share our church worship of Jesus, God's Son and Savior of sinners--we are doing what Jesus wants.

v.14

▸ Lydia, whose livelihood came from selling purple dye, worshiped the true God but had not yet heard that Jesus was the Messiah who had already finished the work of redemption.

▸ *"The Lord Jesus opened her heart to heed the things (gospel) spoken by Paul."*

▸ So simple sounding, but the greatest marvel in all God's creation that the inner sanctuary of the human soul is made to open at the message of God's surpassing love, is moved to contemplate this wondrous revelation and becomes convinced of its truth and integrity!

v. 15

▸ Because she had been brought to faith in Jesus' blood and righteousness, she received holy baptism for the assurance that her sins had been washed away, that she was adopted by God into His family, and that she was included in the fellowship of believers in Christ.

▸ Others in the household (whether children or servants we do not know) who were converted were also baptized, and thus a new Christian congregation was formed and already growing!

▸ It was a fruit of her faith and love for Jesus that she was eager to serve her new friends by offering free housing and meals.

▸ Serving the Lord is a two-way street for Christians; as we freely give, we receive freely from others. Jesus knew this from His own experience and encourages us to discover it also. "Give, and it will be given to you: good measure, pressed down, shaken together, and running over will be put into your bosom. For with the same measure that you use, it will be measured back to you." Luke 6:38

▸ What a contrast to the next event--God's way of getting Paul into contact with the warden of the local jail (perhaps the man of the vision).

v. 16-24

▸ The next step in God's plans was to get Paul into prison, for from that position he could unlock the warden from a worse prison, his fear of God's punishment for his sins.

▸ Paul certainly spoke from personal experience, "How unsearchable are His judgments and His ways past finding out!" (Rom.11:33) We discover that when one door is shut, another opens to a corridor we didn't notice, and thus to another door that awaits our hand. What you and I do today is part of a pattern that God is weaving for you and me and the salvation of others.

▸ So in order to get Paul into an advantageous position for serving the warden, God put this slave girl into Paul's path.

v.16

▸ She was a psychic, whose skill at fortune-telling (if it was a gift from God that she misused we do not know) was at the time under the control of a satanic spirit, a demon.

▸ People who don't allow God to direct their lives try to manipulate their own future, sometimes by use of psychics. Today's psychics have capitalized on television's power to spread their cult. Christians will beware of this Satan-sponsored attraction, rather relying on their loving Father in heaven to be in control of their future.

v.17

▸ When Paul and company came within range, God took temporary control of her demon so that it was forced to tell the truth: *"These men are the servants of the Most High God, who proclaim to us the way of salvation."*

▸ The name she used is one that the gentiles could grasp, even though the *LORD Jehovah* is a title more meaningful to Bible people.

▸ The Muslims have invented one-hundred-and-one names for their deity (Allah), some of which they have smuggled over from our Scriptures. What is the name you use for God when you pray--or when you speak of Him to others? We note that the demon did not preach the gospel message, just identified the messengers and the general purpose of their message. From this we deduce that Jesus does not authorize anyone but His disciples to serve souls with the gospel.  In other words, God does not enlist anyone but the Christian to represent Him with His saving Word.

v.18
▸ After a few days of observing her torment, Paul decided he should exorcize the spirit that was victimizing her, an action that would get him into trouble with her masters, but he knew he had to come to her aid.
▸ Thus the Lord Jesus with His superior power (Mark 3:27) got rid of the evil spirit so that her soul could respond to the Holy Spirit's influence.
▸ We gladly recognize that Jesus has control over the worst of demons, including Satan;  our lives and future are secure if we abide in Him.

v.19
▸ These businessmen had no heart for the girl, but only for their own profit.
▸ They saw Paul and Silas as either business competition or agents of a superior demon.

v.20
▸ Hoping to put a good face on their wickedness, they accused Paul of causing civil unrest.

v.21
▸ This was a misrepresentation, of course, for God's servants do not incite civil disobedience (Rom.13).
▸ The calling of Christian missionaries is spiritual, to deliver souls from Satan's dominion into God's kingdom of grace and salvation.
▸ In foreign countries controlled by Muslims, the government is protective of Mohammedanism but hostile to Christianity.  We must be "harmless as doves, but wise as serpents" in our efforts to reach such people.

v.22-23
▸ Soon the mob coerced the magistrates to come down hard on the "foreigners."
▸ Romans were brutal in dealing with Jews, so our innocent missionaries were whipped with (bamboo?) canes, probably until they collapsed.
▸ Thus deprived of his legal rights, Paul the Roman citizen was unjustly arrested, condemned, punished, and imprisoned.
▸ Paul might wonder how all this could serve to help the man in the vision who had begged them to come to his aid.

v. 24
▸ Handled like the most dangerous criminals, they were dumped into a cell block with the tightest security; in addition, they were immobilized in stocks designed for restraint and torture.

v.25
▸ Despite their pain they considered the whole ordeal in the light of God's love for them and for the other prisoners, so the disciples loudly rejoiced in being on God's side and at His disposal.  "No such sounds had ever before been heard in that prison."

v.26
▸ At midnight God gave a little shove to the foundations under the prison, the walls shifted enough to dislocate doors, and the chains that fastened every prisoner were pulled apart.
▸ Thus God created a way for the warden's heart to be opened and delivered from the chains of Satan.

v.27
▸ The earthquake jolted the warden awake, and seeing that the lock-up system was ruined, the deduction hit him that the prisoners were gone.
▸ By Roman standards he was responsible, so he was ready to take his own life as self-punishment, the "honorable and heroic" thing to do.

v.28
▸ His suicide attempt was seen and stopped by Paul with a loud shout, for Paul was hoping to intervene in the man's soul-life and bring him to the Savior for eternal life.
▸ Comment here on the horror of suicide--the sin from which you can never return to God, the sin from which you can never return to the love of other humans; the self-murder from which there is no opportunity to repent.

v.29
▸ The warden welcomed the reprieve, and when he discovered Paul had something to do with everybody being still safe in jail, he realized that somehow Paul was in control of what had just happened.
▸ Impressed by Paul's concern for his well-being, he *"fell down trembling before Paul and Silas."*
▸ God had done everything necessary to prepare his heart for this moment when he could throw himself on the mercy of a man who obviously had some close connections with the Almighty.

v.30
▸ His question, *"What must I do to be saved?"* was not a concern for his mortal body--for the prisoners were all in custody--rather, he was concerned for his immortal soul, and so...

v.31
▸ Paul directed him to Jesus the Messiah for the salvation of his soul; *"Believe on the Lord Jesus Christ."*
▸ Paul's doctrinal position on the principles of salvation was always the same: a) by grace alone, without human meriting; b) by faith in Jesus alone, without adding human good deeds; c) at Luther's time the third plank had to be nailed down also: by Scripture alone, without human additives or subtractions.

v.32
▸ Paul also perceived that the warden held his family dear, and so assured the whole household that God loved them one and all and had secured their eternal salvation as well.

v.33
▸ When there was a lull, the warden fed and gave home-care medical aid to his new-found spiritual brothers.
▸ Baptism naturally followed, as Paul wanted them to have the blessed assurance that their sins were indeed washed clean, and that as gentiles they were welcomed into the Christian fellowship.
▸ This membership matter did not have to be cleared with the "front office" in Jerusalem, for <u>God</u> had already cleared them <u>one-hundred percent.</u>

v.35-40
▸ This aftermath deserves some attention: we see that Paul took legal advantage of his Roman citizenship to put the city officials on the defensive for having robbed him of his rights.
▸ Out of concern for the Christians he would leave behind, Paul wanted the magistrates to realize that he could return at any time and make a federal case against them if he so chose.
▸ Unintimidated, our Christian friends revisited Lydia and all the other Christians of the city, encouraging them with the assurance that (also by softening the hostility of the magistrates) the Lord Jesus would support them and bless them, and they could get on with their new lives in His service. Hallelujah!

## APPLICATIONS

1.  We should be ready and willing to answer the plea for help from those calling out from the darkness of unbelief just as Paul answered the plea, "Come and help us!"

2.  We have no Synodical rule book for "How to start a mission." When we speak of our Savior with neighbors, at school, at work, at sports events--or invite people to share our church worship of Jesus, God's Son and Savior of sinners--we are doing what Jesus wants.

3.  Because Lydia had been brought to faith in Jesus' blood and righteousness, she received holy baptism for the assurance that her sins had been washed away, that she was adopted by God into His family, and that she was included in the fellowship of believers in Christ. Others in the household (whether children or servants we do not know) who were converted were also baptized, and thus a new Christian congregation was formed and already growing.

4.  Serving the Lord is a two-way street for Christians; as we freely give, we receive freely from others. Jesus knew this from His own experience and encourages us to discover it also. "Give, and it will be given to you: good measure, pressed down, shaken together, and running over will be put into your bosom. For with the same measure that you use, it will be measured back to you." Luke 6:38

5.  People who don't allow God to direct their lives try to manipulate their own future, sometimes by use of psychics. Today's psychics have capitalized on television's power to spread their cult. Christians will beware of this Satan-sponsored attraction, rather relying on their loving Father in heaven to be in control of their future.

6.  By Roman standards the jailer was responsible for the prisoners and thus for their suspected escape, so he was ready to take his own life as self-punishment, the "honorable and heroic" thing to do. His suicide attempt was seen and stopped by Paul with a loud shout, for Paul was hoping to intervene in the man's soul-life and bring him to the Savior for eternal life. Comment here on the horror of suicide--the sin from which you can never return to God, the sin from which you can never return to the love of other humans; the self-murder from which there is no opportunity to repent.

## STUDENT PRAYER

Lord Jesus, here I am again, this time to tell You thanks for being my Savior. Besides, I need You to fill me up so full with love for You and with concern for other people that I will speak as You wish, and do as You desire. Thanks in advance for this blessing. Amen.

## PRESENTATION

Tell the story with the same emotion and excitement as if you were there. Tell the story in your words, but be faithful to the account that God recorded in Acts.

## PASSAGES

These passages can be assigned as memory work or simply discussed in class as to how they fit the lesson.

<u>Lower</u>

Mt.28:18 - All authority has been given to Me in heaven and on earth. Go therefore and make disciples of all nations, baptizing them in the name of the Father and of the Son and of the Holy Spirit.

Mt. 5:11 - Blessed are you when they revile and persecute you and say all kinds of evil against you falsely for My sake.

<u>Middle</u> any of the above and...

I Jn.2:2 - And he Himself is the propitiation for our sins, and not for ours only but also for the whole world.

Gal.6:6 - Let him who is taught the word share in all good things with him who teaches.

Rom. 2:15a: - Who show the work of the law written in their hearts, their conscience also bearing witness.

<u>Upper</u> any of the above and...

Rom.5:3 - We also glory in tribulations, knowing that tribulation produces perseverance.

I Pet.4:14 - If you are reproached for the name of Christ, blessed are you, for the Spirit of glory and of God rests upon you.

Rom.3:19-20 - Now we know that whatever the law says, it says to those who are under the law, that every mouth may be stopped, and all the world may become guilty before God. Therefore by the deeds of the law no flesh will be justified in His sight, for by the law is the knowledge of sin.

## HYMN CHOICES

"Lord Jesus Christ, Be Present Now" TLH #3
"Lord, Open Thou My Heart to Hear" TLH #5
"On My Heart Imprint Thine Image" TLH #179

Things Needed: a sheet of cardboard (70x45 cm), half-finished crafts of the scenery, scissors, glue, colors, wide Scotch transparent tape, 2 threads 50 cm each, thick needle.

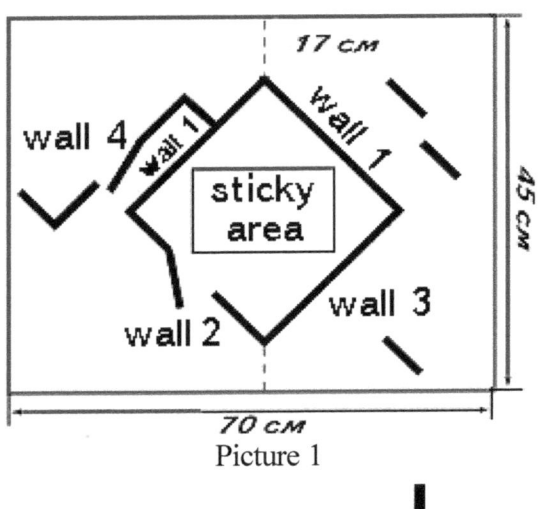

Picture 1

1. Glue fragments of the scenery and figures of people on cardboard, color them and cut them out. Cut out the door in wall 2 and bend this door so that it would open outside.

2. Redraw scheme from Picture 1 to the sheet of cardboard (70x45 cm) which will be the base for the craft.

3. Bend wall 1 in its middle and glue the trees and the bush together;

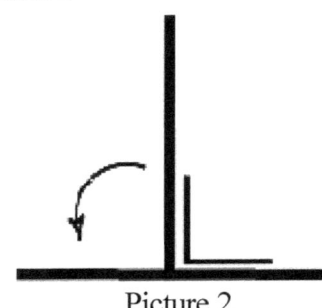

Picture 2

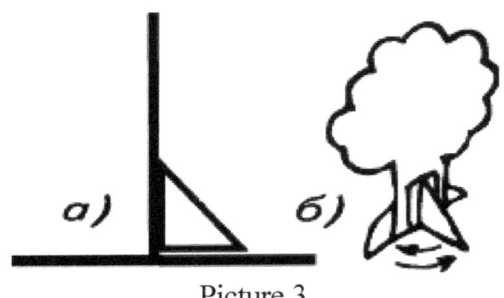

Picture 3

4. **"Falling" walls 2 and 3** glue to the inner side of the prison by wide Scotch transparent tape so that they could easily fall outside (Picture 2). Fortify the trees and the bush with triangles so that they don't fall (see Pictures 3 a,b). You can also add one more supplementary wall.

5. Color the base of the craft. Use some Scotch tape to make a sticky area inside of the prison.

6. Make holes in walls 1, 2, and 3 with a thick needle (see Picture 4). Take 2 needles (preferably of the same color of the walls), make knots at the end of each needle, run the other ends through the holes in the walls (Picture 4). Fasten all the ends of the needles with a clip so that the walls stand firm.

When you are telling about Paul and Silus being arrested open door of the prison, bring the apostles inside, put them on a ky area and tightly close the door. Telling about the earth- ake, start shaking the craft, insensibly take the clip off and pull knotted ends of the needles. The walls will fall down, and you see the apostles standing in the middle of the prison.

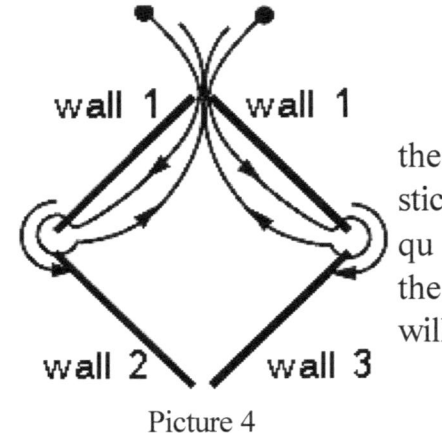

the
stic
qu
the
will

Picture 4

You can keep the craft folded.

*Jailer of Philippi - Lesson 53*

*198*

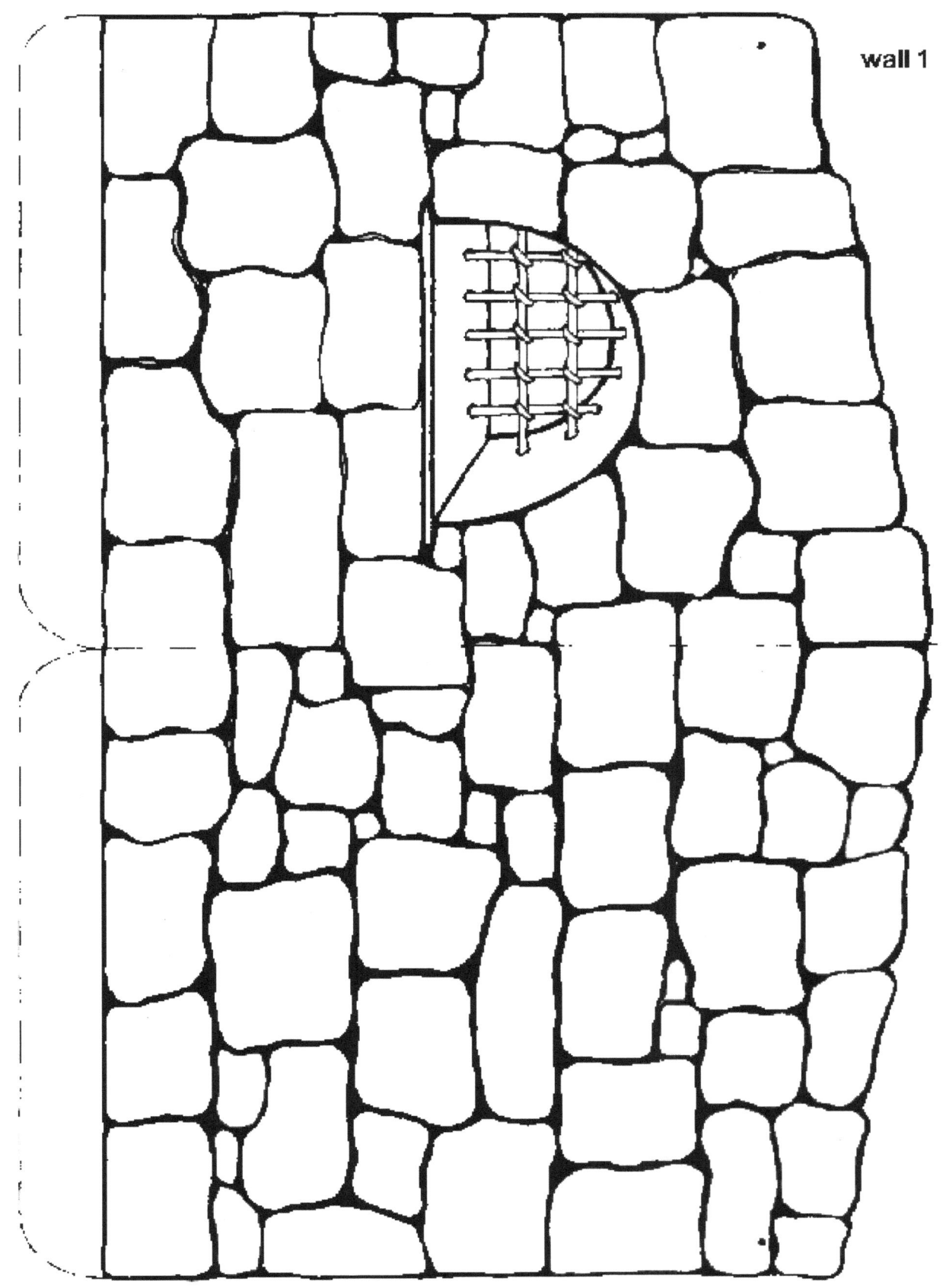

http://www.emmanuel.kiev.ua/Kids/shem_p2gE.html

**wall 2**

http://www.emmanuel.kiev.ua/Kids/shem_p2gE.html

**wall 3**

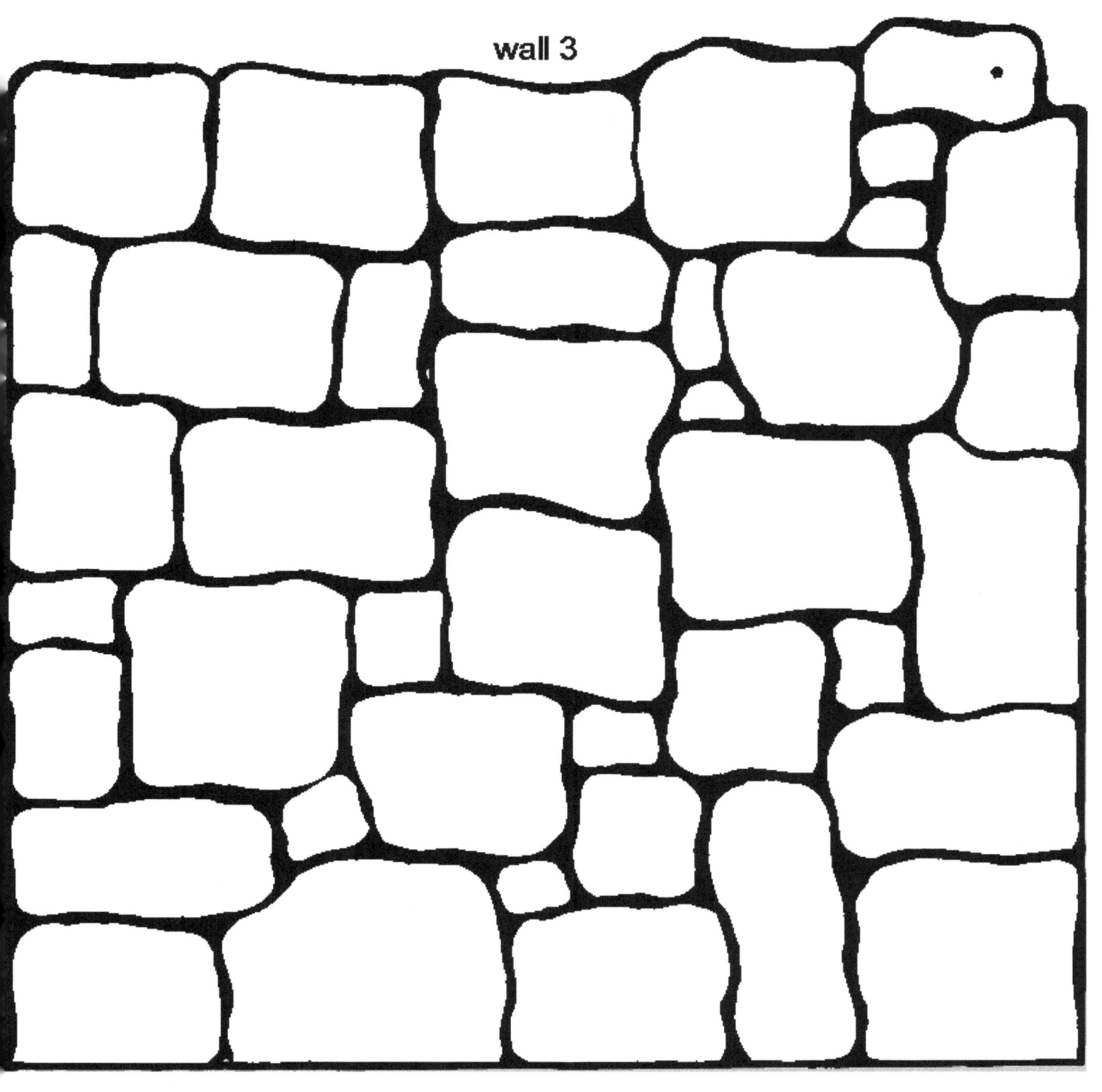

*Jailer of Philippi - Lesson 53*

*Jailer of Philippi - Lesson 53*

http://www.emmanuel.kiev.ua/Kids/shem_p2gE.html

## 54

**STORY**

Paul's First Missionary Journey - Acts 13-14)

**TEACHER PRAYER**

O dearest Jesus, You have called me to "feed Your lambs." As I study Your saving Word and prepare my lesson, enable me to lead the children to You, their Lord and Savior. Help me to share the good news of salvation with them and instill in them a fervent zeal for Your Word and a sincere desire to share it with others. "Your Word is Truth." Amen.

**VOCABULARY**

*synagogue* - a church or place of worship

*sorcerer* - a false prophet who tries to predict the future

*proconsul* - the Roman governor

*proselytes* - converts to the Jewish faith

**OUTER AIM**

The Lord called Paul and Barnabas to preach the Gospel in far-off lands.

**INNER AIM**

The Lord blesses the preaching of the Gospel with fruits.

**BACKGROUND** Rupprecht *Bible History References, Vol. 2,* pp. 539-555.

Paul the apostle, by God's grace, became one of the greatest missionaries of all time. He was once known as Saul, the great persecutor of the church. After his conversion on the road to Damascus, Saul became known as Paul, one of the great missionaries of the church. A Jew by birth, he was called by God to spread the Gospel of Christ to Jew and Gentile alike. He is known to us as the "apostle to the Gentiles." In this lesson, we follow him on his 1st great missionary journey.

Acts 13:1-12  Paul and Barnabas on Cyprus

vs. 1-3  A growing, thriving early Christian congregation was located in Antioch in Syria. Led by the Holy Spirit, this congregation called and sent Saul (Paul) and Barnabas to do foreign mission work. It was at Antioch that Jesus' followers were first called Christians. This church at Antioch had five great prophets and teachers in its midst. The Lord chose Paul and Barnabas to help spread the Gospel to lands and people far away.

vs. 4-12  The island of Cyprus was the first place they went. Cyprus was Barnabas' home. He had originated from there. John Mark accompanied them on their journey. They preached in the synagogue of the Jews. While on Cyprus, a man named Sergius Paulus, the Roman governor of the island, was brought to faith. A Jewish false prophet and sorcerer, named Bar-jesus, or Elymas, was struck with blindness by Paul. The Lord used this miracle together with Paul's testimony to convert the Roman governor.

Acts 13:13-52  Paul and Barnabas in Pisidia

Paul and Barnabas left the island of Cyprus and headed to Asia Minor (present-day Turkey). John Mark left them and returned to Jerusalem. Perhaps he was unwilling to go to the Gentiles with the Gospel at this time. Their first stop was Perga in Pamphylia, then they headed for Antioch in Pisidia.

v. 14  Their first stop was the synagogue of the Jews.

vs. 15-41  The rulers of the synagogue invited Paul and Barnabas to speak.  They stood up and proclaimed Christ Jesus as Savior and Lord.  Paul preached, outlining Israel's long history, God's abundant grace, and His precious promises.  Paul's sermon began with Abraham and touched on such things as Israel's enslavement in Egypt and deliverance, the 40 years in the wilderness, the occupation of Canaan, the period of the judges, kings, and prophets . . .down to the days of John the Baptist and Jesus.  He spoke at length concerning Jesus' bitter sufferings and death and glorious resurrection.  He urged all to repent of their sins and to believe on Jesus as their Lord and Savior.

Some of the Jews were hesitant to believe, but the Gentiles wanted to hear more.  The Jews opposed Paul and Barnabas and their testimony.  Paul and Barnabas announced that they would bring the Gospel to the Gentiles.  The Word of the Lord spread.  Paul and Barnabas were persecuted and moved on to Iconium.

Acts 14:1-7  Paul and Barnabas in Iconium
v. 1  They first spoke at the local synagogue.  Many Jews and Gentiles believed.

v. 2-3  Unbelieving Jews stirred up opposition.  Paul and Barnabas continued preaching and teaching and doing
     miracles there for some time.

v. 4-7  More opposition and persecution came from some Jews and Gentiles.  Paul and Barnabas fled to Lystra and
     Derbe and the surrounding countryside.

Acts 14:8-20  Paul and Barnabas at Lystra
Paul healed a crippled man.  The heathen in that city viewed Paul and Barnabas as gods and prepared to worship them.  Paul proclaimed the true God.  More persecutions arose.  Paul was stoned but miraculously survived.  He and Barnabas departed.

Acts 14:21-28  Paul and Barnabas at Derbe
They preached at Derbe also.  Many believed.  They then retraced their steps and returned to Lystra, Iconium, and Antioch.  They sought to strengthen and confirm the brethren in their faith.  They also labored in other cities and towns along the way, finally coming to Perga.  Then they returned to Antioch in Syria to give a full report to the church.  The door of faith had been opened to the Gentiles.  Their missionary trip had been a great success.  The Lord was building His church.

## STUDENT PRAYER

Dearest Lord Jesus, Your precious gospel is "the power of God unto salvation to everyone that believes."  Therefore, richly bless the preaching of the Gospel far and wide.  "Add to the Church daily such as should be saved."  Help us love Your Word more and more.  Move us to pray for our missionaries and their work.  Move us all to do what we can to "preach the Gospel to every creature and thereby make disciples of all nations."  In Your saving name we pray.  Amen.

## PRESENTATION

The Lord's great Commission is very clear. . ."make disciples of all nations". . ."preach the Gospel to every creature."  Jesus was not only "the Glory of His people Israel, He was a Light to lighten the Gentiles."  In this lesson we see just how true this was.  Paul and Barnabas reached out to Jew and Gentile alike.  Wherever they went, they first sought out the Jews.  Then they reached out also to the Gentiles.

As you present this lesson to your children, a map outlining where Paul and Barnabas went would be very helpful and meaningful. The map would help them pinpoint the places mentioned in this lesson.

As the lesson proceeds, remind your students that the Lord was guiding Paul and Barnabas, and also blessing their efforts.

Note also that the preaching of the Gospel invited opposition from Jews and Gentiles alike. The Lord was with His servants. . .blessing and keeping them.

## APPLICATION

The Lord calls His people to preach the Gospel. He also sends them to the places He Himself has chosen. He opens certain doors; He closes others. "The Lord adds daily to the church such as should be saved."

The Lord called Paul and Barnabas to preach the Gospel at Antioch. He has called each of us into His service as well.

We are called to peach the Gospel. "The Lord will give the increase."

Whenever and wherever the Gospel is proclaimed, opposition is certain to arise. It can be expected. Our Lord has said, "If they have persecuted Me, they will also persecute you."

The Lord will bless and keep His people today, as He did Paul and Barnabas long ago.

## PASSAGES
**These passages can be assigned as memory work or simply discussed in class as to how they fit the lesson.**

Beginners
Mark 16:15 - "Go into all the world and preach the Gospel to every creature."

Romans 10:13 - "For whoever calls on the name of the Lord shall be saved."

Middle
Matthew 28:18-20 - "All authority has been given to Me in heaven and on earth. Go therefore and make disciples of all nations, baptizing them in the name of the Father and of the Son and of the Holy Spirit, teaching them to observe all things that I have commanded you; and lo, I am with you always,"

Romans 8:14 - "For as many as are led by the Spirit of God, these are sons of God."

I Cor. 12:3b - "No one can say that Jesus is Lord except by the Holy Spirit."

Upper
Isaiah 55:11 - "So shall My Word be that goes forth from My mouth; it shall not return to Me void, but it shall accomplish what I please, and it shall prosper in the thing for which I sent it."

I Tim. 2:4 - "God our Savior desires all men to be saved and to come to the knowledge of the truth."

II Pet. 3:9 - "The Lord is not slack concerning His promise . . . but is longsuffering toward us, not willing that any should perish, but that all should come to repentance."

**HYMN CHOICES**
From Greenland's Icy Mountains - TLH #495
Hark! the Voice of Jesus Crying - TLH #496

## 55

## STORY
Paul's Second Missionary Journey - Acts 15:36-18:22)

## TEACHER PRAYER
O dearest Jesus, You have given me the privilege of teaching Your little lambs.  Bless my studies and efforts to share Your Word with them and thereby strengthen their faith in You.  Enable them, too, to share Your Word with others.  Awaken in them a sincere desire to support the preaching of the Gospel far and wide with prayers and offerings.  Amen.

## VOCABULARY
*contention* - a verbal strife, argument, controversy, dispute
*commended* - committed
*foremost* - first
*purple* - purple dye
*spirit of divination* - able to foretell the future and/or do fortune telling
*fair-minded* - noble

## OUTER AIM
The Lord sent Paul and Silas to revisit old churches and open new ones.

## INNER AIM
The Lord uses believers to fulfill the truth that "The Lord gives the increase."

## BACKGROUND   Rupprecht *Bible History References*, *Vol. 2,* pp. 556-573
After their first missionary journey, Paul and Barnabas gave a lengthy report to the brethren in Antioch, Syria.  The early church there had sent them on their journey, called by the Holy Spirit.  Their journey had been very successful and rewarding.  Many doors had been opened.  About a year later, Paul and Barnabas were sent to Jerusalem to consult with the apostles and other brethren over a question that had arisen in Antioch regarding the Old Testament ceremonial law.  The meeting went well.  There was agreement.  About a year later, the Antioch church again sent Paul on a missionary journey which would last three years.

Acts 15:36-41
Paul and Barnabas made plans and preparations to visit the brethren to whom they had preached on their first journey.  Barnabas hoped to take along John, called Mark; but Paul said no.  Barnabas and John therefore went off to Cyprus alone.  Paul chose a man named Silas to accompany him.  They journeyed through Syria and Cilicia, strengthening the churches.

Acts 16:1-11
Paul and Silas stopped at Derbe and Lystra.  They asked a disciple named Timothy to join them on their journey.  "The churches were strengthened in the faith and increased in number daily."  v.5  They then passed through Phrygia and Galatia.  The Holy Spirit prevented them from preaching in the Roman provinces of Asia and Bithynia.  In a vision, the Lord called them to pass over into Europe.

Acts 16:12-40  Paul and Silas in Philippi

This section records their contact with Lydia, the seller of purple, and her conversion. Later Paul and Silas were arrested after casting out an evil spirit. They landed in prison. The Lord subsequently brought the jailer of Philippi and his household to faith.

Acts 17:1-9  Paul and Silas and Timothy at Thessalonica

Acts 17:10-14  Paul and Silas and Timothy at Berea

Acts 17:15-34  Paul in Athens

The idols and idolatry moved Paul to preach to the philosophers of the day. His sermon is recorded for us. Only a few of the hearers believed. They mocked at the resurrection of the dead.

Acts 18:1-17  Paul and his coworkers at Corinth

Here Paul met Aquila and Priscilla. The Lord encouraged him to continue there for some time--over 1 and a half years.

Acts 18:18-22  The journey continued with a stop in Ephesus.

Paul hurried on to Jerusalem to observe the Passover feast. While in Jerusalem he greeted the church. From there he went to Antioch in Syria and reported on his second missionary journey.

## STUDENT PRAYER

O dearest Jesus, the great Shepherd of the Sheep, bless the preaching of the Gospel, both near and far. Be with all our missionaries, pastors, and teachers wherever they labor. Bless their efforts according to Your good and gracious will. Increase our faith. Move us to pray, "Thy Kingdom come." Enable us to do all that we can to help bring Your saving Gospel to lost, dying sinners. Amen.

## PRESENTATION

This lesson follows the last. Again a map of the areas where Paul traveled would be most helpful to teacher and students alike. Following Paul and his companions as they journeyed helps make the account live. Within this bigger lesson there can be found more than one familiar Bible story from Paul's second missionary journey.(cf. The jailer of Philippi)

## APPLICATION

Paul was "the apostle to the Gentiles." His missionary activities remind us that "the Lord is not willing that any should perish, but that all should come to repentance. God our Savior will have all men to be saved and come to the knowledge of the truth." Paul's example and zeal to reach out to the heathen should serve as an inspiration also to us. This is one reason why the Holy Spirit inspired Luke to record the second missionary journey of Paul for us in the Scriptures.

In this story we again see how the Lord is in control. He calls, sends, guides, leads, and blesses. His Word and Spirit are what bring forth fruit.

The fact that Paul and Silas revisited places where they had labored earlier demonstrates the importance of "continuing in the Word" and confirming one another in the faith.

The Lord definitely was with Paul and Silas and those with them. He will also be with us. He has promised: "All authority is given unto Me. . .lo, I am with you always, even unto the end of the age." Mark 28:20

## Levels 1 & 2 - Activity Three Directions

1.  Cut out the patterns and glue them on cardboard; color them and bend them as shown on Picture 1. Make openings where indicated. Bend parts of the cross marked with the dotted lines 90 degrees to the back.

2.  Put the ready craft into an envelope and write on the envelope: "Salvation is found in no one else, for there is no other name under heaven given to men by which we must be saved." Acts 4:12

3.  This craft activity can help you explain your story for today.

**Picture 1**
**God and Man were together.**

**Picture 2**
**Sin separated man from God.**

**Picture 3**
**The sacrifice of Jesus restored the relationship between man and God.**

http://www.emmanuel.kiev.ua/Kids/shem_p2eE.html

**PASSAGES**

**These passages can be assigned as memory work or simply discussed in class as to how they fit the lesson.**

Beginners

Matt. 28:18 - "All authority has been given to Me in heaven and on earth."

2 Tim. 2:19 - "The Lord knows those who are His."

Middle

Matt 18:20 - "For where two or three are gathered together in My name, I am there in the midst of them."

Mark 16:16 - "He who believes and is baptized will be saved; but he who does not believe will be condemned."

John 8:31-32 - "If you abide in My Word, you are My disciples indeed. And you shall know the truth, and the truth shall make you free."

Upper

John 10:16 - "And other sheep I have which are not of this fold; them also I must bring, and they will hear My voice; and there shall be one flock and one shepherd."

John 10:27-28 - "My sheep hear My voice, and I know them and they follow Me. And I give them eternal life, and they shall never perish; neither shall anyone snatch them out of My hand."

2 Tim. 4:18 - "And the Lord will deliver me from every evil work and preserve me for His heavenly Kingdom."

## HYMN CHOICES

Rise, Thou Light of Gentile Nations - TLH #498

O'er the Gloomy Hills of Darkness - TLH #505

Spread, Oh, Spread, Thou Mighty Word - TLH #507

## 56

## STORY

Paul's Third Missionary Journey - Acts 18:23 - 21:14)

## TEACHER PRAYER

Lord God, heavenly Father, "Your Word is a Lamp unto my feet and a Light unto my path." Through Your precious, saving Word strengthen my faith and lead me into all truth. Bless my study and help me to teach Your lambs. Strengthen their faith as well. Bless the teaching of Your Word wherever it is proclaimed, and let Your Kingdom come. In Jesus' Name. Amen.

## VOCABULARY

*itinerant* - traveling from place to place or on a circuit; a person who so travels
*exorcist* - one who casts out demons

## OUTER AIM

Paul's third great missionary journey

## INNER AIM

The Word of God is proclaimed; the Church grows

## BACKGROUND *(Rupprecht, Bible History References, vol. 2, pp. 524-586)*

Acts 18:23-28 Paul left Antioch after some time to revisit the brethren in Asia Minor. He traveled through the provinces of Galatia and Phrygia, "strengthening the disciples." A man named Apollos came to Ephesus. He was an eloquent speaker and well-versed in the Scriptures. Aquilla and Priscilla instructed him more thoroughly. Paul went on to teach in Achaia. *Note:* This third missionary journey of Paul lasted about four years. Three of those years were spent in Ephesus, one of the largest cities of Asia Minor.

Acts 19:1-20 Paul at Ephesus. About 12 disciples were further instructed by Paul. They together with Paul taught in the Jewish synagogues for three months. Then Paul moved to the school of Tyrannus, where he and the disciples taught for two years. Everyone in Asia heard the Word of the Lord. Paul also performed many wonderful miracles.

Acts 19:21-41 Paul labored in Macedonia and Achaia. He planned to go to Jerusalem and then later on to Rome. While still in Ephesus, there was an uproar led by a man named Demetrius, the silversmith.

Acts 20:1-6 Paul again went into Macedonia, then on to Greece. There he labored three months. When the Jews again plotted against him, he headed for Syria. He returned through Macedonia.

Acts 20:7-12 Paul spent seven days in Troas. There Paul raised from the dead the man who had fallen asleep during his late night service and had fallen down from the upper loft.

Acts 20:13-21 - 21:14 Paul is heading for Jerusalem and the feast of Pentecost. He goes by ship. He is in a hurry. He makes various stops along the way. He stops at Miletus and calls for the elders of the church in Ephesus to meet him. He gives them his farewell. He goes on to Jerusalem. He's warned about what awaits him there. He's determined to go anyway.

## STUDENT PRAYER   TLH #507 1 and 6

Spread, oh, spread thou mighty Word,
Spread the kingdom of the Lord,
Wheresoe'er His breath has given
Life to beings meant for heaven.

Lord of Harvest, let there be
Joy and strength to work for Thee
Till the nations far and near
See Thy light and learn Thy fear.  Amen.

## PRESENTATION

A map showing places mentioned in this lesson would again be helpful.  This enables the students to better visualize where Paul and his companions sojourned.

## APPLICATION

Paul the apostle was both pastor and missionary.  He reached out to the unchurched and ministered to the churched. He returned and revisited the churches and brethren seen on earlier missionary journeys.  He also sent pastoral letters to them.  He practiced what he preached.  In his epistles, he stressed the importance of
'continuing in the things once learned' and 'confirming one another in the faith.'  The same is still true today.

In this lesson we continue to see how "the Lord added daily to the church such as should be saved."

The missionary activity of Paul vividly demonstrates the Lord's promise; "So shall My Word be that goes forth from My mouth; it shall not return to Me void, but it shall accomplish what I please, and it shall prosper in the thing for which I sent it."  Is. 55:11

## PASSAGES
**These passages can be assigned as memory work or simply discussed in class as to how they fit the lesson.**

Lower
Mark 16:15 - "Go into all the world and preach the Gospel to every creature."

Rom. 10:13 - "For whoever calls on the name of the Lord shall be saved."

Middle
Prov. 3:5 - "Trust in the Lord with all your heart, and lean not on your own understanding."

Prov. 3:6 - "In all your ways acknowledge Him, and He shall direct your paths."

Upper
Is. 55:11 - "So shall My Word be that goes forth from My mouth; it shall not return to Me void, but it shall accomplish what I please, and it shall prosper in the thing for which I sent it."

Matt. 9:37-38 - "The harvest truly is plentiful, but the laborers are few.  Therefore pray the Lord of harvest to send out laborers into His harvest."

John 15:16 - "You did not choose Me, but I chose you and appointed you that you should go and bear fruit, and that your fruit should remain, that whatever you ask the Father in My name He may give it to you."

## HYMN CHOICES

Saints of God, the Dawn is Brightening - TLH #502
Send Thou, O Lord, to Every Place - TLH #506
Thou Whose Almighty Word - TLH #508

## 57

## STORY
Paul the Prisoner - Acts 21:15 - 26:32

## TEACHER PRAYER
O Lord, Your Almighty Word is very important. Its holy law shows us our many, many sins. Its glorious gospel shows us our dear Savior. Help me to proclaim the whole counsel of God in my classes, "rightly dividing the Word of Truth." Enable my students to treasure Your Word and remain faithful to it all their days. In Jesus' name. Amen.

## VOCABULARY
*mean* - insignificant, small
*thongs* - a narrow strip of leather, used as a lace or strap
*courtesy* - politeness, graciousness

## OUTER AIM
Paul suffered much for the sake of the gospel.

## INNER AIM
The Lord used Paul to advance His Kingdom

## BACKGROUND *(Rupprecht, Bible History References, Vol. 2, pp. 586-598)*
Shortly after his conversion on the road to Damascus, Paul heard that he would suffer many things for the sake of the Gospel and Jesus, his Savior and Lord. In his epistle he describes them. (II Cor. 11:23-27) He often alluded to them in his writings. This story records a series of imprisonments beginning at Jerusalem and extending to Rome.

Acts 21:15-26 As Paul headed to Jerusalem, various disciples warned him not to go there. They spoke of great dangers awaiting him. They even pleaded with him not to go there. (cf. previous verses) Paul knew what lay ahead. He was determined to go and was ready to suffer, if the Lord so willed. Paul met with the apostles and leaders at Jerusalem. He told them of his journeys, and they rejoiced.

Acts 21:27-40 Only a few days later, Paul was arrested in Jerusalem. Jews from Asia Minor stirred up the crowd against Paul and accused him of many things. A tumult followed. Paul was rescued by the Romans. He requested to defend himself and to speak to the people. Permission was granted.

Acts 22:1-30
Paul explained at some length who he was, what he had done, and what he was now doing. He reviewed for them what his life had been before his conversion. He also conveyed to them what happened to him on the day of his conversion and what had been doing since that day. When they heard about the gentiles being a part of his ministry, the Jews could listen no longer. They would have killed him, but the Romans whisked him away. The Romans would have scourged and interrogated him; but when they learned that he had Roman citizenship, they were afraid. They couldn't understand why the Jews hated him so. They hoped to find out.

Acts 23

Paul was placed on trial before the chief priests and the Jewish high council (the Sanhedrin). Paul explained to all present why he was on trial. Since some believed in the resurrection (Pharisees) and some did not (Sadducees), the Council was divided. A great dissension and tumult followed. The Roman commander again rescued Paul from his enemies. The Lord reassured Paul that He was with him and would help him. (v. 11) There was a conspiracy among the Jews to kill Paul. It was revealed to the Roman commander. Paul was kept safe until he could be escorted safely to Caesarea and the Roman governor.

Acts 24:1-27

vs. 1-9  Paul is charged by his accusers from Jerusalem.
Vs. 10-27  Paul is permitted to defend himself before the Roman governor concerning the charges levied against him. Felix was moved by Paul's testimony. (His wife was Jewish.) He postponed a decision concerning Paul until a more convenient time. (v. 25) He hoped to let Paul go free and was hoping for a bribe from Paul's friends. Paul remained a prisoner in Caesarea for two years.

Acts 25:1-12

Festus replaced Felix as governor of Judea. Again there was a plot against Paul at Jerusalem. Festus kept Paul safe in Caesarea. Paul's accusers again came to Caesarea. Many charges were levied against him, but none could be proven. Paul was permitted to defend himself. Festus encouraged Paul to go back to Jerusalem to be tried in the Jewish court. Paul appealed to Caesar to have his case heard.

Acts 25:13-27  Paul's Defense Before King Agrippa

Festus knew Paul had done nothing worthy of death. He told King Agrippa about the case. The king wanted to hear Paul for himself.

Acts 26 - King Agrippa permitted Paul to speak for himself in his own defense. Paul recounted his pre-conversion life and post-conversion life. He used the opportunity to proclaim Christ. Festus thought Paul was mad, out of his mind. King Agrippa was deeply moved and confessed that he was almost persuaded to become a Christian. All those present realized that Paul was innocent of all the charges levied against him and could have been released. Since he appealed to Caesar, he would be sent to Rome.

**STUDENTS' PRAYER**  TLH #498: 1, 5
Rise, Thou Light of Gentile nations, Jesus, bright and Morning Star;
Let Thy Word, the gladsome tidings, Ring out loudly near and far,
Bringing freedom to the captives, Peace and comfort to the slave,
That the heathen, free from bondage, May proclaim Thy power to save.

May our zeal to help the heathen Be increased from day to day
As we plead in true compassion And for their conversion pray.
For the many faithful heralds,  For the Gospel they proclaim,
Let us all be cheerful givers To the glory of Thy name. Amen.

## PRESENTATION

There is more than one Bible story within this lesson. It covers both Paul's imprisonment in Jerusalem and in Caesarea. A number of individuals appear in this lesson, people to whom Paul proclaimed Christ. A listing of these individuals and their titles, together with a map of the places mentioned, might be helpful.

## APPLICATION

The Lord predicted concerning Paul: "He is a chosen vessel of Mine to bear My name before Gentiles, kings, and the children of Israel. For I will show him how many things he must suffer for My name's sake." (Acts 9:15-16) In this lesson we have a graphic fulfillment. Paul appears before a Jewish king and queen, a Roman governor, actually two Roman governors. He appears before both Jews and Gentiles. "The Lord moves in mysterious ways His wonders to perform." Had Paul not become a prisoner, some of these individuals would never have had such an opportunity to hear the Gospel. The Lord opens doors in very special ways today, also. He guides and leads us, as He did Paul.

The Lord was with Paul, blessing and keeping, protecting and defending him . . . so also He is with us.

## PASSAGES
**These passages can be assigned as memory work or simply discussed in class as to how they fit the lesson.**

### Lower
Psalm 50:15 - Call upon Me in the day of trouble; I will deliver you, and you shall glorify Me.

Psalm 124:8 - Our help is in the name of the Lord, who made heaven and earth.

I Peter 5:7 - casting all your care upon Him, for He cares for you,

### Middle
Matt: 16:24 - If anyone desires to come after Me, let him deny himself, and take up his cross, and follow Me.

Acts 14:22 - We must through many tribulations enter the Kingdom of God.

I Peter 1:5 - You are kept by the power of God through faith for salvation ready to be revealed in the last time.

### Upper
Romans 8:28 - and we know that all things work together for good to those who love God, to those who are the called according to His purpose.

Romans 10:17 - So then faith comes by hearing, and hearing by the Word of God.

II Tim. 4:18 - and the Lord will deliver me from every evil work and will preserve me for His heavenly Kingdom: To Him be glory forever and ever. Amen!

I Peter 5:6-7 - Therefore humble yourselves under the mighty hand of God, that He may exalt you in due time, casting all your care upon Him for He cares for you.

## HYMN CHOICES
Awake, Thou Spirit, Who Didst Fire" - TLH #494
There Still Is Room - TLH #509
Jesus Shall Reign Where'er the Sun - TLH #511

## STORY
Paul is Taken to Rome - Acts 27-28

## TEACHER PRAYER
O dearest Jesus, You have said: "I am with you always, even unto the end of the world." What a comforting promise! Be with me now as I ponder Your holy Word in this lesson. Bless my meditation and preparation. Also bless my presentation and application. Enable the children entrusted to my care to see You in this lesson. Strengthen their faith and increase their love for You and Your word. Move them also to share it with others. Amen.

## VOCABULARY
*fast* - the Day of Atonement, late September or early October

*Euroclydon* - a southeast wind that stirs up broad waves, a northeaster

*drive* - be driven

*skiff* - any light rowboat, or a long, narrow rowboat, especially one with a small sail

*fathom* - a nautical unit of depth or length, approximately six feet

*stern* - back end of a ship or boat

*prow* - the forward part of a ship

*reef* - a ridge of rock or sand near or at the surface of the water

## OUTER AIM
Paul is taken to Rome

## INNER AIM
Paul was a "prisoner" of Jesus Christ

## BACKGROUND (Rupprecht, *Bible History References,* Vol. 2, pp. 598-612)
In his epistle to the Romans, Paul mentions his desire to come and preach in Rome. (Romans. 1:9-15) The Lord granted his prayer and request, but not under the most favorable of circumstances. He was brought to Rome as a prisoner since he had appealed to Caesar, the Roman emperor. Paul was a prisoner in Rome for two years. During this time he had plenty of opportunity to proclaim the Gospel of Christ.

Chapter 27
Paul Sails for Rome. Luke records many details concerning the voyage. He reports where they sailed and what they encountered. The Roman centurion on board was sympathetic to Paul and his plight. The weather became a serious problem. Paul advised wintering on the island of Crete. The shipowner and helmsman thought otherwise. They figured they could continue. The ship became engulfed in a terrible storm. It lasted for days and days. The crew and soldiers feared the worst. Paul assured them that all would survive, but the ship would be lost. The Lord saved them. He had plans for Paul in Rome.

Chapter 28:1-10
Paul is Shipwrecked on Malta. The natives regarded Paul as some sort of god. He miraculously survived a deadly snakebite. Paul later healed the father of the island's magistrate. Many others on the island were healed as well. They were sent and were helped on their way.

Chapter 28:11-31

Paul Teaches in Rome. Paul and those with him stayed on the island of Malta for three months. The journey to Rome continued, first by sea, then by land. Finally, Paul arrived in Rome. He was still a prisoner, but he was granted considerable freedom. He spoke to the Jews at Rome. They had heard nothing about Paul or the charges levied against him by the Jews in Jerusalem. They had heard about the Christian faith. They wanted to know more. Paul taught them. Some believed; some didn't. For two years, Paul spoke to all who came to him–Jews and Gentiles alike. He proclaimed Christ and His kingdom. No one interfered.

Note: After two years, Paul's case was finally heard. He was acquitted and released. He continued on with a fourth missionary journey. Following that he was again arrested, tried, and condemned in Rome. He was beheaded for his testimony concerning Jesus Christ.

**STUDENTS' PRAYER** TLH #498:3, 6
If Thou, merciful Redeemer, Hadst not saved us from this plight
In like darkness we should languish Hopeless, helpless, in sin's night.
Lovingly Thou, Lord, didst seek us In the beauty of Thy grace;
Now with joy we freely serve Thee, We, Thy blessed, chosen race.

Savior, shine in all Thy glory On the nations near and far;
From the highways and the byways Call them, O Thou Morning Star.
Guide them whom Thy grace hath chosen Out of Satan's dreadful thrall
To the mansions of Thy Father-There is room for sinners all.

## PRESENTATION

In this lesson, again you will find more than one familiar Bible story. This lesson will take you from Caesarea to Rome.

A map showing the path Paul took will be of considerable help. The student can then trace the routes and places Paul visited.

Keep in mind the overall reason for Paul's trip to Rome. Paul was sent there to have his case brought before the Roman Emperor. He had done nothing wrong, nothing worthy of death, as the Jews claimed. The Lord wanted Paul in Rome so that the Gospel could ring out. Refer to passages such as Acts 9:15-16 and 23:11.

## APPLICATION

In his epistles, Paul describes himself as a servant, slave, even prisoner of Jesus Christ. (Rom. 1:1; Phil. 1:1; Titus 1:1) After his conversion, he devoted his entire life to his Savior, spreading the Gospel of the Kingdom. Wherever he went, no matter what the circumstances, the Lord used Paul to advance His Kingdom. "All things worked together for good." The fact that Paul was in bonds and that he was a prisoner did not hinder the Gospel. If anything, the Lord used the situation to advance it. The Gospel of the Kingdom reached people and places it may never have reached otherwise.

Today, too, the Lord works in a variety of ways to 'let His Kingdom come.'

## PASSAGES
**These passages can be assigned as memory work or simply discussed in class as to how they fit the lesson.**

**Lower**

Matt. 18:11 - The Son of Man has come to save that which was lost.

Mark 16:15 - Go into all the world and preach the Gospel to every creature.

**Middle**

John 3:16 - For God so loved the world that He gave His only begotten Son, that whoever believes in Him should not perish but have everlasting life.

Acts 16:31 - Believe on the Lord Jesus Christ, and you will be saved, you and your household.

**Upper**

Acts 4:12 - Nor is there salvation in any other, for there is no other name under heaven given among man by which we must be saved.

Romans 10:4 - For Christ is the end of the law for righteousness to everyone who believes.

I Cor. 1:18 - For the message of the cross is foolishness to those who are perishing, but to us who are being saved it is the power of God.

## HYMN CHOICES
Look From Thy Sphere of Endless Day - TLH #499
Savior, Sprinkle Many Nations - TLH #510
Jesus Shall Reign Where'er the Sun - TLH #511
O Christ, Our True and Only Light - TLH #512